CODING BASICS

Coding Basics: Medical Billing and Reimbursement Fundamentals

Coding Basics:
Medical Billing and
Reimbursement
Fundamentals

Cynthia A. Richards, CPC

DELMAR
CENGAGE Learning™

Australia • Brazil • Japan • Korea • Mexico • Singapore • Spain • United Kingdom • United States

Coding Basics: Medical Billing and Reimbursement Fundamentals
Cynthia A. Richards, CPC

Vice President, Career and Professional Editorial: Dave Garza

Director of Learning Solutions: Matthew Kane

Senior Acquisitions Editor: Rhonda Dearborn

Managing Editor: Marah Bellegarde

Product Manager: Jadin Babin-Kavanaugh

Editorial Assistant: Chiara Astriab

Vice President, Career and Professional Marketing: Jennifer McAvey

Executive Marketing Director: Wendy Mapstone

Senior Marketing Manager: Nancy Bradshaw

Marketing Coordinator: Erica Ropitzky

Production Director: Carolyn Miller

Production Manager: Andrew Crouth

Content Project Manager: Brooke Greenhouse

Senior Art Director: Jack Pendleton

Technology Product Manager: Mary Colleen Liburdi

Technology Project Manager: Erin Zeggert

Library of Congress Control Number: 2008944318

ISBN-13: 978-1-4283-1802-1

ISBN-10: 1-4283-1802-X

Delmar
5 Maxwell Drive
Clifton Park, NY 12065-2919
USA

Cengage Learning is a leading provider of customized learning solutions with office locations around the globe, including Singapore, the United Kingdom, Australia, Mexico, Brazil, and Japan. Locate your local office at **international.cengage.com/region**

Cengage Learning products are represented in Canada by Nelson Education, Ltd.

To learn more about Delmar, visit **www.cengage.com/delmar**

Purchase any of our products at your local college store or at our preferred online store **www.ichapters.com**

Notice to the Reader

Printed in Canada
1 2 3 4 5 6 7 11 10 09

Contents

Reviewers

The author and publisher would like to thank the following reviewers for their feedback.

Christina Booker
Medial Billing and Coding Department Supervisor
Career Services Coordinator
Antelope Valley Medical College
Lancaster, California

Deborah Fazio, CMAS, RMA
MBC Program Director
Sanford Brown Institute
Cleveland, OH

Deborah K. Forcier, CPC, DIO
Anesthesia Coder II
Moffitt Cancer Center
Tampa, Florida

Rashmi Gaonkar, MS (Chemistry)
Senior Instructor
ASA Institute
Brooklyn, New York

Sharon Imperiale, CMA, AA Science
Instructor
College America
Phoenix, Arizona

Norma Mercado, MAHS, RHIA
Department Chair
Austin Community College
Austin, Texas

Aimée Michaelis, BA, MEd.
Lead Instructor,
Pima Medical Institute
Denver, Colorado

Pat G. Moeck, PhD, MBA, BA, CMA (AAMA)
Director, Medical Assisting Program
El Centro College
Dallas, Texas

Lynn G. Slack, BS, CMA
Kaplan Career Institute – ICM Campus
Pittsburgh, Pennsylvania

TECHNICAL REVIEWERS

Dorothy Anderson, CMRS, CPC
Coordinator
Medical Reimbursement Program
Career Learning Center of the Black Hills

Jeanne L. West, CPC, CMRS
Box Elder
South Dakota

Preface

Careers in the health claim field have grown and will continue to grow by leaps and bounds. It is essential that the learner be grounded in the fundamentals of the medical environment, medical insurances, insurance regulations, coding procedures/services and diagnoses, accurate submission of health claims, and the health claim follow-up. The rapidly changing rules and regulations of the healthcare field require up-to-date information for the prospective reimbursement specialist and medical assistant.

Billing and Reimbursement Fundamentals provides the most current information in the health insurance industry. It is important that the reimbursement specialist have a solid foundation of information in this field and build on the knowledge through experience working in the medical office. Understanding the basic concepts in the health claim field through clear and concise information will ensure this strong foundation of knowledge. Through discussion and practice, these concepts will ensure accurate billing in the physician's office.

FEATURES OF THIS TEXTBOOK

Coding Basics: Billing and Reimbursement Fundamentals is part of the Coding Basics series of books from Delmar, Cengage Learning, designed to provide the basic training for reimbursement specialists and medical assistants needed for employment in a physician's office. These basics can be taught at the vocational, college, and career school level, in either a traditional or modular program.

The objectives of the text are to:

- Explain the job description of the reimbursement specialist
- Provide an overview of the medical office environment
- Provide the basic knowledge of the major health insurances
- Explain many of the essential claim forms used in the healthcare billing industry
- Explain the essentials of health claim submission and follow-up
- Provide an overview of the CPT and ICD-9-CM coding

- Provide important information on obtaining entry-level reimbursement employment
- Opportunity for real-world practice using case studies and SimClaim, Delmar's software for the CMS-1500 form

The concepts are introduced in this text by the use of chapter objectives, key terms, section questions, chapter summaries, and chapter reviews. The text also allows the learner to complete health claim forms either electronically or manually, and expand on practical applications of concepts learned in each chapter.

Conceptual Approach

Billing and Reimbursement Fundamentals was designed to be used in a classroom setting. This text should be used in conjunction with other health care modules including medical terminology, anatomy and physiology, and computer courses.

Development of this text was based on needs in the classroom for a real-life approach to set a solid foundation of knowledge regarding the collection of health claim data, health insurance rules and regulations for submission of the health claim, charge and payment entry, coding, and insurance claim follow-up and collections. Emphasis needs to be placed on the basics of actual concepts needed in the physician's billing office and not on the historical background of the health insurance industry.

Experts in the educations field have indicated a concept needs to be read, seen, and practiced over and over for the learner to retain that concept. This text uses that principal. A concept is introduced in a chapter; the learner reads the chapter and answers the questions associated with the concept. Discussion of the concept is important in the classroom, and any residual questions are answered. The chapter has a practical application for the learner to research and present in the classroom. Many chapters allow the learner to be introduced to forms needed in the reimbursement process. This allows the learner to recognize and properly use the forms, again reinforcing the concept being examined.

As an instructor in the health claim specialist field, I found communication skills to be lacking in the classroom. This is one of the most important skills needed in the health claim specialist field. The text uses short answer questions throughout the chapters; this was designed to increase the learner's ability to explain a concept "in his or her own words". This method helps in the development of communication. A reimbursement specialist must not only understand the steps in billing and reimbursement, he or she must be able to communicate those steps to a patient. Employers in today's healthcare industry are looking for employees who have the knowledge of the reimbursement process and can communicate with the patient, insurance company, co-workers, and clinical staff.

Instructor's Manual, ISBN 1-4283-1803-8

The Instructor's Manual contains answer keys to all textbook and software exercises, as well as Chapter Tests.

ORGANIZATION OF TEXTBOOK

- Chapter 1, The Reimbursement Specialist, outlines the career opportunities, job description, job market and personal and professional qualifications for the reimbursement specialist. This chapter will also outline the professional certifications and credentials available in this career field.

- Chapter 2, Office Procedures, provides an overview of the physician's office. It includes information about office equipment, medical records, training, HIPAA, office policies, and professionalism. Knowledge of the methods used in the medical office are essential to the reimbursement specialist's career.

- Chapter 3, Patient Information, reviews the concepts of a health claim, clinical services, patient check in and out process, and office dynamics.

- Chapter 4, CMS-1500 Form, explains the patient information needed for this claim form, the submission of the claim form, and step-by-step instructions for filling out the CMS-1500 form.

- Chapter 5, Health Insurance, outlines the basic information on health insurance in today's market. The text reviews reimbursement terminology and managed care health insurance.

- Chapter 6, Medicare, outlines one of the most important and complex insurance coverage today. Outlined is a brief history of Medicare, Medicare eligibility, Medicare plans, Medicare reimbursement, Medicare rules and regulations, participating physicians, Medigap policies, and how to submit Medicare claims on the CMS-1500 form.

- Chapter 7, Blue Cross Blue Shield, Medicaid, TRICARE, Commercial and Workers' Compensation Insurances, outlines the major insurance companies the reimbursement specialist will encounter. Information covered for each insurance company may include a brief history, eligibility, plans, claim submission rules and regulations, reimbursement, and covered services/procedures.

- Chapter 8, Coding Overview of CPT and ICD-9-CM Coding, explains the concept of coding procedures/services, and diagnosis coding. This chapter outlines a brief history of coding, the coding manuals, and guidelines of coding.

- Chapter 9, Charge Entry, provides information on the collection of data needed for entering charges into the medical software for submission of health claims. It outlines how the clinical and billing staff work together in the collection of data needed for the health claim, encounter forms, compliance in the medical office, and auditing the medical record for compliance and submission of clean claims.

- Chapter 10, Payment Entry, explains the reimbursement payment entry process. This chapter will outline the importance of correct reimbursement, the explanation of benefits, denials and rejection of claims, and how payment posting is accomplished. This chapter will also explain reimbursement of secondary insurance claims.

- Chapter 11, Problem Solving, introduces the learner to the important concept of understanding reimbursement problems and how to solve any incorrect payment. Included in this chapter is how to talk with insurance companies about problems and appeals.

- Chapter 12, Aged Trial Balance Reports, introduces the learner to how to use the aged trial balance report to accomplish follow-up on unpaid accounts in the medical office. Account Receivable (A/R) is outlined in this chapter as well as the Billing Cycle. These processes are essential concepts to the reimbursement specialist.

- Chapter 13, Collections, outlines the collection process in the physician's office. Explanations of state and federal collection laws, collection agencies, and write-offs are included in this chapter.

- Chapter 14, Résumés and Interviews, outlines the importance of professionalism, writing résumés, cover letters, and thank you letters. Included in this chapter is important information regarding job interviews.

ABOUT THE AUTHOR

Cynthia A. Richards, CPC, has worked in the medical profession for over 30 years. She received her AAS and worked as a radiologic technologist for 15 years. She gained experience in the clinical side of the medical profession both in the physician's office and hospital settings. She worked in the reimbursement sector of the medical office for over 16 years in the specialties of Rheumatology, Anesthesia, Family Practice, Eye Care, Orthopedics, and Radiology. She became a Certified Professional Coder in 2004 while coding for a large radiology billing company in the New Jersey area. Sharing her expertise in the reimbursement and coding fields led her to a teaching position in a local Maine career school. Becoming the lead instructor in the Health Claim Specialist Program was rewarding and challenging. Teaching adult learners the concepts of medical reimbursement, insurances, coding, hospital billing, medical terminology, psychology, math, and English turned into a full-time profession. Working to expand the current program and becoming the externship site coordinator allowed her to help each student gain his or/and her full potential. The most rewarding aspect in the education field for Cynthia was seeing the students graduate and become an important part of the medical community.

How to Use the SimClaim CMS-1500 Student Practice CD-ROM

Main Menu

The Main Menu has an interactive user interface with a desktop motif. Clicking on each tab located down the right-hand side of the file folder opens a new page.

Getting Started

Click on the **Getting Started** tab to see resources available to you:

- **Tutorial**—provides complete instructions for installing and uninstalling the software, completing CMS-1500 claims for various types of payers using the case study sets provided, saving claims, and printing claims

- **Glossary**—click on a term to see the definition

- **Abbreviations**—click on an abbreviation to see the meaning

- **Block Help**—step-by-step instructions for completing each block of the CMS-1500 claim form for Commercial, Blue Cross Blue Shield, Workers' Compensation, Medicare, Medicaid, and TRICARE payers

Access additional resources by clicking on 'Contents' from the pull-down Help menu.

Study Mode

Click on the **Study Mode** tab to access Case Studies 1 through 20, which can also be found in print in Appendix I of the textbook. You can click on the **CMS-1500** claim form to open a blank claim form, and select your Case Study of choice to begin. If you need help entering the correct information in a block, click **Block Help** at any time for block-by-block instructions. In **Study Mode**, feedback is provided as you enter information into each block. Completed claims and summary reports with justification can be printed.

Test Mode

In Test Mode, you can access Case Studies 1 through 20. No feedback is provided as you enter information into each block when in Test Mode. The completed claim is graded, and completed claims can be printed.

Blank Form Mode

You may click on the Blank CMS-1500 tab to complete the Case Studies 1 through 20 or any additional case studies that your instructor chooses. No feedback is provided in this mode, and the completed claim forms can be printed.

System Requirements

Minimum System Requirements:

- Operating System: Microsoft Windows 98 SE, Windows 2000, Windows XP, or Windows VISTA
- Processor: Pentium PC 500 MHz or higher (750 MHz recommended)
- RAM: 64 MB of RAM (128 MB recommended)
- 32 MB free hard drive space
- Monitor Screen Resolution: 800 x 600 pixels
- Color Depth: 16-bit color (thousands of colors)
- Mouse
- Printer: 16 MB memory recommended

The SimClaim Student Practice CD-ROM, found inside the back cover of this textbook, is designed to help you practice completing CMS-1500 claims. The CD-ROM Procedure Manual, along with tutorials for using the Blank Form, Study, and Test Modes, are located on the CD-ROM. They can be viewed on your computer screen or printed. Brief instructions to get you started using the software follow. Install the program using the CD-ROM included with this textbook.

Installing the SimClaim Student Practice CD-ROM Program on Your Computer

1. Insert the CD-ROM into a CD-ROM drive
2. Click Start, then click Run.
3. Enter d:\Setup and click OK (Note: replace "d" with your CD-ROM drive letter if necessary).
4. In a few moments, you will be welcomed to the installation program. Click Next to start the installation.
5. A dialog box will ask for the drive and directory where you want the program installed. To install the program in the default directory at

c:\Program Files\Delmar Applications\SimClaim for Coding Basics, click **Next**. If you want to change this, click **Browse**, and enter the directory and drive where you want the program to be installed.

6. Once the installation begins, it can be cancelled at any time by clicking **Cancel**.

7. A Delmar icon will be added to the **Start** menu under **Programs> Delmar Applications**.

8. The install program will automatically complete the installation process. Click **OK** when you see the **installation is complete** message.

Removing the SimClaim Student Practice CD-ROM Program from Your Computer

To remove the SimClaim for Coding Basics program from your computer, follow this procedure:

1. First, exit the program before attempting to uninstall it.

2. Next, in Windows 2003 or newer, on the Windows task bar, choose **Start> Programs>Delmar Applications>Uninstall SimClaim for Coding Basics**.

3. A prompt will appear asking you to confirm that you want to delete the program. Click **Yes** to continue.

4. When the program uninstall procedure is completed, click **OK**.

Completing Case Study Claims

You can use the Student Practice CD-ROM to:

- **Print** blank CMS-1500 and UB-04 claim forms for manual completion of case studies

- **View** Case Studies 1 through 20

- **Complete** Case Studies 1 through 20 in Blank Form Mode, Study Mode, or Test Mode

- **Save** completed claim forms to your desktop for later, or as PDFs for emailing

General Hints

- Press the **Caps Lock** key on your keyboard before beginning to use the SimClaim program, since the program only accepts capital letters

- **Proofread** each CMS-1500 block entry before moving to the next block

- When you use the numeric keypad on your keyboard to enter numbers, press the **Num Lock** key on your keyboard

Printing, Printing to PDF format, and Emailing Completed Claims

1. Once you have completed a CMS-1500 claim in the Blank Form, Study, or Test mode, click **Print** or **File>Print**.

2. Once the Printing Options window displays, click OK to print the CMS-1500 form, Summary Report with Justifications and Case Study.

3. To print claim forms to **PDF** files, click that option from within the program. Be sure to save your file to a location where you can easily retrieve it, such as your desktop, and to name it according to the case. A PDF file can easily be emailed to your instructor as an attachment; attach the PDF file from within your email browser.

Features and Benefits of EncoderPro

Encoder Pro is the essential code look-up software for CPT®, ICD-9-CM and HCPCS code sets. It gives users fast searching capabilities across all code sets. Encoder Pro can greatly reduce the time it takes to build or review a claim and helps improve overall coding accuracy. If you decide to subscribe to the full version of Encoder Pro, the following tools will be available to you:

- **Powerful Ingenix CodeLogic™ search engine**. Improve productivity by eliminating time-consuming code look up in outdated code books. Search all three code sets simultaneously using lay terms, acronyms, abbreviations and even misspelled words.

- **Lay descriptions for thousands of CPT® codes**. Enhance your understanding of procedures with easy-to-understand descriptions.

- **Color-coded edits**. Understand whether a code carries an age or sex edit, is covered by Medicare, or contains bundled procedures.

- **Quarterly update service**. Rest assured you are always using accurate codes. You can code confidently throughout the year with free code updates.

- **Great value**. Get the content from over 20 code and reference books in one powerful solution.

For more information about EncoderPro software, click on the Help menu from inside the free trial version, then select "Features by Product," or go to www.ingenixonline.com.

How to Use the Encoder PRO 30-Day Trial CD-ROM

The Encoder Pro software included in the back cover of this textbook is a 30-day free trial of Ingenix's powerful medical coding solution that allows you to look up ICD-9-CM, CPT, and HCPCS Level II codes quickly and accurately. This software can be used to assign codes to any of the exercises in the textbook. **Note:** Be sure to check with your instructor before installing the Encoder Pro software because the CD-ROM bundled with your book expires 30 days after installation.

Menus and Toolbars

- Encoder Pro contains a menu that expands to allow you to easily navigate the software. Click on a menu heading to select one of its options, such as View, Code Book Sections, etc. Encoder Pro contains a toolbar with drop-down menus that allow you to select the ICD-9-CM, CPT, or HCPCS level II coding system and new/revised/deleted codes and code book sections.

- Use the coding system drop-down menu on the far left to select a coding system. Then enter a condition (e.g., diabetes) or procedure/service in the Search box. Click the Search button to view Tabular Results, which can be expanded, or click the "See index listing" to use the alphabetic index to locate a code.

- Use the drop-down list on the far right of the black toolbar to quickly access New Codes, Revised Codes, Deleted Codes, and Code Book Sections. Make a selection and click the View button to access the dialog boxes.

- Encoder Pro's toolbar with clickable buttons allows you to use its unique features. Simply mouse over a button to view its title, and a brief description of the button will also appear in the status bar on the bottom left of the screen. Click on the button to use its function.

Features and Benefits of EncoderPro

Encoder Pro is the essential code look-up software for CPT®, ICD-9-CM and HCPCS code sets. It gives users fast searching capabilities across all code sets. Encoder Pro can greatly reduce the time it takes to build or review a claim and helps improve overall coding accuracy. If you decide to subscribe to the full version of Encoder Pro, the following tools will be available to you:

- **Powerful Ingenix CodeLogic™ search engine.** Improve productivity by eliminating time-consuming code look up in outdated code books. Search all three code sets simultaneously using lay terms, acronyms, abbreviations and even misspelled words.

- **Lay descriptions for thousands of CPT® codes.** Enhance your understanding of procedures with easy-to-understand descriptions.

- **Color-coded edits.** Understand whether a code carries an age or sex edit, is covered by Medicare, or contains bundled procedures.

- **Quarterly update service.** Rest assured you are always using accurate codes. You can code confidently throughout the year with free code updates.

- **Great value.** Get the content from over 20 code and reference books in one powerful solution.

For more information about EncoderPro software, click on the Help menu from inside the free trial version, then select "Features by Product," or go to www.ingenixonline.com.

Printing, Printing to PDF format, and Emailing Completed Claims

1. Once you have completed a CMS-1500 claim in the Blank Form, Study, or Test mode, click **Print** or **File>Print**.

2. Once the Printing Options window displays, click OK to print the CMS-1500 form, Summary Report with Justifications and Case Study.

3. To print claim forms to **PDF** files, click that option from within the program. Be sure to save your file to a location where you can easily retrieve it, such as your desktop, and to name it according to the case. A PDF file can easily be emailed to your instructor as an attachment; attach the PDF file from within your email browser.

Acknowledgements

Thank you to my husband, Dave, and son, Nathan, for understanding my passion in going the extra mile in the classroom and writing this textbook. My many thanks to my sister Jan who helped to cross my "t's" and dot my "i's". I also want to acknowledge two of my mentors in the education field, Denis St. Pierre and Deb Casey. I want to thank all of my students who really made the classroom a joy to be in. Their many letters of thanks made it worthwhile.

AVENUE FOR FEEDBACK

Please contact me at ca.richards@live.com if any questions arise.

Chapter 1

The Reimbursement Specialist

OBJECTIVES

Upon completion of this chapter, the student should be able to:

- Describe the job of the reimbursement specialist.
- List the personal qualifications for the reimbursement specialist.
- Describe the professional qualifications for the reimbursement specialist.
- Specify the professional certifications for the reimbursement specialist.
- Discuss the job market for the reimbursement specialist.

KEY TERMS

Accounts receivable (AR)

Ambulatory

Certifications

Charge entry

CMS-1500 billing form

Demographics

Diagnosis

Health claim

Health insurance

Insurance benefits

Medical codes

Medical team

Payment entry

Reimbursement

INTRODUCTION

Understanding what a reimbursement specialist is, and what the job requirements are, will be the first step in choosing this new career. A reimbursement specialist will be a vital part of a medical team. This chapter will discuss the many important job opportunities available to the reimbursement specialist and what the learner will need to achieve to be successful in this very exciting field.

A CAREER AS A REIMBURSEMENT SPECIALIST

A new career in the health care profession will be a challenging but rewarding one. The medical profession is one of the fastest-growing industries in the United States. The expanding technologies in the medical field are helping people live longer lives, thus health care services have increased and health care workers are in high demand. The Department of Labor has predicted employment in this field to increase by 18% through 2016. However, this expansion has altered the insurance industry. The insurance companies are scrutinizing the claims and payments for billed services. For this reason, employers in the health care field are requiring knowledgeable and certified employees.

The reimbursement specialist is an essential part of the **medical team**. This team consists of both the clinical and administrative departments in **ambulatory** facilities. An ambulatory facility is one in which a patient is treated as an outpatient, not formally admitted to a facility overnight. This textbook will be limited to a discussion of the physician's office, an ambulatory (outpatient) facility.

The Job Description

Employers may advertise for a reimbursement specialist, a health claims specialist, or a medical billing specialist. The job skills will be the same for any of these job titles. These job descriptions will require the specialist to be an expert in all aspects of the medical billing department. The job description will include knowledge in collecting patient data, insurance verification, medical coding, charge entry, claim submission, payment entry, insurance follow-up, and collections.

A reimbursement specialist will work directly with the clinical staff to ensure the services performed for the patient are billed correctly and efficiently. The medical facility must collect **reimbursement** for those services performed in the clinical area in order to remain solvent as a business. Reimbursement is defined as: to compensate another for services rendered. This reimbursement may come from many sources: the patient, the insurance companies, or private sources.

ACCOUNTS RECEIVABLE

According to the United States Census, 85% of Americans have **health insurance**. Health insurance is a contract between an individual and an insurance company. This contract states the insurance company will pay a predetermined payment for medical costs when that person is sick or injured and requires medical treatment. Before medical costs are paid, health insurance companies require a bill from the medical facility. The reimbursement specialist is the employee who collects the information required by the insurance company for this bill. The **health claim** or insurance bill is generated by a computer using specialized billing software, and is formatted to a **CMS-1500 billing form**. The CMS-1500 form is a universal billing form used by all insurance companies. The reimbursement specialist collects the patient's **demographics**, which is important information regarding the patient. Demographics include the patient's name, date of birth, address, insurance information, marital status, employment information, and reason for treatment. Not all insurance companies require the same information on a claim. It is important for the reimbursement specialist to know the local health insurance companies that they work with, to collect the correct reimbursement.

Each service and/or procedure performed on the patient then must be medically coded with nationally recognized numeric and alphanumeric **medical codes** to identify each service performed. These codes are used by all of the insurance companies, making communication between physicians' offices and insurance companies uniform. By using numeric and alphanumerical codes, it is also easier for computer programs to be established (medical coding will be discussed in more detail in Chapter 6). The billing department assigns the medical codes and enters them into computer software programs developed specifically for billing the insurance claims. This process is called **charge entry**. Keyboarding will be an important skill to master for the reimbursement specialist when this stage of billing is done.

Once the information regarding each service is entered into the billing software, a claim can be computer-generated. The reimbursement specialist's job is to ensure the information is correct and to submit it electronically to the insurance company for reimbursement. The **insurance benefit** or payment is determined by the insurance company as set by the contract each patient has within their policy. The payment is then received by the physician's billing office and the reimbursement specialist will enter (post) the payment to the patient's account. This is called **payment entry**. In the payment-entry stage, skills in 10-key operation of an adding machine are needed. Speed and accuracy are very important.

All insurance companies do not pay the same reimbursement and the patient's insurance benefits also differ, which leads the reimbursement specialist to the next phase of their job. This is insurance payment follow-up. A reimbursement specialist must recognize when the insurance company does not pay correctly on a claim or a denial is received on a claim. If ignored, these denials and incorrect payments lead to loss of income for the medical facility.

The important skills of written and oral communications with the insurance companies will be discussed in later chapters.

The final phase in the reimbursement process is collections. The remainder of the patient's bill, after their health insurance pays, may now be their responsibility. Or if the patient does not have insurance coverage, they are responsible for the entire bill. A bill will be generated by the computer and sent out to the patient. The collection process is not always an easy one. Many patients cannot afford health care costs. Knowing the process of collecting unpaid debts will be a part of the reimbursement specialist's job. Each facility will have its own rules regarding the collection process.

This complete process of reimbursement is called **accounts receivable (AR)**. This textbook will be discussing in detail each of these stages in the account receivable process in later chapters.

STOP AND PRACTICE

Exercise 1-1

Short answer: Answer each question with a short statement.

1. Describe the job description of a reimbursement specialist.

   _____

   _____

2. Why are careers in the reimbursement specialist field growing today?

   _____

   _____

3. What information is needed from the clinical and administrative medical teams for the health claim?

   _____

   _____

4. Explain reimbursement.

   _____

   _____

5. Explain health insurance.

   _____

   _____

PERSONAL QUALIFICATIONS

The career as a reimbursement specialist can be complicated and challenging. With the wealth of new information flooding into the medical field, it is constantly changing. There are personal qualifications that will help the specialist become a valuable member of the medical team. Following is a list of qualifications that can be developed now, while learning the professional skills needed for this new career. All of these attributes are important and should be studied carefully.

PERSONAL QUALIFICATIONS

1. Communication skills

2. Positive attitude

3. Moral and ethical behavior

4. Detail-oriented

5. Critical thinking skills

6. Honest and reliable

7. Confident

8. Quest for learning

Communication is a skill that can be developed as we proceed through the exercises, chapter reviews, and group activities. Communication skills can only be developed by practicing both in the classroom and in everyday activities. It is important to remember that learning all the information necessary to become a reimbursement specialist is a must, but being able to communicate that knowledge is equally important. There must be a line of communication with the physician, other members of the medical team, the patient, and the insurance companies.

The patients are often very sick. A reimbursement specialist must project a positive and caring attitude at all times. Keeping in mind the physical condition of the patient will help keep these attitudes at the forefront. Being detail-oriented is always important when working in the medical billing department. The codes chosen represent people: mothers, fathers, or children. They are not just numbers on paper.

STOP AND PRACTICE

Exercise 1-2

Short answer: Answer each question with a short statement.

1. Why is communication an important personal qualification for a reimbursement specialist?

    _____

    _____

2. List at least six personal qualifications for the reimbursement specialist.

    _____

    _____

3. Explain why being detail-oriented is important in your new career.

    _____

    _____

4. Why is it important to have a positive attitude in the medical profession?

    _____

    _____

PROFESSIONAL QUALIFICATIONS

The following represents a list of professional qualifications the reimbursement specialist will need to develop while studying for this new career. These skills can be challenging and will come with concentrated study. They will also develop with time as the learner gains experience working within the reimbursement field.

PROFESSIONAL QUALIFICATIONS

1. **Communication skills**
2. **Computer skills**
3. **Accounting skills**
4. **Knowledge of health insurances**

5. Knowledge of the CMS-1500 health claim form

6. Medical coding

7. Knowledge of professional certifications

8. Knowledge of medical terminology

9. Knowledge of anatomy and physiology

10. Troubleshooting skills with excellent follow-through

A reimbursement specialist will need to know the specific accounting software the medical office uses. Insurance knowledge is essential to this career, as well as understanding the clinical side of the medical office. Knowing the types of services and procedures the clinical staff performs for the patient is important to correctly code and bill the services. Recognizing what illness or injury the patient has is important in assigning a **diagnosis** to the procedures. Understanding medical terminology, anatomy, and physiology will help with the assignment of the services, procedures, and diagnoses. We will be exploring all of these skills in later chapters.

There are many resources available to the reimbursement specialists, aiding in medical coding and billing. They include medical dictionaries, coding manuals, anatomy and physiology reference books specifically for medical billing, and the Internet. This may seem overwhelming, but before long the learner will understand the basics needed for the career as a reimbursement specialist.

STOP AND PRACTICE

Exercise 1-3

Matching: Assign personal qualification (PQ) and/or professional qualification (PRQ) to each skill.

1. Communication skills   _____

2. Detail-oriented   _____

3. Medical coding   _____

4. Quest for learning   _____

5. Computer skills   _____

6. Positive attitude   _____

7. Medical terminology   _____

8. Office procedures   _____

9. Honest and reliable   _____

10. Accounting skills   _____

CERTIFICATIONS

Becoming a certified reimbursement specialist is important, though not a requirement at the present time. However, many employers are looking for medical billing specialists with a **certification**. Nationally recognized associations award certifications in many aspects of the medical reimbursement field. These certifications acknowledge expertise in reimbursement and coding within the ambulatory, hospital, and insurance company environments. Medical insurance billing is very complex; the changes in insurance regulations happen very quickly. Becoming certified lets the employer know the reimbursement specialist has successfully completed formal schooling in this career and passed a national exam. This credentialing measures the knowledge and dedication in the area of medical reimbursement and coding.

It is very important to choose the certification exam carefully. Many companies will offer certifications in this field, but are not nationally recognized. It is important to spend certification dollars wisely. Following is a list of some of the best credentialing associations. Their exams are best researched online. See Appendix II for a list of current Web sites.

CREDENTIALING ASSOCIATIONS

Credentialing for reimbursement specialists can be accomplished through:

- **American Medical Billing Association (AMBA) offers the CMRS exam for certification of the reimbursement specialist.**
- **Medical Association of Billers (MAB) offers the certified medical billing specialist (CMBS) exam.**
- **American Academy of Professional Coders (AAPC) offers the exams for medical coders. The CPC-H exam is for coders working in the hospital environment, while the CPC-P exam is for coders working in the insurance environment. The AAPC also offers specialty certifications, including anesthesia, ambulatory surgical centers, cardiovascular and thorasic surgery, general surgey, ob/gyn, gastroenterology, family practice, e/m auditors, internal medicine, pediatrics, orthopedics, urology, and plastic and reconstructive surgery.**
- **American Health Information Management Association (AHIMA) offers multiple exams for coding. These include the Registered Health Information Administrator (RHIA), the Registered Health Information Technician (RHIT), the Certified Coding Associate (CCA), the Certified Coding Specialist (CCS), and the Certified Coding Specialist, Physician Based (CCS-P).**

Employers will quickly recognize and hire employees with nationally known credentials.

These associations also offer many other services, such as continuing education, newsletters, and links to medical billing resources. Keeping credentials current yearly requires documentation on continuing education units, ensuring knowledge and growth in the billing profession. It cannot be stressed enough: continual learning is vital due to the quickly changing insurance regulations. Many of the associations have local chapters that can be joined to better network and learn the latest advances in the medical profession.

STOP AND PRACTICE

Exercise 1-4

Short answer: Answer each question with a short statement.

1. Why is credentialing so important for a reimbursement specialist?

   _____

   _____

   _____

2. Name at least two associations that administer certification exams.

   _____

   _____

   _____

3. Why choose a nationally recognized association for certification?

   _____

   _____

   _____

4. What important services do the certification associations offer?

   _____

   _____

   _____

THE JOB MARKET

The job market for a reimbursement specialist is one that can encompass many career opportunities. We will be discussing the ambulatory, or outpatient, facility in this textbook, specifically the physician's office. Reimbursement specialists can also be employed in hospitals within the medical records department, admission department, and the financial office. Other job opportunities can be found in ambulatory surgical centers, specialty clinics, nursing homes, pharmacies, rehab centers, and insurance companies.

The job description for a reimbursement specialist may depend on the size of the facility. Small medical offices may employ only one or two specialists and all of the skills learned will be necessary. Larger facilities may employ many billers to do very specific jobs. Figure 1-1 is an example of an advertisement for employment as a reimbursement specialist.

The Department of Labor has listed the reimbursement specialist in the top-10 fastest-growing jobs in the nation. What an excellent career choice!

Medical Reimbursement Specialist

Job Category: Healthcare

Description: We have an immediate need for a number of customer service individuals that will be supporting multiple stages of the reimbursement process. This position is directly involved in the communication and processing of claims, including benefit investigations and answering all reimbursement related questions. The main responsibilities of the position include:

- Understanding billing software, customer contract implementation, information gathering and benefit verification
- Manage and process reimbursement information from potential customers
- Handle necessary documentation, including: obtaining a letter of Medical Necessity, assignment of benefits and prescriptions, and verifying insurance eligibility.
- Obtain and verify all required information for billing
- Answer incoming calls from customers, payors, providers, and insurance inquires.
- Document all appropriate customer information accurately to ensure timely verification of benefits and billing.
- Deliver superior frontline customer service
- Strictly maintain a high level of integrity and confidentiality/ patient privacy per HIPAA
- Knowledge of the reimbursement processing cycle
- Knowledge of managed care industry is required
- Competencies desired are: Medical reimbursement, customer care/call center, managed care, and benefits/health insurance

If you are qualified, please contact Jane Smith at 335-123-4567.

Figure 1-1. Example of an advertisement for employment as a reimbursement specialist

Exercise 1-5

Short answer: Answer each question with a short statement.

1. Name at least three places of employment for a reimbursement specialist.

2. Explain why the job description for a reimbursement specialist may be different for small and large facilities.

3. Explain why YOU have made a great career choice.

CHAPTER SUMMARY

- The medical reimbursement specialist's career is one of the fastest-growing careers in America.

- Whatever the job title is—reimbursement specialist, health claims specialist, or medical billing specialist—the skills needed are the same.

- The reimbursement specialist is a vital member of the medical team.

- The medical reimbursement specialist's job description is to correctly and efficiently billing the services and procedures performed in the medical office.

- A medical reimbursement specialist will become an expert in collecting demographic information, insurance verification, medical billing software, medical coding, charge entry, claim submission, payment entry, insurance follow-up/denials, and collections.

- Reimbursement is the monetary payment for services rendered.

- Health insurance is a contract between an insurance company and the insured for payment when sickness or injury strikes.

- The health claim is produced with information collected from the patient and the clinical team, billed on a CMS-1500 form, and sent to the insurance company.

- Personal qualifications for the job of reimbursement specialist include communication skills, positive attitude, moral and ethical characteristics, being detail-oriented, critical thinking skills, being honest and reliable, having confidence, and having a quest for learning.

- Professional qualifications for the reimbursement specialist include communication skills, computer skills, accounting skills, knowledge of medical insurances, medical coding, medical terminology, anatomy and physiology, and office procedures.
- Certification from nationally recognized associations can bring higher paying jobs.
- The job market for the reimbursement specialist includes physicians' offices, hospitals, specialty clinics, ambulatory surgical centers, and insurance companies.

REVIEW QUESTIONS

Fill in the blank for each statement.

1. The medical profession is one of the fastest-growing industries in the United States because _____ and because of new _____.

2. The increase in the demand for health care services have altered insurance companies to _____ the claims for these services, thus increasing the demand for _____ health care workers.

3. A reimbursement specialist is a part of the medical team made up of _____ and _____ departments.

4. Approximately _____ percent of Americans have health insurance.

5. The name of the claim form used in the ambulatory setting is _____.

Short answer: Answer each question with a short statement.

6. What are some other job titles for a reimbursement specialist?

_____

_____

7. Define reimbursement.

_____

_____

8. Define health insurance.

_____

_____

9. Define health claim.

_____

_____

10. List the demographic information needed for a medical claim.

_____

_____

11. Explain medical coding/diagnoses.

_____

_____

12. Explain the skills needed for charge entry.

_____

_____

13. Explain the skills needed for payment entry.

_____

_____

14. Explain insurance follow-up and why is this so important.

_____

_____

15. List the personal qualifications and explain why these are important in becoming a reimbursement specialist.

_____

_____

16. List the professional qualifications for a reimbursement specialist.

_____

_____

17. Name four associations that measure your knowledge in the medical billing field.

_____

_____

PRACTICAL APPLICATION

Divide into teams of two. Start developing good communication skills by researching online one of the certification associations. Write a short report on this association and present it orally to the rest of the class. Possible topics could include certification exams, continuing education, the pros and cons of becoming certified, or additional resources provided by the association.

Chapter 2

Office Procedures

OBJECTIVES

Upon completion of this chapter, the student should be able to:

- Specify the importance of training in the medical office.
- Discuss the important office equipment used by the reimbursement specialist.
- Define HIPAA and the importance of patient privacy.
- Define what professionalism means to the reimbursement specialist.

KEY TERMS

Clearing house

Collate

Compliance

Cover sheet

Disclaimer

Electronic Medical Record (EMR)

Electronic swipe device

Explanation of benefits (EOB)

Fax

Health Insurance Portability and Accountability Act (HIPAA)

Medical record

National Provider Identifier (NPI)

Preauthorizations

Professionalism

Release of information

INTRODUCTION

Understanding medical office procedures will make the transition from formal schooling to employment an easier one. Every office has its unique policies and procedures but the basics common to all offices will be easy to learn. We will explore the more important policies in this chapter.

OFFICE TRAINING

Understanding the variety of office equipment is an essential part of medical office training today. Treating the sick and injured effectively requires information from many sources. We are working in an age that requires instantaneous communication. Because of today's technology, physicians are treating patients with a quicker and more effective outcome. Being a part of the medical team requires training in many areas.

Whether it's the clinical or administrative departments, a medical office can obtain information for or about a patient with the click of a button. Let's first look at the flow of a basic physician's office. The interactions between the clinical and administrative teams will demonstrate how important office training is and how important sharing patient information is. Figure 2-1 will give you an idea of how the patient flows through a medical office.

Each area of the medical office has a specific job to perform, but must all work together to ensure quality healthcare. The process of the billing cycle begins when the patient first calls the office for an appointment, then check-in collects the patient demographics and starts the insurance verification process. The clinical team of physicians, nurses, medical assistants, and diagnostic personnel sees the patient and documents all encounters. The last step for the patient in the office dynamics is seeing the reimbursement specialist for checkout. Their job continues long after the patient leaves the office with coding, claim submission, insurance follow-up, and collections.

Information Exchange

The clinical staff can receive important medical information regarding a patient's history from other physicians' offices, hospitals, laboratories, or radiology departments. The clinical staff can also send information to these sources regarding their patients. The administrative team (billing office) can receive or send referrals to specialists. They can acquire **preauthorizations**, which are promises of reimbursement from insurance companies. The billing department can verify insurance benefits and resolve benefit denials quickly and efficiently.

How is all this information exchanged so quickly? It is done electronically using office equipment. The essential tools include facsimile, or fax, machines, photocopy machines, computers, and electronic scanning/swipe devices. The standard equipment in the medical office will still include the telephone, pagers, and postal services. A reimbursement specialist will utilize all of these

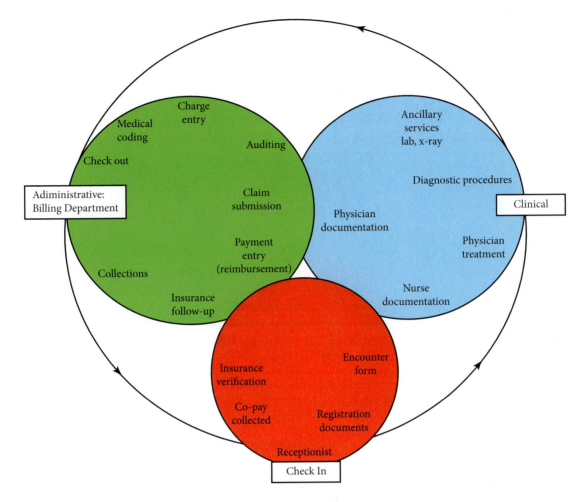

Figure 2-1. Office dynamics chart

communication systems to make the billing process effective. They will be exchanging information with other physicians' offices, insurance companies, clearing houses, and governmental agencies. A **clearing house** is a centrally located entity (business) that links together the physicians' office and insurance company to exchange information regarding claims. Clearing houses reformat health claims for each insurance company. This concept will be discussed in later chapters.

The Medical Record

All treatment and administrative processes must be documented and saved in the patient's **medical record**. This is important because the medical record is a legal document. These documents must be complete, including current illnesses, dates of services, medications, allergies, results of diagnostic testing, and history of any previous illness. These records must be unaltered from the original documents and legible. Expanding technology is introducing the **electronic medical record (EMR)**. EMRs are medical records in digit format (paperless records).

Office Equipment

Medical office equipment can be a little different depending on the models purchased. We will examine briefly how the machines work and their importance in the billing process. Much of the information for treatment and reimbursement comes from many different sources. For this reason, the fax and photocopy machines are invaluable.

Fax Machine

The **fax**, or facsimile, machine utilizes a phone line and photo sensors to scan and send documents instantly over the telephone line. Medical office employees must be very careful when using the fax machine. The risk of sending private information electronically to a wrong destination is great. Keeping the patient's information confidential is essential.

When sending any information via the fax machine, it is important to include a **cover sheet**. The cover sheet is the first page of any information sent. See Figure 2-2 for an example of a cover sheet. It should include your medical office name, address (street, city, and state), telephone number, and fax number. The receiving facility's information should be clearly marked, with the number of pages being sent (including the cover sheet).

A **disclaimer** should always be printed at the bottom of the cover letter. A disclaimer is a statement explaining:

[Street Address]
[City, ST Zip Code]
[phone]
[fax]
[Web address]

[Company Name]

Fax

To: _____   From: _____

Fax: _____   Pages: _____

Phone: _____   Date: _____

Re: _____   cc: _____

☐ Urgent   ☐ For Review   ☐ Please Comment   ☐ Please Reply   ☐ Please Recycle

● Disclaimer: This facsimile transmission contains information that is confidential and/or privileged. This information is intended for use only by the addressee indicated above. If you are not the intended recipient, please be advised that any disclosure, copying, distribution, or use of the contents of this information is strictly prohibited, and that any misdirected or improperly received information must be returned to this company immediately. Your cooperation in phoning us of erroneous receipt is requested.

Figure 2-2. Sample fax cover sheet

1. The faxed information is confidential

2. The faxed information is intended only for the addressee

3. Use of the faxed information is strictly prohibited if recipient not the addressee

4. Please notify the sender if recipient received the fax in error

The fax machine should be located where only authorized personnel can access the information.

EXAMPLE OF A DISCLAIMER

This facsimile transmission contains information that is confidential and/or privileged. This information is intended for use only by the addressee indicated above. If you are not the intended recipient, please be advised that any disclosure, copying, distribution, or use of the contents of this information is strictly prohibited, and that any misdirected or improperly received information must be returned to this company immediately. Your cooperation in phoning us of erroneous receipt is requested.

Photocopy Machine

The photocopy machine is an essential tool in the billing process. Technology today has allowed these machines to copy, **collate** (assembling in proper order), and even staple the copies. This will make the reimbursement specialist's job much easier and more efficient. Some common uses for a photocopy machine in a billing department include: copying referrals, **explanation of benefits (EOB)**, and claim forms. An EOB is a document from the insurance company relaying reimbursement information on a claim. Copying insurance cards, both front and back, on each patient will save time, resolving many insurance questions. Information contained on the front of an insurance card will include the patient's policy information. The information found on the back of the insurance card will be claim submission addresses that are essential to keep on file for the reimbursement process.

Computer

The medical office would not be as efficient as it is today without the computer. As a reimbursement specialist, you must be completely comfortable with all aspects of the office computer. It is not only an informational tool, but essential to electronically submitting health claims for reimbursement. The use of the computer has revolutionized the billing process. Not only can claims be sent electronically to the insurance company, saving time, but the insurance companies' payments can also be sent electronically to the physician's office. With the computer, the reimbursement specialist has the ability to access the Internet, thus networking with many sources. Quickly checking the patient's insurance benefits and checking the status of their claims is important to the reimbursement process.

Electronic Swipe Devices

Some insurance companies are issuing insurance cards that can be used with scanning/swipe devices. **Electronic swipe devices** look very much like credit card point-of-service devices. This gives the physician's office the ability to check patients' insurance eligibility instantly and have an immediate overview of their benefits. Instant information regarding the patient's benefits allows the reimbursement specialist to knowledgeably explain to the patient what will be a covered service. Communication with the patients regarding their possible costs is very important in the billing department.

Electronic office equipment makes the reimbursement process more efficient. Saving time helps lower health care costs for the physician and the patient. Familiarization with specific office equipment is an important aspect in your office training. The equipment will be unique for different offices, but the basic functions are the same.

OFFICE POLICIES AND HIPAA

Knowledge of office policies is essential to the reimbursement specialist. These office policies are set up for good office management and should be respected and followed. All offices should have policies regarding **compliance** with governmental regulations. Compliance is defined as a disposition to yield to a rule. **The Health Insurance Portability and Accountability Act (HIPAA)** is a compliance policy set by the US Dept. of Health and Human Services that establishes national standards for the protection of health information. Every medical office must adhere to these standards, and violators can be fined. HIPAA improves the efficiency and effectiveness in the medical facility. HIPAA was enacted on August 21, 1996. Title I of the act protects health insurance coverage for workers when they change jobs or lose their jobs. Title II of the act is known as the Administrative Simplification provision. This part of HIPAA sets the national standards for electronic health care transactions, national identifiers for providers, insurance plans, and employers. Title II also sets the standards for the security and privacy of health data. HIPAA was enacted to improve the efficiency and effectiveness of the health care system through electronic data interchange.

The privacy rule of HIPAA took effect April 14, 2003. The goal of HIPAA's privacy rule is to ensure the patient's health information is protected while still allowing needed health information exchange for quality health care. A balance must be achieved to protect patient rights and still allow for the correct sharing of health information.

STOP AND PRACTICE

Exercise 2-1

Fill in the blank for each statement.

1. Because of today's technology, physicians are treating patients with a/an _____ and more _____ outcome.

2. The clinical staff can receive instantaneous information on a patient from _____ and _____.

3. The billing department will be exchanging information to _____ and _____.

4. All treatment and administrative processes must be _____ and saved in the patient's medical record.

5. EMR is the _____ a paperless medical record.

Short answer: Answer each question with a short statement.

6. Describe what is required on the fax cover sheet.

   _____

   _____

   _____

7. Describe a fax disclaimer.

   _____

   _____

   _____

8. Name three uses for the photocopy machine in the billing department.

   _____

   _____

   _____

9. Describe three uses for the computer in the billing department.

   _____

   _____

   _____

The Privacy rule of HIPAA applies to health plans, clearinghouses, and health care providers who transmit health information electronically. Protected Health Information (PHI) is protected by the privacy rule whether information is transmitted electronically, by paper, or orally.

HIPAA requires all providers, healthcare clearinghouses, and large health plans use only the **National Provider Identifier (NPI)** on all electronic transactions. The NPI replaces all other identifiers used by health plans, such as Medicare's UPIN. The NPI does not replace the provider's DEA number, state license number, or tax identification number. The NPI is 10 digits (it can be alphanumeric), unique, and used nationally. You can read this act in its entirety on the US Dept. of Health and Human Services Web site.

What does all this mean for the reimbursement specialist? Whenever information is sent on a patient, particularly electronically, you must obtain a **release of information** form signed by your patient. This release form gives the medical office authorization to send private medical information to the insurance company. This exchange of information is essential for the reimbursement process. Any additional exchange of patient information, such as attorneys' requests or liability case requests, requires additional releases from the patient. Patients must know where and how their private medical information is being used. See Figure 2-3 for a common release of information.

There will be other specific office protocols. Telephone calls regarding patients' bills should be carefully screened. Knowing whom the billing office is talking with should be carefully examined. If possible, the billing specialist should talk only with patients themselves, and check to verify the patient's identity. Asking specific questions only the patient would know is one way to verify identity. Social Security numbers, telephone numbers, or treatment specifics are personalized questions you can use to verify the speaker's identity.

STOP AND PRACTICE

Exercise 2-2

Define the following key terms.

1. HIPAA

_____

_____

2. Compliance

_____

_____

3. Release of information

_____

_____

Authorization for Release of Medical Record Information

Name: _____   Date of Birth: _____

Address: _____   Medical Record No.: _____

City: _____   State: _____ Zip: _____

Telephone No.: _____

I hereby authorize:

Name: _____   Address: _____

City: _____   State: _____ Zip: _____

to disclose information from my / my minor child's medical records to (name and address):

Name: _____   Address: _____

City: _____   State: _____ Zip: _____

I hereby authorize redisclosure of this information to:

Name: _____   Address: _____

City: _____   State: _____ Zip: _____

This information is needed for the following reason:

The specific information I wish to have released is (included dates of treatment):

I understand that I may revoke this consent at any time, except where information has already been released. This authorization is valid for a sixty (60) day period from the date it is signed.

          Signature: (Parent or Legal Guardian if Minor Child)   Date:

Expires:

Witness:

This medical record may contain information about drug abuse, alcoholism, alcohol abuse, venereal disease, abortion, or mental health treatment. Separate consent must be given before this information can be released.

☐ DO consent to have this information disclosed.
☐ DO NOT consent to have this information disclosed.

          Signature: (Parent or Legal Guardian if Minor Child)   Date:

This medical record may contain information concerning HIV testing and/or AIDS diagnosis treatment. Separate consent must be given before this information can be released.

☐ DO consent to have this information disclosed.
☐ DO NOT consent to have this information disclosed.

          Signature: (Parent or Legal Guardian if Minor Child)   Date:

Figure 2-3. Sample release of information

PROFESSIONALISM

All of the training involved in medical billing can seem challenging. Attention to detail skills will be put to the test. Always remember the reimbursement specialist is a part of a very important health care team. Working together ensures an office will run smoothly and efficiently, keeping health care costs down, while administering quality care for the patient. Treating patients with care and respect is the common goal for all members of the health care team. Remembering many sick or injured patients can become irritable; keeping a positive attitude should be first and foremost.

What is **professionalism**? It is how the specialist will look, talk, write, act, and work. Professionalism is a behavior that must be learned. It will determine your success as a reimbursement specialist. This includes technical knowledge as well as interpersonal relationships within the medical office. Following is a list of the characteristics of professionalism. Notice how closely they match the personal and professional qualifications discussed in Chapter 1.

CHARACTERISTICS OF PROFESSIONALISM

1. **Skill based on technical knowledge**

2. **Professional associations**

3. **Education**

4. **Competence testing**

5. **Code of conduct and ethics**

6. **Positive attitude**

Developing these characteristics not only for medical careers but in everyday life is essential. It is a matter of attitude and behavior. Willingness to learn, knowledge of the job, getting along with other members of the medical office, respect, integrity, and living up to commitments will help the reimbursement specialist be successful in this new profession.

STOP AND PRACTICE

Exercise 2-3

Fill in the blank for each statement.

1. Working in a medical team ensures an office will run _____ and _____.

2. An important goal in the medical office is to keep health care _____ down while administering _____ care for the patient.

3. Treating patients with _____ and _____ is a common goal for all members of the medical team.

4. Professionalism is how you _____ and _____.

5. Professionalism will determine your _____ as a reimbursement specialist.

Short answer: Answer each question with a short statement.

6. Identify the six characteristics of professionalism.

   _____

   _____

   _____

   _____

7. Professionalism is a matter of attitude and behavior, describe some of these behaviors.

   _____

   _____

   _____

   _____

CHAPTER SUMMARY

- Following office procedures and policies ensures effective and efficient office management.

- Technology today allows instantaneous exchange of medical information electronically.

- Office equipment helps the reimbursement specialist with efficient claim submission.

- Essential office equipment includes: fax machine, photocopy machine, computer, and electronic swipe devices.

- The patient's medical record is a legal document and must be unaltered and legible. Some facilities are using the electronic medical record (EMR).

- Faxes require a cover sheet with a disclaimer; care must be used for confidential reasons.

- The photocopy machine is the most-used piece of office equipment in the office. The billing department uses it for referrals, copying EOBs, and claim forms.

- Computers have revolutionized the submission of health claims. They are important tools for informational uses.

- HIPAA's privacy rule protects the patient's private health information.

- Release of information documents are required by HIPAA. This gives the patient control over their own health information.

- Professionalism is a behavior learned in the medical field. It includes skill and technical knowledge, professional associations, proficiency testing, code of conduct and ethics, and positive attitude.

REVIEW QUESTIONS

Short answer: Answer each question with a short statement.

1. Why is instantaneous information so important in the medical office today?

   _____

   _____

   _____

   _____

   _____

2. Describe the flow of the medical office and how the clinical and administrative departments interact together.

   _____

   _____

   _____

   _____

   _____

3. Name the essential office equipment and how it is used in the medical billing department.

   _____

   _____

   _____

   _____

4. Explain the patient's medical record.

   _____

   _____

   _____

   _____

Matching: Match the office equipment with its use.

_____ 5. Facsimile machine A. Important tool for claims submission

_____ 6. Computer B. A standard informational tool

_____ 7. Electronic swipe device C. Credit-card-type point of service device

_____ 8. Telephone D. Electronic exchange of information using photo sensors and a phone line

True or False: Choose the correct answer for each question.

_____ 9. The fax disclaimer is optional for the medical office.

_____ 10. The fax cover sheet includes the sender's name, address, phone number and fax number.

_____ 11. The computer cannot check the status of health claims.

_____ 12. Electronic swipe devices check the patient's insurance eligibility.

_____ 13. HIPAA was created as a possible answer to insurance denials.

_____ 14. HIPAA stands for Health Information Policy and Accountability Act.

Multiple choice: Pick the best answer to each question.

15. The Privacy Rule indicates you should scrutinize telephone calls by:
    A. asking for the callers Social Security number
    B. asking the caller for their phone number
    C. asking the caller for treatment specifics
    D. all of the above

16. A reimbursement specialist should always treat the patient with:
    A. care and respect
    B. a positive attitude
    C. business-like coolness
    D. both A and B

17. Professionalism is:
    A. not important in the medical field
    B. a characteristic you were born with
    C. how you look, talk, write, act and work
    D. only for physicians

18. Characteristics of professionalism include:
    A. being detail-oriented
    B. skill based on technical knowledge
    C. working independently without regard to the medical team
    D. all of the above

19. HIPAA stands for:

    A.   Help in Professional Attitude and Accountability

    B.   Healthcare Initiative for Positive Attitude and Accountability

    C.   Health Insurance Portability and Accountability Act

    D.   none of the above

PRACTICAL APPLICATION

Research and write a short report on one of the following topics:

- HIPAA

- Medical Office Technology

- Professionalism

Do a formal presentation to the class on the research.

CODING BASICS

Chapter 3

Patient Information

OBJECTIVES

Upon completion of this chapter, the student should be able to:

- Outline medical office dynamics.
- Define the collection of patient demographics.
- Define clean claims.
- Outline the CMS-1500 form.

INTRODUCTION

Understanding how a medical office flows and how the reimbursement specialist fits into the team environment will help in collecting the correct information from the patient. This is the first and most important step in the reimbursement process. Correct information will save time and money in the medical billing department. We will explore how and what kind of information is important to this concept of clean claims.

REVIEW

We explored some important information in the first two chapters of this textbook. The learner should now understand the reimbursement specialist's job description and the personal and professional qualifications needed for the job. The learner has studied the kind of certifications needed for this new career, and what professionalism is. We have briefly explained the terms health insurance, health claims, and medical reimbursement. Let's review some of this important information.

Health insurance is a written contract, or policy, between an individual (or **policyholder**) and an insurance company. The policyholder pays the insurance company a **premium**, a monthly payment. The insurance company will pay medical costs as set up in the written contract. Not all contracts or policies are the same. The **policy** is a certificate of coverage that outlines what medical costs are covered and what services are not covered.

There are three parties involved in this contract: the policyholder, the insurance company, and the physician. The policyholder is the **first party**, the physician is the **second party**, and the **third party** is the insurance company.

CLEAN CLAIMS

When a patient is treated by the physician, it is up to the reimbursement specialist to send a bill or claim to the insurance company for services rendered. This claim is the most important first step in the reimbursement process. A reimbursement specialist will collect all the necessary information from the patient and clinical staff to send in a clean claim. A **clean claim** is a claim that has all of the necessary and correct information the insurance company needs for a full and correct reimbursement. The information will be compiled and entered into the offices' medical billing software, which is formatted to the universal outpatient billing claim form, the **CMS-1500 form**. Figure 3-1 is the CMS-1500 form. We will be working with this form in detail throughout this textbook.

All of the information collected and formatted to the CMS-1500 form is then submitted to the third-party payer (the insurance company) for payment (reimbursement). Without the correct information on the CMS-1500 form, the insurance company will pay incorrectly or not at all. With the correct

STOP AND PRACTICE

Exercise 3-1

Matching: Match the key terms.

1. _____ Policyholder   A.   Certificate of coverage
2. _____ Premium   B.   Insurance company
3. _____ Policy   C.   Policy holder's payment for benefits
4. _____ First party   D.   The patient
5. _____ Second party   E.   The insured
6. _____ Third party   F.   The physician

Define the following key terms.

7. Insurance policy

_____

_____

_____

8. Premium

_____

_____

information collected and submitted, the insurance companies should pay the claim in 30 days or less. This correct and timely reimbursement of the claim will save the reimbursement specialist time and effort in the insurance follow-up phase of their job.

What information is required by the insurance company? First, they require patient-demographic information. As we discussed in Chapter 1, this is personal information about the patient. The insurance companies require an **authorization** to bill this claim, or a release of information statement, signed by the patient. This release-of-information statement was discussed in Chapter 2. It authorizes the physician's office to release private medical information to the insurance company. The patient is also asked to sign an **assignment of benefit** statement. This statement authorizes the insurance company to pay the provider directly. Payment for services rendered will not be paid to the patient. It is important for the medical office to receive and process all payments for fast and efficient reimbursement.

The insurance company will require the medical codes that represent the services and procedures performed for the patient by the physician. The last piece of the CMS-1500 claim form requires information about the physician: his or her name, address, and tax information. All this information is required by the insurance company in order to recognize the policyholder, what benefits (services) the company will reimburse, and where to send the payment.

1500

HEALTH INSURANCE CLAIM FORM

APPROVED BY NATIONAL UNIFORM CLAIM COMMITTEE 08/05

PICA   PICA

1. MEDICARE	MEDICAID	TRICARE CHAMPUS	CHAMPVA	GROUP HEALTH PLAN	FECA BLK LUNG	OTHER	1a. INSURED'S I.D. NUMBER	(For Program in Item 1)
(Medicare #)	(Medicaid #)	(Sponsor's SSN)	(Member ID#)	(SSN or ID)	(SSN)	(ID)		

2. PATIENT'S NAME (Last Name, First Name, Middle Initial)

3. PATIENT'S BIRTH DATE MM DD YY   SEX   M   F

4. INSURED'S NAME (Last Name, First Name, Middle Initial)

5. PATIENT'S ADDRESS (No., Street)

6. PATIENT RELATIONSHIP TO INSURED   Self   Spouse   Child   Other

7. INSURED'S ADDRESS (No., Street)

CITY   STATE

8. PATIENT STATUS   Single   Married   Other

CITY   STATE

ZIP CODE   TELEPHONE (Include Area Code) (   )

Employed   Full-Time Student   Part-Time Student

ZIP CODE   TELEPHONE (Include Area Code) (   )

9. OTHER INSURED'S NAME (Last Name, First Name, Middle Initial)

10. IS PATIENT'S CONDITION RELATED TO:

11. INSURED'S POLICY GROUP OR FECA NUMBER

a. OTHER INSURED'S POLICY OR GROUP NUMBER

a. EMPLOYMENT? (Current or Previous)   YES   NO

a. INSURED'S DATE OF BIRTH MM DD YY   SEX   M   F

b. OTHER INSURED'S DATE OF BIRTH MM DD YY   SEX   M   F

b. AUTO ACCIDENT?   PLACE (State)   YES   NO

b. EMPLOYER'S NAME OR SCHOOL NAME

c. EMPLOYER'S NAME OR SCHOOL NAME

c. OTHER ACCIDENT?   YES   NO

c. INSURANCE PLAN NAME OR PROGRAM NAME

d. INSURANCE PLAN NAME OR PROGRAM NAME

10d. RESERVED FOR LOCAL USE

d. IS THERE ANOTHER HEALTH BENEFIT PLAN?   YES   NO   *If yes*, return to and complete item 9 a-d.

READ BACK OF FORM BEFORE COMPLETING & SIGNING THIS FORM.

12. PATIENT'S OR AUTHORIZED PERSON'S SIGNATURE I authorize the release of any medical or other information necessary to process this claim. I also request payment of government benefits either to myself or to the party who accepts assignment below.

SIGNED _____   DATE _____

13. INSURED'S OR AUTHORIZED PERSON'S SIGNATURE I authorize payment of medical benefits to the undersigned physician or supplier for services described below.

SIGNED _____

14. DATE OF CURRENT: MM DD YY   ILLNESS (First symptom) OR INJURY (Accident) OR PREGNANCY(LMP)

15. IF PATIENT HAS HAD SAME OR SIMILAR ILLNESS. GIVE FIRST DATE MM DD YY

16. DATES PATIENT UNABLE TO WORK IN CURRENT OCCUPATION FROM MM DD YY   TO MM DD YY

17. NAME OF REFERRING PROVIDER OR OTHER SOURCE

17a.
17b. NPI

18. HOSPITALIZATION DATES RELATED TO CURRENT SERVICES FROM MM DD YY   TO MM DD YY

19. RESERVED FOR LOCAL USE

20. OUTSIDE LAB?   YES   NO $ CHARGES

21. DIAGNOSIS OR NATURE OF ILLNESS OR INJURY (Relate Items 1, 2, 3 or 4 to Item 24E by Line)

1. ___.___   3. ___.___

2. ___.___   4. ___.___

22. MEDICAID RESUBMISSION CODE   ORIGINAL REF. NO.

23. PRIOR AUTHORIZATION NUMBER

24. A. DATE(S) OF SERVICE						B. PLACE OF SERVICE	C. EMG	D. PROCEDURES, SERVICES, OR SUPPLIES (Explain Unusual Circumstances)		E. DIAGNOSIS POINTER	F. $ CHARGES	G. DAYS OR UNITS	H. EPSDT Family Plan	I. ID. QUAL.	J. RENDERING PROVIDER ID. #
From MM	DD	YY	To MM	DD	YY			CPT/HCPCS	MODIFIER						
1														NPI	
2														NPI	
3														NPI	
4														NPI	
5														NPI	
6														NPI	

25. FEDERAL TAX I.D. NUMBER   SSN   EIN

26. PATIENT'S ACCOUNT NO.

27. ACCEPT ASSIGNMENT? (For govt. claims, see back)   YES   NO

28. TOTAL CHARGE $

29. AMOUNT PAID $

30. BALANCE DUE $

31. SIGNATURE OF PHYSICIAN OR SUPPLIER INCLUDING DEGREES OR CREDENTIALS (I certify that the statements on the reverse apply to this bill and are made a part thereof.)

SIGNED _____   DATE _____

32. SERVICE FACILITY LOCATION INFORMATION

a. NPI   b.

33. BILLING PROVIDER INFO & PH # (   )

a. NPI   b.

NUCC Instruction Manual available at: www.nucc.org

APPROVED OMB-0938-0999 FORM CMS-1500 (08-05)

CARRIER

PATIENT AND INSURED INFORMATION

PHYSICIAN OR SUPPLIER INFORMATION

Figure 3-1. CMS-1500 form

STOP AND PRACTICE

Exercise 3-2

Short answer: Answer each question with a short statement.

1. Explain what a clean claim is.

   _____

   _____

   _____

   _____

   _____

2. What is a third-party payer?

   _____

   _____

   _____

   _____

   _____

3. What is a release-of-information statement?

   _____

   _____

   _____

   _____

   _____

Fill in the blanks for each statement.

4. Most insurance companies will pay a claim in _____ days or less.

5. The _____ form is a universal outpatient health claim form.

6. A clean claim will save you _____ and _____ if the correct information is collected from the patient.

7. Patient _____ information includes his or her name, address, telephone number, and insurance information.

8. Patient information is collected and _____ to the CMS-1500 form and _____ to the insurance company.

OFFICE DYNAMICS

Before we look at the detailed information required by the insurance company, let's look at the office dynamics or flow of the office. This will help clarify how the information collection process starts. In Chapter 2, Figure 2-1 demonstrates the flow of the office. Let's look at this illustration again and expand on this flow through the office.

1. The patient calls the medical office for an appointment.

2. The patient checks in at the reception area in the office.

3. The patient fills in a registration form and insurance is verified at check in.

4. The patient's co-pay is collected.

5. The patient is seen in the clinical area of the medical office.

6. The patient sees the nurse, medical assistant, or physician. Any ancillary services are performed.

7. The physician and his assistant document services performed.

8. Using the patient's encounter form and physician documentation, medical codes are assigned.

9. The patient's demographic information and medical codes are entered into the billing software.

10. The patient's claim is submitted electronically to the insurance company.

11. Insurance follow-up occurs, if needed.

12. Collections process (from the patient).

Making the Appointment

The patient's first contact with the medical office is his or her telephone call to set up an appointment. The efficiency of medical office schedulers is very important. They perform the first step in the account-receivable process by collecting the initial patient demographics. The scheduler should ask the patient his or her legal name, complete address, telephone number, and insurance information. This initial information is very important. Only with the correct information will a clean claim result.

Exercise 3-3

Short answer: Answer each question with a short statement.

1. Explain why an efficient medical scheduler is so important to the collection of patient demographics.

_____

_____

_____

_____

2. Explain the 12 steps that illustrate the office flow for the patient.

_____

_____

_____

_____

_____

_____

_____

_____

_____

_____

_____

_____

_____

_____

Check-in

Explaining the steps of the check-in process is very important. This process will be the medical offices' first face-to-face contact with the patient. Collecting the patient's demographic information is essential to billing the clean claim.

The Patient Registration Form

Many offices will send information to new patients ahead of their scheduled appointment, including a **patient registration form**. A patient registration form will help collect information for both the reimbursement specialist and the clinical staff. Figure 3-2 illustrates a common registration form used in the medical office. Offices may use different registration form formats, but the information collected will be the same.

For the billing department, the registration form is important but, interviewing the patient and double-checking this information is a must. This will be the opportunity for the reimbursement specialist to have the patient sign the release of information statement. Again, the release of information

Patient Registration Form

Patient's Name:_____ SS #: _____

First Name   Middle   Last Name

Date of Birth:_____ ☐ Male ☐ Female   ☐Single ☐Married ☐Widowed ☐Divorced ☐Separated

Street Address: _____

City/State/Zip Code: _____   Home Phone w/Area Code: _____

    Cell Phone w/Area Code: _____   Fax w/Area Code: _____

Spouse's Name: _____   SS #: _____

Spouse's Employer: _____   Spouse's Work Phone #:_____

Patient's Employer:_____   Work Phone w/Area Code:_____

Credit: (Circle) MC Visa # _____ Exp __/__/___ Name on card _____

Responsible Party: _____   Relationship: ☐Self ☐Spouse ☐Parent ☐Other

If patient is a Minor, are parents ☐Married ☐Divorced Custodial Parent:_____

    Custodial Parent's Home Phone w/Area Code:_____ Work Phone w/Area Code:_____

    Custodial Parent's SS #: _____ Date of Birth: _____

In case of emergency, contact (not living with you): _____

    Phone Number w/Area Code: _____ Relationship to Patient:_____

Is this injury work-related?☐Yes☐No If yes, date of injury?_____ Claim #:_____

    How did this injury happen?_____

Referring Physician's Name & Phone Number:_____

<u>PLEASE PRESENT INSURANCE CARD(S) & PHOTO ID FOR COPYING AND COMPLETE THE REQUESTED INFORMATION</u>

Insurance Company # 1:_____   Phone Number: _____

    Primary Insured's Name: _____   Date of Birth:_____

    Policy #:_____   Group #: _____   Relationship:_____

Insurance Company # 2:_____   Phone Number: _____

    Primary Insured's Name: _____   Date of Birth:_____

    Policy #:_____   Group #: _____   Relationship:_____

If you do not have insurance, have you applied for Medicaid?☐Yes ☐No If yes, what is the name and phone number of the social worker with whom you are working?

_____

- I hereby authorize the payment of medical benefits to _____ for services rendered. I understand that I am financially responsible for any services not covered by my insurance carrier.
- I further agree to pay all collections costs, attorney fees, and other collections costs that may be incurred to enforce the collection of any amounts outstanding.
- I hereby authorize _____to release any medical information necessary to complete and process my insurance claims.

Patient's OR Insured's Signature (If patient is a Minor, must have Responsible Party Signature)   Date

I authorize Dr._____ to treat me and use my personal health information for healthcare operations.

Patient's Signature (OR Parent if patient is a Minor)   Date

Figure 3-2. Sample patient registration form

statement is an authorization signed by the patient allowing the billing information to be sent the insurance company.

The patient is authorizing the release of only the information that pertains to the current visit with the physician. The following demonstrates a common release used for this purpose. This release can be incorporated on the encounter form and kept on file in the billing department.

- I authorize the payment of medical benefits to _____ for services rendered.

- I authorize _____ to release any medical information necessary to bill my insurance claim.

- I understand I am financially responsible for any services not covered by my insurance carrier.

The Encounter Form

The **encounter form**, or **super bill**, is a billing document used by the medical office to document clinical information on each patient at each visit or encounter. The patient demographic information is always printed on the form as well. Common office services and diagnoses are preprinted on the encounter form for the physician and medical assistant to check off as the patient is seen in the office. The encounter form will include office visit level, any procedure performed, **ancillary charges** (e.g., lab or x-ray), and diagnosis for the current visit. When the patient checks out at the end of the visit, the encounter form is presented to the reimbursement specialist. This makes the exchange of information from the clinical team to the billing department quick and efficient. The encounter form will be discussed in depth later in the textbook. See Figure 3-3 for an example of an encounter form.

Insurance Verification

Insurance verification is a crucial step during the check-in process. This will ensure that the reimbursement specialist has all the correct information required by the insurance company. **Insurance verification** involves checking the patient's eligibility for insurance benefits with their insurance company. Insurance verification should involve making a copy of the patient's insurance card. A copy of both the front and back of the card will ensure that the reimbursement specialist has the correct **certificate and group numbers**. The certificate number is issued to the policy holder by the insurance company as a method to recognize the benefits in the insurance contract for the patient. The policy holder's group number will help the insurance company identify benefits if the policy holder is covered under a group policy through their place of employment. Insurance verification can be accomplished using the telephone, Internet, or electronic swipe box devices. Another important item on the insurance card is the address and telephone number of the insurance company, which should be located on the back of the insurance card.

Outpatient Encounter Form

Patient Information		Payment Method		Visit Information	
Patient ID number		**Primary**		Visit date	
Patient name		Primary ID number		Visit number	
Address		Primary group number		Rendering physician	
City/State		**Secondary**		Referring physician	
Social Security number		Secondary ID number		Reason for visit	
Phone number		Secondary group no.			
Date of birth		Cash/credit card			
Age		Other billing			

E/M Modifiers	Procedure Modifiers	Other Modifiers
24 — Unrelated E/M service during postop.	22 — Unusual, excessive procedure	
25 — Significant, separately identifiable E/M	50 — Bilateral procedure	
57 — Decision for surgery	51 — Multiple surgical procedures in same day	
	52 — Reduced/incomplete procedure	
	55 — Postop. management only	
	59 — Distinct multiple procedures	

CATEGORY	CODE	MOD	FEE	CATEGORY	CODE	MOD	FEE
Office Visit — New Patient				**Wound Care**			
Minimal office visit	99201			Debride partial thick burn	11040		
20 minutes	99202			Debride full thickness burn	11041		
30 minutes	99203			Debride wound, not a burn	11000		
45 minutes	99204			Unna boot application	29580		
60 minutes	99205			Unna boot removal	29700		
Other				Other			
Office Visit — Established				**Supplies**			
Minimal office visit	99211			Ace bandage, 2"	A6448		
10 minutes	99212			Ace bandage, 3"–4"	A6449		
15 minutes	99213			Ace bandage, 6"	A6450		
25 minutes	99214			Cast, fiberglass	A4590		
40 minutes	99215			Coban wrap	A6454		
Other				Foley catheter	A4338		
General Procedures				Immobilizer	L3670		
Anascopy	46600			Kerlix roll	A6220		
Audiometry	92551			Oxygen mask/cannula	A4620		
Breast aspiration	19000			Sleeve, elbow	E0191		
Cerumen removal	69210			Sling	A4565		
Circumcision	54150			Splint, ready-made	A4570		
DDST	96110			Splint, wrist	S8451		
Flex sigmoidoscopy	45330			Sterile packing	A6407		
Flex sig. w/biopsy	45331			Surgical tray	A4550		
Foreign body removal—foot	28190			Other			
Nail removal	11730			**OB Care**			
Nail removal/phenol	11750			Routine OB care	59400		
Trigger point injection	20552			OB call	59422		
Tympanometry	92567			Ante partum 4–6 visits	59425		
Visual acuity	99173			Ante partum 7 or more visits	59426		
Other				Other			

Vitals:
B/P _____
Pulse _____
Temp. _____
Height _____
Weight _____

Other Visit Information:
Lab Work to Order: _____
Referral to: _____
Provider Signature: _____
Next Appointment: _____

Fees:
Total Charges: $_____
Copay Received: $_____
Other Payment: $_____
Total Due: $_____

Company Name, Street Address, City, State ZIP Code, phone number

Figure 3-3. Sample outpatient encounter form

STOP AND PRACTICE

Exercise 3-4

Multiple choice: Pick the best answer to each question.

1. The patient registration form:

    A. is an authorization for the release of information

    B. assigns benefit payment to the physician

    C. helps collect important patient demographic information

    D. none of the above

2. The release of information statement is:

    A. an authorization signed by the patient to send billing information to the insurance company

    B. collects clinical information for the billing department

    C. lists the services, procedures, and ancillary charges

    D. a statement of insurance benefits

3. Insurance verification involves:

    A. interviewing the patient for past medical illnesses

    B. checking the patient's eligibility for insurance benefits

    C. entering information into medical billing software

    D. all of the above

4. Insurance verification can be accomplished by using:

    A. the telephone

    B. the Internet

    C. swipe box devices

    D. all of the above

5. The super bill is a/an:

    A. large medical bill

    B. a special bill for procedures performed by the physician

    C. encounter form

    D. both A. and C.

Clinical Services

At this point, the patient will be taken to the clinical area of the medical office to see the physician. All services and procedures, as well as any ancillary services, will be marked on the encounter form. The physician will also mark the diagnosis for the patient encounter. These are represented by medical codes and we will examine these codes in Chapter 6.

The most important point for the reimbursement specialist in this phase of the billing process is the physician documentation. Every encounter with a patient must be documented by the physician and the documentation must support the services performed. Medical insurance companies may **audit** a medical office for documentation to support the level of service billed to them. An audit involves the insurance company examining the medical records for the claim they are processing.

Checkout

As the patient finishes his visit with the physician, he or she will be directed to the check-out section of the billing office. The reimbursement specialist will again have contact with the patient and the opportunity to talk with him or her regarding the insurance information. The reimbursement specialist will be checking the co-pay that was collected for the visit and answering any questions the patient may have regarding the payment process. A **co-pay** is a monetary payment predetermined by his or her insurance contract for a physician's visit.

Claim Submission

As each patient is checked out after the office visit, it is important to collect the encounter form. This form has vital information regarding the patient's visit, billing information, and release of information signed by the patient. The day after the patient's visit, all encounter forms for that date are checked against a list of patients seen. It is an important routine to double-check this list, making sure the billing department has all the encounter forms for that date of service. This is done to ensure a patient did not accidentally take the encounter form out of the office. Encounter forms can also be lost in the check-out process.

Once all the encounter forms are accounted for, the medical coder will check the codes for accuracy, audit some of the services, and authorize the charges to be entered into the billing software (charge entry). Accuracy at the charge entry level is a must. As stated previously, these are not just codes on paper; they represent a person. The billed code submitted to a health insurance company becomes a legal record. As a reimbursement specialist, you would not want a patient having an incorrect diagnosis recorded on a legal document.

The medical billing software program compiles all the information you have carefully recorded and formats the information to the CMS-1500 form, either on paper or to the electronic format. The reimbursement specialist can then download all of the claims recorded and send them to the insurance company. This is called **claim submission**.

Exercise 3-5

True or False: Choose the correct answer for each question.

_____ 1. An audit is done by an insurance company to check the documentation that supports a level of service performed and billed.

_____ 2. At checkout, a reimbursement specialist will have the opportunity to collect for the bill in full.

_____ 3. Claim submission is done on the encounter form.

_____ 4. Charge entry is the process of entering medical codes into a medical software program.

_____ 5. The CMS-1500 form is the universal health claim billing form.

_____ 6. On the CMS-1500 form, patient information is always the same as the insured's information.

Cash Flow

The collection of patient information for a health claim can be a laborious but worthwhile process. Making sure all the information is correct from the beginning will ensure the health claim is a clean claim. The clean claim will save time and money in the account receivable process if it is minimally handled by the reimbursement specialist and insurance company.

Let's look closer at all the important information you have collected. Patient demographics identify the patient for correct insurance benefit recognition. It is also important to remember the patient is not always the **insured** (or policy holder). Many families are covered by health insurance under a family member who is the insured. Carefully entering the correct information regarding the patient and the insured is important.

If children are covered under an insurance policy, different rules will apply. If only one parent is covered by an insurance policy, they are the insured and the child will be the patient. If both parents have insurance policies, the primary insurance (first insurance billed) will be determined by the birthday rule. Gender no longer plays a part in the determination of the primary insurance. Whichever parent's birthday comes first *in the year* will be the primary policy holder for the children covered by the insurance company. As an example, suppose Jane and Ron Smith have a child, Jessica, who is covered by both parents' insurance policies. Jane's birthday is Feb. 3, 1965 and Ron's birthday is Aug. 30, 1964. Jane's insurance policy would be the primary insurance for Jessica.

Collecting the patient's or insured's name appears to be an easy task, but it can be tricky. Many people use a nick-name or shortened versions of their legal name. It is important to remember the name used on the health claim form must exactly match the name on the insurance policy. If it does not, the insurance company will deny the claim. A correction must be made, which takes time, effort, and a delay in reimbursement for your physician. The encounter form information will be discussed in detail in the charge entry chapter.

Insurance companies want to know information regarding the patient, the insured, and the physician. They require data regarding any accident information, as well as a signed release of information from the patient per governmental regulations (HIPAA). Why is all this information required? Insurance companies need to know all of this information to determine the correct reimbursement based on their contract with the patient. The important items to remember when collecting patient information for a clean claim are:

- Take the time to collect all information from the start.
- Ask appropriate questions to get the correct information.
- Know what information is required for each payer (insurance company).

Remember, a clean claim will save your physician time and money.

When the reimbursement specialist has successfully collected the required patient information, a clean claim has been produced. Remember, a clean claim equals cash flow for your physician.

STOP AND PRACTICE

Exercise 3-6

Short answer: Answer each question with a short statement.

1. Explain the birthday rule.

    _____

    _____

    _____

    _____

2. What is a clean claim and why is it important?

    _____

    _____

    _____

    _____

CHAPTER SUMMARY

- Health insurance is a contract between a policy holder/insured and an insurance company for predetermined benefits.

- The policy holder pays a premium to the insurance company for the predetermined benefit payments.

- An insurance policy involves the first party (patient), the second party (physician), and the third party (insurance company).

- Health claims are billed on a CMS-1500 form.

- The health claim requires correct patient demographic information, the insured's information, clinical information, and a release of information.

- Understanding the flow of a medical office helps the reimbursement specialist collect the correct patient information.

- An encounter form, or super bill, is used to document correct office visit information.

- Insurance verification is essential to every office encounter.

- The physician must document each visit and this documentation is a legal document.

- A clean claim is the correct billing information collected by the reimbursement specialist. A clean claim equals cash flow.

REVIEW QUESTIONS

Fill in the blank for each statement.

1. Health insurance is a/an _____ between the insured and an insurance company.

2. The _____ is a payment to the insurance company for health care reimbursement.

3. An insurance policy involves the first party, or _____, the second party, or _____, and the third party, or _____.

4. The health claim requires correct patient _____ information.

5. The _____ form is used to document correct office visit information.

6. A/An _____ claim equals _____ flow.

Short answer: Answer each question with a short statement.

7. Describe the information found on an encounter form.

_____

_____

_____

_____

_____

_____

8. Explain insurance verification and how this might be accomplished.

_____

_____

_____

_____

_____

_____

9. Why is the correct collection of patient demographics important for reimbursement?

_____

_____

_____

_____

_____

_____

10. Why would an insurance company audit a physician's documentation?

_____

_____

_____

_____

_____

PRACTICAL APPLICATION

The learners should be in groups of two. Collect the pertinent information from each other as if you were new patients entering a physician's office. Using the forms in the back of the textbook, make out a new patient registration form, an encounter form, and a release-of-information form.

Chapter 4

CMS-1500 Form

OBJECTIVES

Upon completion of this chapter, the student should be able to:

- Define the importance of collecting correct patient demographic information for a clean claim.
- Specify who developed the health claim billing form.
- Identify each block on the CMS-1500 form.
- Explain the recent changes to the CMS-1500 form.
- State some common errors submitted on the CMS-1500 form.

KEY TERMS

CMS-1500 claim form

Coordination of benefits

Electronic claim submission (ECS)

Electronic data interchange (EDI)

Health Care Financing Administration (HCFA)

Health Insurance Portability and Accountability Act (HIPAA)

National Provider Number (NPI)

National Standard Format (NSF)

Scrubber

The American National Standard Institute (ANSI)

INTRODUCTION

It is essential for the reimbursement specialist to be an expert in the information required for every insurance claim. Understanding every single block on the CMS-1500 form and each insurance company's requirements will produce a clean claim. The clean claim will ensure the correct reimbursement, which is the ultimate goal for every medical billing department.

PATIENT INFORMATION

Collecting the correct information from the patient as discussed in Chapter 3 of this text is the first step in the claim submission process. Entering this important information into the medical billing software program on the computer is equally important. All demographic information, medical codes for services, and provider information are used for billing each date of service to the insurance company. This is accomplished by the medical billing software compiling the information and producing a claim on a standardized **CMS-1500 claim form**.

STOP AND PRACTICE

Exercise 4-1

Short answer: Answer each question with a short statement.

1. What information is important to collect and enter for the CMS-1500 billing form?

   _____

   _____

2. What is the standardized health claim billing form?

   _____

   _____

CMS-1500 FORM

The CMS-1500 form (universal billing form), originally developed by the **Health Care Financing Administration (HCFA)** standardized the billing systems for Medicare claims. Other healthcare payers accepted the form as well. The original form was called the HCFA 1500 form adopted by the American Medical Association in 1975.

Over the years, Medicare has revised this HCFA form and it is now called the CMS-1500 form. CMS is the Centers for Medicare & Medicaid Services. The paper format of the CMS-1500 form has also undergone many changes. The most recent format change was released and was effective July 1, 2007. See the CMS-1500 form shown in Figure 4-1.

CODING BASICS

1500

HEALTH INSURANCE CLAIM FORM

APPROVED BY NATIONAL UNIFORM CLAIM COMMITTEE 08/05

| (Medicare #) | (Medicaid #) | (Sponsor's SSN) | (Member ID#) | (SSN or ID) | (SSN) | (ID) |

PICA | | PICA

CARRIER

1. MEDICARE   MEDICAID   TRICARE CHAMPUS   CHAMPVA   GROUP HEALTH PLAN   FECA BLK LUNG   OTHER
(Medicare #)   (Medicaid #)   (Sponsor's SSN)   (Member ID#)   (SSN or ID)   (SSN)   (ID)

1a. INSURED'S I.D. NUMBER   (For Program in Item 1)

2. PATIENT'S NAME (Last Name, First Name, Middle Initial)

3. PATIENT'S BIRTH DATE   MM DD YY   SEX   M   F

4. INSURED'S NAME (Last Name, First Name, Middle Initial)

5. PATIENT'S ADDRESS (No., Street)

6. PATIENT RELATIONSHIP TO INSURED   Self   Spouse   Child   Other

7. INSURED'S ADDRESS (No., Street)

CITY   STATE

8. PATIENT STATUS   Single   Married   Other

CITY   STATE

ZIP CODE   TELEPHONE (Include Area Code)   (   )

Employed   Full-Time Student   Part-Time Student

ZIP CODE   TELEPHONE (Include Area Code)   (   )

PATIENT AND INSURED INFORMATION

9. OTHER INSURED'S NAME (Last Name, First Name, Middle Initial)

10. IS PATIENT'S CONDITION RELATED TO:

11. INSURED'S POLICY GROUP OR FECA NUMBER

a. OTHER INSURED'S POLICY OR GROUP NUMBER

a. EMPLOYMENT? (Current or Previous)   YES   NO

a. INSURED'S DATE OF BIRTH   MM DD YY   SEX   M   F

b. OTHER INSURED'S DATE OF BIRTH   MM DD YY   SEX   M   F

b. AUTO ACCIDENT?   PLACE (State)   YES   NO

b. EMPLOYER'S NAME OR SCHOOL NAME

c. EMPLOYER'S NAME OR SCHOOL NAME

c. OTHER ACCIDENT?   YES   NO

c. INSURANCE PLAN NAME OR PROGRAM NAME

d. INSURANCE PLAN NAME OR PROGRAM NAME

10d. RESERVED FOR LOCAL USE

d. IS THERE ANOTHER HEALTH BENEFIT PLAN?   YES   NO   If yes, return to and complete item 9 a-d.

READ BACK OF FORM BEFORE COMPLETING & SIGNING THIS FORM.

12. PATIENT'S OR AUTHORIZED PERSON'S SIGNATURE I authorize the release of any medical or other information necessary to process this claim. I also request payment of government benefits either to myself or to the party who accepts assignment below.

SIGNED _____   DATE _____

13. INSURED'S OR AUTHORIZED PERSON'S SIGNATURE I authorize payment of medical benefits to the undersigned physician or supplier for services described below.

SIGNED _____

14. DATE OF CURRENT: MM DD YY   ILLNESS (First symptom) OR INJURY (Accident) OR PREGNANCY(LMP)

15. IF PATIENT HAS HAD SAME OR SIMILAR ILLNESS. GIVE FIRST DATE   MM DD YY

16. DATES PATIENT UNABLE TO WORK IN CURRENT OCCUPATION   MM DD YY   FROM   TO   MM DD YY

17. NAME OF REFERRING PROVIDER OR OTHER SOURCE   17a.   17b. NPI

18. HOSPITALIZATION DATES RELATED TO CURRENT SERVICES   MM DD YY   FROM   TO   MM DD YY

19. RESERVED FOR LOCAL USE

20. OUTSIDE LAB?   YES   NO $ CHARGES

21. DIAGNOSIS OR NATURE OF ILLNESS OR INJURY (Relate Items 1, 2, 3 or 4 to Item 24E by Line)

1. _____ . _____   3. _____ . _____

2. _____ . _____   4. _____ . _____

22. MEDICAID RESUBMISSION CODE   ORIGINAL REF. NO.

23. PRIOR AUTHORIZATION NUMBER

PHYSICIAN OR SUPPLIER INFORMATION

24. A. DATE(S) OF SERVICE						B. PLACE OF SERVICE	C. EMG	D. PROCEDURES, SERVICES, OR SUPPLIES (Explain Unusual Circumstances)		E. DIAGNOSIS POINTER	F. $ CHARGES	G. DAYS OR UNITS	H. EPSDT Family Plan	I. ID. QUAL.	J. RENDERING PROVIDER ID. #
From MM	DD	YY	To MM	DD	YY			CPT/HCPCS	MODIFIER						
1														NPI	
2														NPI	
3														NPI	
4														NPI	
5														NPI	
6														NPI	

25. FEDERAL TAX I.D. NUMBER   SSN   EIN

26. PATIENT'S ACCOUNT NO.

27. ACCEPT ASSIGNMENT? (For govt. claims, see back)   YES   NO

28. TOTAL CHARGE $

29. AMOUNT PAID $

30. BALANCE DUE $

31. SIGNATURE OF PHYSICIAN OR SUPPLIER INCLUDING DEGREES OR CREDENTIALS (I certify that the statements on the reverse apply to this bill and are made a part thereof.)

SIGNED _____   DATE _____

32. SERVICE FACILITY LOCATION INFORMATION   a. NPI   b.

33. BILLING PROVIDER INFO & PH # (   )   a. NPI   b.

NUCC Instruction Manual available at: www.nucc.org

APPROVED OMB-0938-0999 FORM CMS-1500 (08-05)

Figure 4-1. CMS-1500 form

CMS-1500 Form Layout

Each block of the standardized CMS-1500 form requires specific information that the insurance companies need to process each claim. The CMS-1500 form is divided into three distinct sections: Top: patient information, Middle: coding information and Bottom: Physician billing information.

The latest revision of this billing form includes split provider identifier fields to accommodate Medicare's new **National Provider Identifier number (NPI)**. The NPI is a number that identifies all providers. Other changes include an eight-digit date in blocks 3, 9b, and 11a. Each block or field on the CMS-1500 form will be explained later in this chapter.

Instructions for Completing the Form

This universal health claim in paper form must be printed on an original red form: no photocopies will be accepted. This red form is easy to optically scan. The form must be perfectly aligned in the printer; rejections will result if misaligned. The computer should print in 10 characters per inch and be all uppercase letters. You cannot use any punctuation except for a hyphen in a compound name. Use only Jr. or Sr. if it is on the insurance card. No designations for physicians (MD) or lawyers (Esq.) are allowed. The comma, decimal point or dollar sign are not used; they are incorporated into the form. For example, the decimal point in the diagnosis code block is there already. Writing in the upper-right corner on the claim form is prohibited. This space is used by the insurance companies.

Block-by-Block instructions are:

- Block 1: Check the appropriate box for the type of health insurance applicable to the claim, Medicare, Medicaid, Tricare, Champva, Group Health Plan, Black Lung program, or other.

- Block 1a: Enter the insured's insurance id number from their insurance policy card.

1a. INSURED'S I.D. NUMBER	(For Program in Item 1)

- Block 2: Enter the patient's last name, first name, and middle initial, exactly how it appears on their insurance card (remember, sometimes the patient is different than the insured).

2. PATIENT'S NAME (Last Name, First Name, Middle Initial)

- Block 3: Enter the patient's date of birth in the format MM DD YYYY, and check the box for the patient's sex.

- Block 4: Enter the insured's last name, first name and middle initial. If the patient is the same as the insured, type "same". Note that for Medicare, you can leave this block blank, (the patient is always the insured with Medicare).

- Block 5: Enter the patient's address–street; city, state, and zip code (remember this must match the address on file with the insurance company).

- Block 6: Enter the patient's relationship to the insured.

- Block 7: Enter the insured's address and telephone number, if it is the same as the patient's write "same". Note that for Medicare, you can leave this block blank (the patient is always the insured with Medicare).

- Block 8: Enter the patient's marital status and employment status.

- Block 9: Enter the name of the insured if there is a secondary insurance, for Medicare the name of the insured in a Medigap policy if applicable.

- Block 9a: Enter the insured's policy or group number of the secondary policy. For Medicare enter the Medigap policy or group number followed by "Medigap", "MG", or "MGAP".

- Block 9b: Enter the insured's DOB for the secondary insurance in the format of MM DD YYYY, for Medicare this is the Medigap enrollees DOB. Also check the sex of the patient.

- Block 9c: Enter the secondary insurance insured's employers name, for Medicare if the Medigap payer ID number is entered into 9d leave this blank, if no Medigap payer ID is listed, enter the claims processing address of the Medigap insurance. (enter street, city, state, and zip code).

a. EMPLOYER'S NAME OR SCHOOL NAME

- Block 9d: Enter the secondary insurance plan name. For Medicare enter the Medigap payer ID number.

d. INSURANCE PLAN NAME OR PROGRAM NAME

- Block 10a: Enter information regarding whether the patient's condition is related to employment (check yes or no).

- Block 10b: Enter information whether the patient's condition is related to auto accident (check yes or no).

- Block 10c: Enter information regarding whether the patient's condition is related to another type of accident (check yes or no).

- Block 10d: Use this item exclusively for Medicare–reporting Medicaid MCD information. Enter the patient's secondary Medicaid identification number followed by MCD.

- Block 11: Enter the insured's policy group number. For Medicare leave this blank.

- Block 11a: Enter the insured's DOB in the format of MM DD YYYY unless the patient is the insured, in which case you can leave this blank. Check the insured's sex. For Medicare leave this blank.

- Block 11b: Enter the insured's employer. For Medicare, enter "Retired" with the retirement date in the format of MM DD YYYY.

- Block 11c: Enter the insured's insurance plan name. For Medicare leave blank.

- Block 11d: Enter Yes or No to "is there another health benefit plan (secondary insurance)"? for Medicare leave this blank.

- Block 12: Enter Signature on file SOF. This indicates the patient has signed an authorization for the release of any medical or information necessary to process this claim, and the patient has assigned benefits to the provider.

- Block 13: Enter SOF signature on file for authorization of payment of medical benefits to the provider.

- Block 14: Enter a six- or eight-digit date of current illness (first symptom), injury, or pregnancy.

- Block 15: Enter date if patient has had same or similar illness, Medicare leave blank.

- Block 16: Enter a six- or eight-digit date when the patient is employed and unable to work.

- Block 17: Enter the name of the referring or ordering physician. Referring physician is one who had requested the treating physician to see the patient.

  Ordering physician (or non physician) is the physician who orders services for the patient: lab, X-ray, etc.

- Block 17a: Enter the ID qualifier and provider number for the specific insurance company of the physician in block 17.

- Block 17b: Enter the NPI for Medicare.

- Block 18: Enter six- or eight-digit dates of hospitalization.

- Block 19: Enter any additional information for the claim; Medicare limits this space to three items. Examples of information would include: modifiers when 99 is used for multiple modifiers on claim, workers comp information, dates a patient was last seen by a physician for physical therapy.

```
19. RESERVED FOR LOCAL USE
```

- Block 20: Enter Yes or No for any purchased lab tests billed for on this claim.

```
20. OUTSIDE LAB?          $ CHARGES
      □ YES   □ NO  |
```

- Block 21: Enter up to 4 ICD-9 codes for diagnosis. Enter in priority order. Medicare can capture and process up to 8 diagnoses.

```
21. DIAGNOSIS OR NATURE OF ILLNESS OR INJURY (Relate Items 1, 2, 3 or 4 to Item 24E by Line)
   1. |____.____            3. |____.____
   2. |____.____            4. |____.____
```

- Block 22: Enter for Medicaid only, resubmission code and original reference no.

```
22. MEDICAID RESUBMISSION
    CODE          ORIGINAL REF. NO.
```

- Block 23: Enter any insurance company prior authorization number, for Medicare enter the quality improvement organization prior authorization number if needed, or investigational device exemption number, or clinical laboratory improvement act number.

```
23. PRIOR AUTHORIZATION NUMBER
```

- Block 24: Enter possible 6 services performed. The shaded top portion in each line is for reporting supplemental info; example would be anesthesia start and stop times.

- Block 24A: Enter six- or eight-digit date of service, enter only the "from" date unless billing for a series of identical services.

- Block 24B: Enter the 2-digit place of service codes, different insurance companies may require different codes, for Medicare some common codes are:

  - 11 Office
  - 12 Home
  - 13 Assisted Living Facility
  - 20 Urgent Care Facility
  - 21 Inpatient Hospital
  - 22 Outpatient Hospital
  - 23 Emergency Room–Hospital
  - 24 Ambulatory Surgical Center

- Block 24C: Enter Y for yes if the service is deemed an emergency only if individual payers require this block, Medicare does not require this.

- Block 24D: Enter the CPT/HCPCS code and any modifier for the service being billed; any unlisted service code should have a description in Block 19.

- Block 24E: Enter the diagnosis pointer number (reference from Block 21). Do not list an ICD-9 code, just the appropriate reference number from Block 21. The diagnosis from Block 21 should be the primary diagnosis for the services being billed in Block 24D. The diagnosis must show medical necessity.

- Block 24F: Enter the charge in dollar amount for the billed service (S) in total for this line.

- Block 24G: Enter the number of days billed on this line or the units being billed.

- Block 24H: Enter Y or N for yes or no for Medicaid only if the claim relates to early and periodic screening, diagnosis and treatment, or for family planning.

- Block 24I: Enter into top shaded portion the id qualifier or NPI number in bottom portion for rendering provider if billing for an individual provider (not a group practice).

- Block 24J: Enter providers pin in top shaded portion or NPI in the bottom portion if the provider is in a group practice.

- Block 25: Enter the provider-of-service- Federal Tax ID number or social security number.

- Block 26: Enter the patient's account number assigned by the provider.

26. PATIENT'S ACCOUNT NO.

- Block 27: Enter Yes or No for accept assignment. This block indicates for governmental claims, but all insurance companies want this filled in. This will indicate to the insurance company that the physician is accepting the fees paid by the patient's policy (not including co-pay's or co-insurance or deductible).

- Block 28: Enter total amount of all six lines of the claim.

- Block 29: Enter any amount paid by the patient, deductible or co-pay.

- Block 30: Leave blank.

- Block 31: Enter the signature of the physician or provider of service and date in a six- or eight-digit format. Acceptable is signature on file, or a computer-generated signature if the physician is contracted with the insurance company.

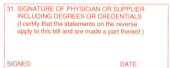

- Block 32: Enter the facility location information if services were performed outside the physician's office: name, address, zip, such as hospital, nursing home, etc.

- Block 32a: Enter the NPI number for the service facility.

- Block 32b: Enter the ID qualifier and PIN number for the service facility.

- Block 33: Enter the physician's billing entity (legal billing name, address, zip code and telephone #).

33. BILLING PROVIDER INFO & PH #   (   )

- Block 33a: Enter the NPI number for the billing entity.

a.   NPI

- Block 33b: Enter the ID qualifier and PIN number for the billing entity.

b.

STOP AND PRACTICE

Exercise 4-2

Define the following key terms.

1. HCFA

_____

_____

2. NPI

_____

_____

Short answer: Answer each question with a short statement.

3. Explain the history of the universal health claim form.

_____

_____

4. List the printing rules for the CMS-1500 form.

_____

_____

5. Explain what the three distinct sections of the CMS-1500 form.

_____

_____

1500

HEALTH INSURANCE CLAIM FORM

SAMPLE ONLY: NOT APPROVED FOR USE

| | PICA | | | | | | | | | | | | PICA | |

CARRIER

1. MEDICARE	MEDICAID	TRICARE CHAMPUS	CHAMPVA	GROUP HEALTH PLAN	FECA BLK LUNG	OTHER	1a. INSURED'S I.D. NUMBER (For Program in Item 1)
(Medicare #)	(Medicaid #)	(Sponsor's SSN)	(Member ID#)	(SSN or ID)	(SSN)	X (ID)	XX321654

2. PATIENT'S NAME (Last Name, First Name, Middle Initial)	3. PATIENT'S BIRTH DATE MM DD YY	SEX	4. INSURED'S NAME (Last Name, First Name, Middle Initial)
SMITH, JANE, E	08 30 1955	M X F	SAME

5. PATIENT'S ADDRESS (No., Street)	6. PATIENT'S RELATIONSHIP TO INSURED	7. INSURED'S ADDRESS (No., Street)
29 COURT STREET	Self X Spouse Child Other	SAME

CITY	STATE	8. PATIENT STATUS	CITY	STATE
CENTURY	NC	Single X Married Other		

ZIP CODE	TELEPHONE (Include Area Code)		ZIP CODE	TELEPHONE (Include Area Code)
37777	(335)9991111	Employed X Full-Time Student Part-Time Student		( )

PATIENT AND INSURED INFORMATION

9. OTHER INSURED'S NAME (Last Name, First Name, Middle Initial)	10. IS PATIENT'S CONDITION RELATED TO:	11. INSURED'S POLICY GROUP OR FECA NUMBER

| a. OTHER INSURED'S POLICY OR GROUP NUMBER | a. EMPLOYMENT? (Current or Previous) YES X NO | a. INSURED'S DATE OF BIRTH MM DD YY   SEX M F |

| b. OTHER INSURED'S DATE OF BIRTH MM DD YY SEX M F | b. AUTO ACCIDENT? PLACE (State) YES X NO | b. EMPLOYER'S NAME OR SCHOOL NAME JONES LANDING |

| c. EMPLOYER'S NAME OR SCHOOL NAME | c. OTHER ACCIDENT? YES X NO | c. INSURANCE PLAN NAME OR PROGRAM NAME UNITED HEALTHCARE |

| d. INSURANCE PLAN NAME OR PROGRAM NAME | 10d. RESERVED FOR LOCAL USE | d. IS THERE ANOTHER HEALTH BENEFIT PLAN? YES X NO If yes, return to and complete item 9 a-d. |

READ BACK OF FORM BEFORE COMPLETING & SIGNING THIS FORM.

12. PATIENT'S OR AUTHORIZED PERSON'S SIGNATURE I authorize the release of any medical or other information necessary to process this claim. I also request payment of government benefits either to myself or to the party who accepts assignment below.

SIGNED ___SOF___ DATE ___091020XX___

13. INSURED'S OR AUTHORIZED PERSON'S SIGNATURE I authorize payment of medical benefits to the undersigned physcian or supplier for services described below.

SIGNED ___SOF___

| 14. DATE OF CURRENT: MM DD YY ◄ ILLNESS (First symptom) OR INJURY (Accident) OR PREGNANCY (LMP) | 15. IF PATIENT HAS HAD SAME OR SIMILAR ILLNESS, GIVE FIRST DATE MM DD YY | 16. DATES PATIENT UNABLE TO WORK IN CURRENT OCCUPATION MM DD YY   MM DD YY FROM   TO |

| 17. NAME OF REFERRING PROVIDER OR OTHER SOURCE JOHN BERRY MD | 17a. 17b. NPI 1234567891 | 18. HOSPITALIZATION DATES RELATED TO CURRENT SERVICES MM DD YY   MM DD YY FROM   TO |

| 19. RESERVED FOR LOCAL USE | 20. OUTSIDE LAB? YES X NO | $ CHARGES |

| 21. DIAGNOSIS OR NATURE OF ILLNESS OR INJURY (Relate Items 1, 2, 3 or 4 to Item 24E by Line) 1. 354 0   3.   2.   4. | 22. MEDICAID RESUBMISSION CODE   ORIGINAL REF. NO. 23. PRIOR AUTHORIZATION NUMBER |

PHYSICIAN OR SUPPLIER INFORMATION

24. A. DATE(S) OF SERVICE From MM DD YY To MM DD YY	B. PLACE OF SERVICE	C. EMG	D. PROCEDURES, SERVICES, OR SUPPLIES (Explain Unusual Circumstances) CPT/HCPCS	MODIFIER	E. DIAGNOSIS POINTER	F. $ CHARGES	G. DAYS OR UNITS	H. EPSDT Family Plan	I. ID. QUAL.	J. RENDERING PROVIDER ID. #
1	091020XX		11	99203		1	90 00			NPI	1234567891
2										NPI	
3										NPI	
4										NPI	
5										NPI	
6										NPI	

| 25. FEDERAL TAX I.D. NUMBER SSN EIN 111223456 X | 26. PATIENT'S ACCOUNT NO. SMITHJA | 27. ACCEPT ASSIGNMENT? (For govt. claims, see back) X YES NO | 28. TOTAL CHARGE $ 90 00 | 29. AMOUNT PAID $ | 30. BALANCE DUE $ 90 00 |

| 31. SIGNATURE OF PHYSICIAN OR SUPPLIER INCLUDING DEGREES OR CREDENTIALS (I certify that the statements on the reverse apply to this bill and are made a part thereof.) JOHN BERRY MD SIGNED   DATE 031620XX | 32. SERVICE FACILITY LOCATION INFORMATION a. b. | 33. BILLING PROVIDER INFO & PH # ( ) JOHN BERRY MD 3 PARK STREET CENTURY NC 37777 a. 1234567891 b. |

NUCC Instruction Manual available at: www.nucc.org

Figure 4-2. Completed CMS form–Smith

1500

HEALTH INSURANCE CLAIM FORM

SAMPLE ONLY NOT APPROVED FOR USE

1. MEDICARE	MEDICAID	TRICARE CHAMPUS	CHAMPVA	GROUP HEALTH PLAN	FECA BLK LUNG	OTHER	1a. INSURED'S I.D. NUMBER (For Program in Item 1)
(Medicare #)	(Medicaid #)	(Sponsor's SSN)	(Member ID#)	(SSN or ID)	(SSN)	[X] (ID)	111119999

2. PATIENT'S NAME (Last Name, First Name, Middle Initial)
JONES, SANDY, F

3. PATIENT'S BIRTH DATE MM 06 DD 23 YY 20XX SEX M [X] F

4. INSURED'S NAME (Last Name, First Name, Middle Initial)
SAME

5. PATIENT'S ADDRESS (No., Street)
52 SUNRISE AVE

6. PATIENT'S RELATIONSHIP TO INSURED
Self [X] Spouse Child Other

7. INSURED'S ADDRESS (No., Street)
SAME

CITY
CENTURY STATE NC

8. PATIENT STATUS
Single [X] Married Other
Employed [X] Full-Time Student Part-Time Student

CITY STATE

ZIP CODE 37777 TELEPHONE (Include Area Code) (335) 3321144

ZIP CODE TELEPHONE (Include Area Code) ( )

9. OTHER INSURED'S NAME (Last Name, First Name, Middle Initial)

10. IS PATIENT'S CONDITION RELATED TO:

11. INSURED'S POLICY GROUP OR FECA NUMBER

a. OTHER INSURED'S POLICY OR GROUP NUMBER

a. EMPLOYMENT? (Current or Previous) YES [X] NO

a. INSURED'S DATE OF BIRTH MM DD YY SEX M F

b. OTHER INSURED'S DATE OF BIRTH MM DD YY SEX M F

b. AUTO ACCIDENT? PLACE (State) YES [X] NO

b. EMPLOYER'S NAME OR SCHOOL NAME
SMITH AUTO

c. EMPLOYER'S NAME OR SCHOOL NAME

c. OTHER ACCIDENT? YES [X] NO

c. INSURANCE PLAN NAME OR PROGRAM NAME
AETNA

d. INSURANCE PLAN NAME OR PROGRAM NAME

10d. RESERVED FOR LOCAL USE

d. IS THERE ANOTHER HEALTH BENEFIT PLAN?
YES [X] NO If yes, return to and complete item 9 a-d.

READ BACK OF FORM BEFORE COMPLETING & SIGNING THIS FORM.

12. PATIENT'S OR AUTHORIZED PERSON'S SIGNATURE I authorize the release of any medical or other information necessary to process this claim. I also request payment of government benefits either to myself or to the party who accepts assignment below.
SIGNED SOF DATE 103020XX

13. INSURED'S OR AUTHORIZED PERSON'S SIGNATURE I authorize payment of medical benefits to the undersigned physcian or supplier for services described below.
SIGNED SOF

14. DATE OF CURRENT: MM DD YY ILLNESS (First symptom) OR INJURY (Accident) OR PREGNANCY (LMP)

15. IF PATIENT HAS HAD SAME OR SIMILAR ILLNESS, GIVE FIRST DATE MM DD YY

16. DATES PATIENT UNABLE TO WORK IN CURRENT OCCUPATION MM DD YY FROM TO MM DD YY

17. NAME OF REFERRING PROVIDER OR OTHER SOURCE
JOHN BERRY MD
17a.
17b. NPI 1234567891

18. HOSPITALIZATION DATES RELATED TO CURRENT SERVICES MM DD YY FROM TO MM DD YY

19. RESERVED FOR LOCAL USE

20. OUTSIDE LAB? YES [X] NO $ CHARGES

21. DIAGNOSIS OR NATURE OF ILLNESS OR INJURY (Relate Items 1, 2, 3 or 4 to Item 24E by Line)
1. 789 00
2.
3.
4.

22. MEDICAID RESUBMISSION CODE ORIGINAL REF. NO.

23. PRIOR AUTHORIZATION NUMBER

24. A DATE(S) OF SERVICE From MM DD YY	To MM DD YY	B. PLACE OF SERVICE	C. EMG	D. PROCEDURES, SERVICES, OR SUPPLIES (Explain Unusual Circumstances) CPT/HCPCS | MODIFIER	E. DIAGNOSIS POINTER	F. $ CHARGES	G. DAYS OR UNITS	H. EPSDT Family Plan	I. ID. QUAL.	J. RENDERING PROVIDER ID. #
1 10 30 20XX		11		99203	1	90 00			NPI	1234567891
2									NPI	
3									NPI	
4									NPI	
5									NPI	
6									NPI	

25. FEDERAL TAX I.D. NUMBER SSN EIN
111223456 [X]

26. PATIENT'S ACCOUNT NO.
JONESSA

27. ACCEPT ASSIGNMENT? (For govt. claims, see back)
[X] YES NO

28. TOTAL CHARGE $ 90 00

29. AMOUNT PAID $

30. BALANCE DUE $ 90 00

31. SIGNATURE OF PHYSICIAN OR SUPPLIER INCLUDING DEGREES OR CREDENTIALS (I certify that the statements on the reverse apply to this bill and are made a part thereof.)
JOHN BERRY MD
SIGNED DATE 091020XX

32. SERVICE FACILITY LOCATION INFORMATION
a. b.

33. BILLING PROVIDER INFO & PH # ( )
JOHN BERRY MD
3 PARK STREET
CENTURY NC 37777
a. 1234567891 b.

NUCC Instruction Manual available at: www.nucc.org

Figure 4-3. Completed CMS form—Jones

CMS-1500 FORM SUBMISSION

The CMS-1500 form is always computer generated on paper or in electronic format. The reimbursement specialist should never fill in this document manually. Most insurance companies will reject any hand written claim form.

Common errors made in completing the CMS-1500 form include:

- **Incorrect patient demographic information, especially insurance certificate numbers**

- **Incorrect medical coding-CPT, modifiers, ICD-9 codes**

- **Absence of the referring/rendering physician and PIN or NPI numbers**

- **Incorrect or duplicate dates of service**

- **Incorrect provider information, NPI numbers and tax ID numbers**

Understanding all the information required for each payer (insurance company), attention to detail in entering all the required information, and checking each claim for errors is a must in producing a clean claim. It cannot be stressed enough; producing the clean claim will ensure a quick and correct reimbursement.

The two ways of submitting a claim to the payer are: 1. paper claims that are optically scanned into the insurance companies, processing system. 2. **Electronic claims submission (ECS)**. The electronic claim is submitted by direct computer download, modem, fax, or through clearinghouses. A clearinghouse can download any physician's computer-generated claims and send the correct format to each individual insurance company. They are the middleman to ensure the electronic claim is submitted cleanly as well; they edit all the claims for technical errors and missing information.

The **National Standard Format (NSF)**, is the format seen on the computer screen in the CMS-1500 format. **The American National Standard Institute (ANSI)** approves the electronically formatted claim in encrypted form for security and confidentiality of patient information.

The electronic claim submission or **Electronic Data Interchange (EDI)** is the process of exchanging data between two or more computers. **The Health Insurance Portability and Accountability Act (HIPAA)** regulates the format of this electronic exchange of data.

When the claim is electronically submitted directly to the insurance company or through a clearinghouse, a **scrubber** report is generated. It reports

Exercise 4-3

Short answer: Answer each question with a short statement.

1. List some common errors in filling out the CMS-1500 form.

_____

_____

_____

2. Explain two ways of submitting a CMS-1500 claim form.

_____

_____

_____

Define the following key terms.

3. Scrubber report

_____

_____

_____

4. EDI

_____

_____

_____

all the claims submitted, total amount of the claims in dollar amounts, and any claims that were rejected and not submitted do to any edits for errors and missing information. This allows the reimbursement specialist to correct the error and resubmit the claim more efficiently.

Electronic claims have advantages over the old paper submission of claims. Postal submission is much slower and costs are higher. However, there are still instances where paper claims are being used. Secondary claims, and claims with attachments, are still submitted on paper. Electronic claims produce a faster reimbursement, reduce errors, and provide proof the claim was submitted (date and time).

The practical application of electronic submission of claims for the reimbursement specialist is quick and easy. As with the patient encounter form and registration form, the billing office can review them for correct or missing information. Correct coding is double-checked and audited. The information is entered into the billing software; many software packages have their own edit program to further check the claim form.

The day after this information is entered into the computer, the reimbursement specialist downloads all the claims produced from this information into an electronic batch. Through the electronic program this data is electronically downloaded to the insurance company or to a clearing-house. The scrubber report will be printed for the reimbursement specialist to keep on file and check for any rejected claims from the clearinghouse edits. The report will serve as proof of submission and allow the errors to be corrected immediately. The corrected claims from the scrubber report will be resubmitted along with the next day's electronic batch.

The computer billing software will post a submission date on each claim sent, helping to track unpaid claims. With the technology of claim edits, the submission of clean claims electronically has made the job of the reimbursement specialist much easier, and reimbursement quicker.

MULTIPLE INSURANCES

Many patients have more than one insurance policy. Therefore more than one claim may have to be submitted for the same date of service. They are the primary insurance, the secondary insurance and sometimes the tertiary insurance. Reimbursement is made and if there is a balance due, the claim is sent to the secondary insurance policy for payment, and on to the third policy if necessary. As explained in Chapter 3, for children covered by both parents' insurance policies, the birthday rule applies.

The secondary insurance company requires a copy of the EOB from the primary insurance. This is called **coordination of benefits** between insurance companies. Reimbursement cannot be more than 100% of the billed amount.

The attachment of the primary insurance EOB often requires a paper claim to be sent to the secondary insurance. Once the payment from the primary insurance is posted to the patients account the payment poster must be aware of the secondary insurance possibility. The payment poster will produce the next claim to be printed. The claim is printed out on paper, the EOB attached and the claim is sent to the secondary insurance. The secondary claim will have the exact same information as the primary claim, except the payment received from the primary insurance will be listed in Block 29 with the claim balance in Block 30.

Many of the insurance companies are linked and the primary insurance company will electronically send their reimbursement information to the secondary insurance company. One of the major links is between Medicare and Medicaid. This automatic link saves the reimbursement specialist time, is more efficient, and reimbursement is faster. Care must be taken in the follow-up of this automatic electronic data exchange. Insurance follow-up is extremely important to check that the link was correctly made.

For this automatic exchange of data to happen however, the reimbursement specialist must be sure all the correct secondary insurance information is included on the primary claim (Blocks 9-9d).

Because all of the correct information is entered on the CMS-1500 form for the different insurance companies, a clean claim is produced, sent, and reimbursed. Knowledge of the CMS-1500 form is essential for this correct reimbursement.

STOP AND PRACTICE

Exercise 4-4

True or False: Choose the correct answer for each question.

_____ 1. Medicare and Blue Cross Blue Shield HMO are linked to electronically share claim information.

_____ 2. The primary insurance will automatically know when the patient has a secondary insurance.

_____ 3. It is important to follow-up on electronically linked insurance companies, making sure reimbursement is received by both companies.

_____ 4. When submitting a claim to the secondary insurance by paper, an EOB from the primary insurance is attached.

_____ 5. Coordination of benefits is when the patient coordinates his treatment with the insurance company.

CHAPTER SUMMARY

- Correct patient information collected and put into the billing software will help to produce a clean claim.

- The universal health claim billing form is the CMS-1500 form.

- The CMS-1500 form was originally developed by HCFA.

- The CMS-1500 form is maintained by The Centers for Medicare and Medicaid Services (CMS).

- The CMS-1500 form is divided into three distinct sections: patient information, coding information, and physician billing information.

- A recent revision of the CMS-1500 form includes space for the new NPI, National Physician Identifier.

- All CMS-1500 forms are printed in capital letters, at 10 characters per inch. No commas, decimal points or dollar signs are used. Hyphenate only for names, and the form must be perfectly aligned in the printer.

- Each block or field on the CMS-1500 form requires very specific information for the insurance companies to make a correct reimbursement.

- CMS-1500 forms may be submitted by paper or electronically.

- Electronic claim submission (EDI) has been standardized and formatted by CMS and regulated by HIPAA.

- Claim edits can be put in place to ensure a clean claim.

- Coordination of benefits ensures that if more than one insurance company is paying a claim, the multiple reimbursements do not exceed 100% of the billed amount.

- If multiple insurance companies are reimbursing a claim, the primary insurance EOB must be sent to the secondary insurance company.

REVIEW QUESTIONS

Fill in a CMS-1500 form for the following cases located in Appendix I.

1. Case Study #1

2. Case Study #2

3. Case Study #5

4. Case Study #8

5. Case Study #14

6. Case Study #18

PRACTICAL APPLICATION

Pair into groups of two. Each group should produce two CMS-1500 forms. Each learner will be the patient on these forms. Hand-write these claims, this will help you to familiarize yourself with the CMS-1500 form. Choose what insurance company, demographic information, and physician to use.

For coding: diagnoses: 250.00 diabetes 354.0 carpal tunnel syndrome

Procedures: 99203 office visit

Chapter **5**

Health Insurance

OBJECTIVES

Upon completion of this chapter, the student should be able to:

- Define the basics of insurance terminology.
- Define the basics of managed care.
- Outline the information found on the insurance card.
- Outline the information required for physician credentialing.

KEY TERMS

Capitation

Co-insurance

Co-pay

Deductible

Fee-for-service

Fee schedule

Health maintenance organization (HMO)

Indemnity plans

Managed care

National Committee for Quality Assurance (NCQA)

Participating physician

Point-of-service (POS)

Preferred provider organization (PPO)

Primary care physician (PCP)

INTRODUCTION

Knowledge of medical insurances is imperative for the reimbursement specialist. Each physician's office will have patients with many different kinds of health insurance. We will discuss the most common insurance companies in the next few chapters. Understanding managed care and indemnity plans will help the reimbursement specialist collect the correct reimbursement for the physician.

REIMBURSEMENT TERMINOLOGY

Insurance companies reimburse the physician for services and procedures according to the patient's insurance policy benefits. Reimbursement is also based on specific contracts between the insurance company and the physician. Knowledge of both the patient's benefits and the contracts with the insurance company will help the reimbursement specialist in the billing process.

The physician may choose to be a **participating physician** (enter into a contract) with the insurance company or be a non-participating physician. If the physician is participating, a fee schedule is set up based on common CPT codes. CPT codes are discussed in Chapter 8; they represent the services and procedures performed. A **fee schedule** is the amount of reimbursement the physician will expect for each service or procedure in the treatment of patients. The contract will also outline the patient's co-pay or co-insurance. A **Co-pay** is the set amount of payment due from the patient, and is paid at the time of service. The **co-insurance** is usually a percentage of the charge, billed by the physician after the reimbursement comes from the insurance company. If the physician is non-participating, payment in full is expected from the patient by the medical office.

Many insurance company policies have a yearly deductible. A **deductible** is a pre-set amount of money the patient must pay before the insurance company will reimburse any charges. The deductible will be different for each patient and depends on the policy the patient purchased from the insurance company. It is important for the reimbursement specialist to check the patient's deductible, and ask for payment at the time of the service.

MANAGED CARE

The most common types of health insurance include Medicare, Medicaid, Blue Cross Blue Shield, TRICARE, commercial insurances, and Workers' Compensation insurance. Within these major insurance companies, different policies may be purchased. These policies might include managed care; HMO, PPO, POS, or indemnity policies.

Managed care provides subscribers with affordable health care while maintaining quality of care from the physician. The physicians and medical facilities are offered incentives for their part in maintaining quality care, and at the

STOP AND PRACTICE

Exercise 5-1

Define the following key terms.

1. Fee schedule.

   _____

   _____

2. Co-pay

   _____

   _____

3. Co-insurance

   _____

   _____

4. Deductible

   _____

   _____

same time reducing health care costs for the insurance company. **Managed care** policies require a **primary care physician (PCP)**. This physician manages the patient's health care. The PCP's job is to provide efficient and effective health care while keeping the medical costs at a minimum. The PCP will treat the patient and make referrals to specialists only when necessary.

In 1955, the first nationally recognized HMO was created, and in 1973 the Health Maintenance Organization Assistance Act was passed. The HMO act of 1973 awarded grants and loans to develop private HMOs. The Omnibus Budge Reconciliation Act of 1981 helped provide HMOs for Medicare and Medicaid. In 1985, the Preferred Provider Health Care Act allowed preferred provider organizations to allow subscribers to find health care from providers outside the PPO network.

Some managed care organizations pay the provider (physician, facility, or hospital) through a **capitation** payment method. A predetermined amount of money is paid to the provider for services rendered for a certain time span (usually per month or year). During that time, the provider of care must treat all enrollees in the managed health plan. If the provider treats patients efficiently for under the capitation amount, he makes a profit. However, if the services rendered are over the capitation amount, the provider will lose his profit.

Types of Managed Care

The **Health Maintenance Organization (HMO)** seeks to control medical costs and improve the quality of health care. The patient pays the premium for the health care coverage and must use physicians and hospitals approved by their HMO system. The HMO promotes well care or preventative services, hoping to lower health care costs. Patients usually have a co-payment with the HMO.

The **preferred provider organization (PPO)** is another type of managed care system. In this health care coverage, the patient may choose to see any physician or hospital, but the PPO has a list of network-preferred physicians. If utilized, these physicians will save the patient money. Referrals are required to see out-of-network physicians.

The **point-of-service (POS)** system is a kind of managed care system that minimizes the restrictions to the patient in choosing a physician. A referral is not necessary to see a physician. Again, the patient will save money if they choose to see a network physician.

The **National Committee for Quality Assurance (NCQA)** will evaluate all managed care organizations. The NCQA accredits the managed care organizations and shows that the plan meets the standards beyond what is required by law. The NCQA will monitor the physician for quality of care and patient satisfaction through reviews, patient surveys, and grievance procedures.

The **indemnity plans** are also called **fee-for-service** plans. These plans are straight forward. The charges are billed by the physician and reimbursement is paid per the benefit schedule by the insurance company. The patient pays for any remaining balance.

Each patient with insurance will have a health insurance identification card. Knowledge of what is listed on the identification card is important for the

INFORMATION ON IDENTIFICATION CARDS SHOULD INCLUDE:

- The name of the insurance company, address, claim submission address, and telephone number

- The policy holder's name (subscriber, insured) as well as the patient's name if different from the policy-holder

- The identification number

- The group number (not all insurance companies have this number)

- The plan type (PPO, HMO)

- The deductible, co-pay, co-insurance amounts

reimbursement specialist. Every insurance company's identification card will look different but the information on the cards is similar.

Making a copy of both sides of the health insurance identification card is important in the registration process.

DIFFERENT KINDS OF HEALTH INSURANCE COVERAGE INCLUDE:

- Individual private policies
- Employment policies
- Spousal coverage
- Parent/child coverage
- Family coverage
- Governmental programs

Credentialing

Managed care organizations require physician credentialing. Many reimbursement specialists can be responsible for the credentialing of the physician in their office. Each insurance company may require separate credentialing applications to be submitted on all participating physicians. Credentialing is the formal recognition of the physician's competence and performance. This would include clinical review and monitoring of the physician's adherence to the managed care policies. The credentialing also includes verification of the physician's license, experience, certifications, education, training, clinical judgment, technical capabilities, malpractice monitoring, and character.

Each insurance company will require an application, with supporting documentation, submitted to them in a timely manner. Many will require these credentialing applications yearly. Most applications ask for the physician's practice address, the curriculum vita (type of professional resume), date of birth, Social Security number, tax identification number, DEA number, medical license number, name and addresses of all educational institutions, hospital affiliations, practice specialty, work history, and malpractice claim history.

The reimbursement specialist may become a certified credentialing specialist. One association offering this certification is the Certification Commission of the National Association of Medical Staff Services (NAMSS). Experience and a written test are required.

STOP AND PRACTICE

Exercise 5-2

Short answer: Answer each question with a short statement.

1. Name the most common insurance companies.

    _____

    _____

    _____

2. Explain managed care policies.

    _____

    _____

    _____

3. Name the different types of health insurance policies.

    _____

    _____

    _____

4. List the information found on a policy holder's insurance card.

    _____

    _____

    _____

CHAPTER SUMMARY

- Knowledge of reimbursement terminology is essential to the reimbursement specialist.

- A participating physician is one who contracts with an insurance company to accept a predetermined reimbursement for services provided according to the contracted fee schedule.

- The co-pay, co-insurance, and deductible are predetermined monies paid by the patient to the physician according to their insurance policy or contract.

- Managed health care was developed to lower health care costs and still provide quality care to enrollees in an insurance network of providers.

- Many managed care policies require a PCP, or primary care physician, who directs the patients' health care.

- Some common managed care policies include the HMO, PPO, and POS.

- The NCQA evaluates and monitors managed care health plans.

- An indemnity or fee-for-service health plan pays the physician a predetermined reimbursement for each service or procedure performed.

- Credentialing is a procedure set up for many insurance companies to establish standards for physicians in their participating network of providers.

- Important information is contained on all insurance cards and maintained by the insurance company for each enrollee according to their policies.

REVIEW QUESTIONS

Define the following key terms.

1. Participating physician

   _____

   _____

2. Co-pay and co-insurance

   _____

   _____

3. Deductible

   _____

   _____

4. Managed health care

   _____

   _____

5. Fee schedule

   _____

   _____

6. Capitation payment

   _____

   _____

Short answer: Answer each question with a short statement.

7. List three types of managed care policies and explain the differences.

   _____

   _____

   _____

   _____

8. What is credentialing and why is it so important in the managed health care organizations?

   _____

   _____

   _____

   _____

9. Why is it essential to understand the information listed on the patient's insurance card?

_____

_____

_____

_____

10. How do managed-care plans help lower the cost of health care?

_____

_____

_____

_____

PRACTICAL APPLICATION

Investigate what kind of impact participating in a managed health care plan will have on the physician's office. List the pros and cons for both the physician and the reimbursement specialist. Present your findings to the class and discuss whether managed care really lowers the cost of health care.

Chapter 6

Medicare

OBJECTIVES

Upon completion of this chapter, the student should be able to:

- Summarize the history of Medicare.
- Outline the Medicare plans and eligibility requirements.
- Distinguish between participating and non-participating Medicare providers.
- Define Medicare's Medigap and Medicare as a secondary payer concepts.
- Recognize the Medicare insurance card.
- Apply the basics of Medicare reimbursement.
- Summarize some basic forms required by Medicare billing.

KEY TERMS

Abuse

Accept assignment

Advance Beneficiary Notice (ABN)

Centers for Medicare and Medicaid (CMS)

Corrective Coding Initiative (CCI)

Downcoding

Durable medical equipment (DME)

Fraud

Limiting charge

Local Coverage Determination Manual (LCD)

Medicare

Medicare beneficiary

INTRODUCTION

Patients covered by Medicare may very well make up the largest part of a medical office (with a few exceptions). The Medicare program is also the most complicated insurance plan. The rules and regulations can change seemingly daily. It is imperative to constantly monitor the updates for Medicare. This chapter outlines the basics needed to understand Medicare and how to stay updated with these rules and regulations.

MEDICARE OVERVIEW

Medicare is the largest governmental health insurance program in the United States. Medicare is a federally funded health insurance program for people over the age of 65 and some qualified disabled patients. Medicare is run by the **Centers for Medicare and Medicaid Services (CMS)**. They set the regulations but allow independent Medicare carriers to administer the processing of claims. The Medicare carriers are often Blue Cross Blue Shield (Anthem) insurance companies. The Medicare local carriers process claims for individual states or groups of states. Medicare regional carriers process claims for **durable medical equipment (DME)**. Durable medical equipment includes supplies furnished to the patient during treatment. These supplies include crutches, wheelchairs, canes, injections, and many more. If a physician treats a patient and supplies durable medical equipment, two claims will be produced and sent to the two different Medicare carriers. Claims are submitted to Medicare electronically according to HIPAA standards. Physicians may choose to participate with Medicare or not.

History of Medicare

Listed are just a few significant dates in Medicare's history:

- In 1945, President Harry Truman asked Congress to establish a national health insurance plan.

- On July 30, 1965, President Lyndon Johnson signed into law the federal programs of Medicare and Medicaid. They were enacted as a part of the Social Security Act. Harry Truman was the first to enroll in Medicare.

- In 1966, Medicare was implemented and more than 19 million Americans enrolled.

- In 1972, Medicare was extended to persons under the age of 65 who were disabled and those who had end-stage renal disease. Payments were also authorized to HMOs.

- The Health Care Financing Administration (HCFA) was set up to administer Medicare in 1977.

- In 1980, Medigap policies were set up.

- In 1992, Medicare based physicians' reimbursement on fee schedules.

- In 1996, HIPAA was enacted.

- In 1997, some Medicare changes included new Medicare managed care and expanded preventive benefits.

- In 1998, Medicare developed the Internet site Medicare.gov.

- In 1999, Medicare developed the Medicare beneficiary handbook, *Medicare & You*. *Medicare* opened a national toll-free number 1-800-Medicare.

- In 2003, President George W. Bush signed into law an outpatient drug prescription plan for Medicare.

- In 2008, a new provider identifying number goes into effect called the National Provider Identifier (NPI).

Because of the ever-changing rules and regulations for Medicare, the reimbursement specialist must be comfortable with navigating Medicare's Web site, newsletters, seminars, and national updates for specific billing practices.

Medicare Eligibility

Medicare requires individuals or their spouses to have worked in a Medicare-covered job for at least 10 years. They must be 65 years old and be citizens or permanent residents of the United States. Individuals under 65 may also qualify for Medicare if they have a long-term disability or end-stage renal disease. Medicare defines a long-term disability as one that lasts longer than a year. The disability must prevent the individual from working, even with adjustments to the job, due to medical reasons.

End-stage renal disease is permanent kidney failure resulting in a regular course of dialysis or kidney transplant.

Individuals are either automatically enrolled in Medicare or must apply for coverage. If they already receive Social Security, Railroad Retirement Board, or disability benefits, they will be automatically enrolled in Medicare on their 65th birthday or on the 24th month of their disability. All other individuals must apply for Medicare benefits. The individual must contact the Social Security Administration three months before the month of their 65th birthday. Once an individual has applied for Medicare, a seven-month initial enrollment period begins. During this time, the individual may choose Medicare Part A and/or Part B benefits. If the individual waits too long to apply, they will have to wait for the general enrollment period. The general enrollment period is from January 1 to March 31 of each year. In this case, Medicare will become effective July 1 of the enrollment year. Medicare Part B premiums will be 10% higher for these individuals.

STOP AND PRACTICE

Exercise 6-1

Short answer: Answer each question with a short statement.

1. Explain some important events in Medicare's history.

   _____

   _____

   _____

   _____

2. Explain the enrollment process for Medicare.

   _____

   _____

   _____

   _____

3. Who is eligible for Medicare benefits?

   _____

   _____

   _____

   _____

4. What is the difference between local and regional Medicare carriers?

   _____

   _____

   _____

   _____

MEDICARE PLANS

Part A covers inpatient hospital benefits, skilled nursing facilities, hospice care, respite care, and home health care. Part A does not require the patient to pay a premium for this coverage.

Part B covers medical professional services, outpatient hospital care, diagnostic tests, durable medical equipment, ambulance services, anesthesia, radiology, pathology, mental illness, some preventive services, physical therapy, occupational therapy, and nursing services. The elderly must sign up for Part B. It requires a monthly premium paid by the insured (patient). Medicare Part B benefits are paid at a rate of 80% of the Medicare fee schedule. Medicare's fee schedule is revised annually and is based on **relative value units (RVUs)**. The RVUs are based on physician work, practice expenses, and malpractice expense. This relative value unit also is based on geographic location. Patients are expected to pay the remaining 20% of charges. Many Medicare policy holders supplement this coverage with a secondary **Medigap** insurance. Medigap insurance is a supplemental insurance that will pay the remaining 20% that Part B does not pay. This will be discussed later in this chapter.

The following is a summary of the covered services for parts A, B, C and D with Medicare:

			Medicare	Plans
Medicare	Part			
	A	In-patient services		
		Hospice		
		Respite		
		Home health services		
		Skilled nursing facilities		
	B	Physician services		
		Outpatient hospital services		
		Diagnostic testing		
		Durable medical equipment		
		Anesthesia		
		Radiology		
		Lab		
		Pathology services		
		Physical therapy		
		Occupational therapy		
		Ambulance services		
	C	Managed care program		
		Medicare Advantage Plans		
	D	Prescription drug plan		

Part C is called Medicare Advantage Plans. They are similar to managed health care plans, so they will require referrals, and have network physicians. These plans are managed by private companies and must be approved by Medicare. The plans cover all Parts A and B benefits.

Part D is the Medicare Drug Prescription plan. The drug prescription plan for Medicare can be very confusing for patients. They must choose a plan from many different insurance companies according to their prescription needs. The prescription drug plans are administered by other insurance companies but must be approved by Medicare.

Medicare's original plan is the **fee-for-service plan**. Patients have a yearly deductible with billed services reimbursed according to the Medicare fee schedule. Railroad employees are covered under their own Medicare program, Railroad Medicare.

MEDIGAP

Patients may be responsible for a portion of each claim that is submitted to Medicare. Many individuals purchase a Medigap or supplemental insurance policy that will fill in the "gap" of the unpaid amounts. The patient pays a premium and the Medigap insurance pays the percentage due by the patient and any deductibles. These policies are administrated by private insurance companies approved by Medicare. The Medigap information can be entered on the claim when it is initially billed. Medicare will automatically forward reimbursement information to the secondary Medigap insurance company. Payment is then sent directly to the physician's office. Medicare will also automatically crossover claim information to Medicaid as a secondary payer.

Medicare beneficiaries (enrollees) may choose instead to purchase secondary policies not approved by Medicare. These secondary policies may also be billed for the amount due by the patient, but Medicare will not automatically forward the secondary claim.

MEDICARE AS A SECONDARY PAYER

In most circumstances Medicare will be the primary insurance coverage for the patient. There are some exceptions to this rule. Therefore, it is vital for the reimbursement specialist to know the primary insurance to bill.

Medicare will be a secondary insurance if:

- The patient is employed and covered under a group health plan.

- The patient's spouse is working and covers the patient under their group health plan (employer must have more than 20 employees).

- The patient is covered under workers' compensation.

- The patient is covered under liability insurance (auto accident).

- The patient is covered under veteran's benefits.

The medical office will ask the patient to fill out a questionnaire (see Figure 6-1) to help the reimbursement specialist determine whether Medicare is the primary or secondary payer.

Medicare Secondary Payer Questionnaire

All Medicare patients must complete this questionnaire before this medical office can submit your Medicare claim. Medicare law requires this information to determine if your Medicare coverage is your primary or secondary insurance policy.

1. I am working full time _____, part time _____.

2. I retired on this date _____.

3. I had a job-related injury _____ Date _____.

4. I have had treatment for an injury relating to a car accident _____ Date _____.

5. I have had treatment for another kind of accident (liability) _____ Date _____.

6. I am on kidney dialysis _____ Dates _____.

7. I have had an organ transplant _____ Date _____.

8. I am enrolled in Medicare HMO _____ Date _____.

9. I am a veteran _____ I have a fee card _____

10. I have Black Lung Benefits _____ Date _____.

11. I am covered by an employer group policy by a company with more than 20 employees, by either myself or my spouse _____ Insurance company _____.

12. I have an insurance policy to supplement my Medicare _____ Insurance company _____.

13. I am covered by an employer-sponsored health plan for retirees _____ Insurance company _____.

14. I am covered by Medicaid _____ Date _____ ID # _____.

Patient signature _____ Date _____

Figure 6-1. Sample Medicare Secondary Payer Questionnaire

STOP AND PRACTICE

Exercise 6-2

Short answer: Answer each question with a short statement.

1. Describe benefit coverage for the different Medicare plans.

   _____

   _____

   _____

   _____

2. Explain why Medigap coverage is so important to the Medicare beneficiary.

   _____

   _____

   _____

3. When is Medicare considered the secondary payer?

   _____

   _____

   _____

   _____

MEDICARE REIMBURSEMENT

Knowledge of the rules and regulations set by CMS for the submission of Medicare claims will make the reimbursement specialist invaluable to the physician's medical billing office.

The Medicare health insurance identification card, as shown in Figure 6-2, is easy to recognize.

The Medicare card has red and blue stripes at the top. It contains the policy holder's name, signature, sex, effective date, and identification number. The card will indicate the benefit coverage, Part A and/or Part B. The Medicare identification number used to be the patient's Social Security number followed by a letter. Due to identity theft problems, Medicare no longer uses the Social Security number. The letters following the numeric id will indicate

This is the patient's health insurance number. It must be shown on all Medicare claims exactly as it is shown on the card, *including the letter at the end.*

This shows hospital insurance coverage.

This shows medical insurance coverage.

The date the insurance starts is shown here.

Figure 6-2. Copy of a Medicare card

information to Medicare. The following is a short list on some of the most common letters used:

- A is for the retired worker
- B is the wife of the retired worker
- B1 is the husband of the retired worker
- C is the child of the retired or deceased worker
- D is a widow
- D1 is a widower
- HA is a disabled worker
- M is Part B only with no SSA benefit
- W is a disabled widow
- WA is railroad retirement

PARTICIPATING PHYSICIANS

A physician may elect to participate with the Medicare program or be non-participating.

A participating physician will **accept assignment** on all Medicare claims. Accepting assignment means the physician agreed to accept Medicare's allowed charges (fee schedule), of which they pay 80% and the patient pays 20% of the charges. The participating physician's fee schedule will be 5% higher than non-participating physicians. By participating with Medicare, physicians will enjoy some benefits. Their claims will be processed faster. Medicare will automatically forward claims to the patient's secondary insurance, and the physician will be listed in the Medicare carrier's online directory. The non-participating physician can collect up to the limiting charge from the patient, submit the claim to Medicare, and Medicare will reimburse the patient. Medicare's **limiting charge** on the non-participating physician is 115% of the fee schedule.

Non-participating physicians must accept assignment on certain services, which include: ambulance services, physician lab services, clinical diagnostic lab services, medications, ambulatory surgical center services, home dialysis supplies, and equipment. Some providers must accept assignment and they include: anesthesiologist assistants, certified registered nurse anesthetists, physician assistants, nurse practitioners, clinical psychologists, clinical social workers, clinical nurse specialists, certified nurse midwives, and registered dietitians.

Figure 6-3 is a comparison of some par and non-par physician charges and their reimbursement amounts.

Par Physician						
	fee schedule	80%	20%			
Charged amount	Medicare allowed amount	Medicare reimburses	Patient pays	Physician	
$ 100.00	$ 80.00	$ 64.00	$ 16.00	$ 20.00	
$ 165.00	$115.00	$ 92.00	$ 23.00	$ 50.00	
$ 55.00	$ 40.00	$ 32.00	$ 8.00	$ 15.00	
$1,250.00	$995.00	$796.00	$199.00	$255.00	
Non Par Physician						
	fee schedule	115% of allowed amount	80%		Physician
Charged amount	Medicare allowed amount	Medicare limiting amount	Medicare pays patient	Patient pays	adjust
$ 100.00	–5% $ 76	$ 87.40	$ 60.80	$ 26.60	$ 12.60
$ 165.00	–5% $109.25	$ 125.63	$ 87.40	$ 38.23	$ 39.37
$ 55.00	–5% $ 38.00	$ 43.70	$ 30.40	$ 13.30	$ 11.30
$1,250.00	–5% $945.25	$1087.03	$756.20	$330.83	$162.97

Figure 6-3. Reimbursement comparisons between participating and non-participating physicians

STOP AND PRACTICE

Exercise 6-3

Short answer: Answer each question with a short statement.

1. How will you recognize the Medicare card and what information is listed on the card?

   _____

   _____

   _____

2. What does it mean to "accept assignment" on a health claim?

   _____

   _____

   _____

3. Describe the differences between a participating and non-participating physician with Medicare.

   _____

   _____

   _____

Fill in the blanks.

4. Compare the same service.

   Par physician

charged amount	Allowed amount	Medicare pays physician	Patient co-insurance
$100	$60	_____	_____

   Non-par physician

charged amount	Allowed amount	Limiting amount	Medicare pays	Patient pays
$100	_____	_____	_____	_____

Matching: Match the letter designation on the Medicare card with its meaning.

5. _____ A   A. Wife of retired worker

6. _____ B   B. Widow

7. _____ C   C. Railroad retirement

8. _____ D   D. Child of deceased worker

9. _____ WA   E. Retired worker

                          F. Disabled widow

                          G. Disabled worker

MEDICARE RULES AND REGULATIONS

The reimbursement specialist must understand the extensive and often confusing rules and regulations set up by CMS. It is important to remember that reimbursement by Medicare depends on medical necessity. Medicare guidelines require the treatment to be appropriate for the diagnosis (ICD-9 code). The diagnosis must support the need for the service. Treatment cannot be cosmetic, experimental, or investigative. The treatment must be essential and must be billed for the appropriate level of care.

The regulations for Medicare change quickly and frequently. The reimbursement specialist must keep abreast on all Medicare changes.

Excluded Services

Medicare requires the physician's office to inform the patient of any non-covered service they may require. The participating physician will be denied reimbursement if the physician's billing office does not keep the patient informed of non-covered charges. The patient will not be held liable for this charge.

Some of the excluded services for Medicare Part B that are not medically necessary are:

- **Routine physical exams**

- **Most immunizations except influenza, hepatitis B, and pneumococcal vaccines**

- **Routine dental**

- **Foot care (except for diabetic patients)**

- **Hearing exams**

- **Eye exams**

- **Custodial care**

- **Long-term care**

- **Cosmetic surgery**

- **Acupuncture**

Medicare does allow the physician's office to bill the patient for any possible non-covered service or procedure if the patient is informed in writing before the service is performed. If the patient wishes to proceed and pay for this service, an **Advance Beneficiary Notice (ABN)** must be signed and on file in the patient's medical record chart. An ABN is a document explaining that the service might not be a covered service, due to medical necessity. The advance beneficiary notice may not be obtained on every procedure, "just in case." This is fraudulent.

Figure 6-4 shows an Advance Beneficiary Notice.

When billing Medicare for the non-covered service, a **modifier** is attached to the CPT code to alert Medicare that an ABN is on file. A modifier is a two-digit alphanumeric or numeric code that alerts the insurance company of an unusual circumstance.

The GZ modifier is used to indicate the billing office believes that the service will be denied and an ABN is not on file. This is possibly due to an emergency situation.

The GA modifier indicates to Medicare a waiver of liability, or an ABN is on file.

With the use of these modifiers, Medicare will process the claim and remit an EOB to the physician and patient. The payment is the responsibility of the patient. If the billing office did not obtain a necessary ABN, Medicare will process the claim and deny the claim. They will require the physician's office to adjust off the total charged amount, making the patient non-liable for the charges.

Medicare providers must also inform their patients in writing of the possible out-of-pocket costs of any elective surgery and non-covered procedures if the charge is $500 or more. This form is the **Medicare Surgical Disclosure Notice**. The Omnibus Budget Reconciliation Act of 1986 states that the patient must be informed in writing of: the estimated cost of the surgery, the estimated Medicare reimbursement, the patient's out-of-pocket expense, any co-insurance amount, and the difference between the provider's charged amount and the Medicare approved amount of reimbursement. Figure 6-5 is an example of the Medicare Surgical Disclosure Notice.

Rules and Regulations Resources

All of the Medicare rules and regulations from CMS are published in the Federal Register. Medicare also issues newsletters and manuals for billing offices. The manuals define the guidelines for Medicare policies, billing processes, and reimbursement.

These are important manuals. These include The **Medicare Claims Processing Manual**, **National Coverage Determination Manual (NCD)**, the **Corrective Coding Initiative (CCI)**, and **Local Coverage Determinations Manual (LCD)**. It is important for the reimbursement specialist to know how to access and understand these manuals. They can be found on the Internet through the Medicare Web site. Learning how to navigate and obtain information through the Medicare Web site is imperative for the reimbursement specialist.

(*A*) Notifier(s):

(*B*) Patient Name: (*C*) Identification Number:

ADVANCE BENEFICIARY NOTICE OF NONCOVERAGE (ABN)

<u>*NOTE*:</u> If Medicare doesn't pay for (*D*)_____ below, you may have to pay.

Medicare does not pay for everything, even some care that you or your health care provider have good reason to think you need. We expect Medicare may not pay for the (*D*) _____ below.

(*D*) _____	(*E*) Reason Medicare May Not Pay:	(*F*) Estimated Cost:

WHAT YOU NEED TO DO NOW:

- Read this notice, so you can make an informed decision about your care.
- Ask us any questions that you may have after you finish reading.
- Choose an option below about whether to receive the (*D*) _____ listed above.

    Note: If you choose Option 1 or 2, we may help you to use any other insurance that you might have, but Medicare cannot require us to do this.

(*G*) OPTIONS: Check only one box. We cannot choose a box for you.
☐ **OPTION 1.** I want the (*D*) _____ listed above. You may ask to be paid now, but I also want Medicare billed for an official decision on payment, which is sent to me on a Medicare Summary Notice (MSN). I understand that if Medicare doesn't pay, I am responsible for payment, but **I can appeal to Medicare** by following the directions on the MSN. If Medicare does pay, you will refund any payments I made to you, less co-pays or deductibles.
☐ **OPTION 2.** I want the (*D*) _____ listed above, but do not bill Medicare. You may ask to be paid now as I am responsible for payment. **I cannot appeal if Medicare is not billed**.
☐ **OPTION 3.** I don't want the (*D*) _____ listed above. I understand with this choice I am **not** responsible for payment, and **I cannot appeal to see if Medicare would pay**.

(*H*) Additional Information:

This notice gives our opinion, not an official Medicare decision. If you have other questions on this notice or Medicare billing, call **1-800-MEDICARE** 1-800-633-4227/**TTY: 1-877-486-2048).**

Signing below means that you have received and understand this notice. You also receive a copy.

(*I*) Signature:	(*J*) Date:

According to the Paperwork Reduction Act of 1995, no persons are required to respond to a collection of information unless it displays a valid OMB control number. The valid OMB control number for this information collections is 0938-0566. The time required to complete this information collections is estimated to average 7 minutes per response, including the time to review instructions, search existing data resources, gather the data needed, and complete and review the information collections. If you have comments concerning the accuracy of the time estimate or suggestions for improving this form, please write to: CMS, 7500 Security Boulevard, Attn: PRA Reports Clearance Officer, Baltimore, Maryland 21244-1850.

Form CMS-R-131 (03/08)   Form Approved OMB No, 0938-0566

Figure 6-4. Advance Beneficiary Notice. *(Courtesy of the Centers for Medicare & Medicaid Services. http://www.cms.hhs.gov)*

Medicare Surgical Disclosure Notice

Medicare beneficiary:

Name _____ Date _____

Medicare regulations require that all non-participating physicians provide the following

information to patients having elective surgery with a cost of $500.00 or more. I am a

non-participating physician and will not be accepting assignment on your surgery charge.

Surgery _____

Name of physician _____

Estimated charge _____

Estimated Medicare reimbursement _____

Patient's estimated payment _____

Acknowledged and agreed by:

_____ signature of Medicare beneficiary or legal representative

_____ date

_____ signature of physician

_____ date

Figure 6-5. Sample Surgical Disclosure Notice

The National and Local Coverage Determination Manuals will link many CPT codes with medically necessary ICD-9 codes. This will help the medical billing office determine if a service or procedure will be deemed medically necessary, which will result in correct reimbursement. The Corrective Coding Initiative reports bundled codes; if one code will describe the service or procedure, multiple codes cannot be billed. Also listed are mutually exclusive codes, codes that cannot be billed together on the same date of service. These manuals help prevent improper coding. Learning how to use these manuals will help the medical billing office submit clean claims, and receive correct reimbursement.

Fraud and Abuse

It is of the utmost importance to correctly bill and code all services for Medicare according to their rules and regulations. Medicare monitors for fraud and abuse in health claim billing. **Fraud** is knowingly filing an improper health claim. **Abuse** is unknowingly filling an improper health claim. Ignorance is not an excuse for filing these improper claims. Some common coding errors on a Medicare claim include:

Upcoding or **downcoding**: Incorrectly coding what the physician has documented. Up-coding is coding a higher-level service than was performed, and down-coding is coding for a lower-level service than was performed.

Reporting services that are not documented.

Altering documents after services are reported.

Not coding diagnoses to the highest specificity.

Changing the diagnoses to collect reimbursement.

Unbundling codes for higher reimbursement.

Avoiding these problems will be straightforward if the reimbursement specialist has knowledge of Medicare rules and regulations and stays current with the rules through continuing education. Keep current through:

Utilizing all newsletters and publications on policy updates.

Learning and understanding previously received denials.

Effectively navigating the Medicare Web site.

Reimbursement Process

Once a claim is submitted to a Medicare carrier, the claim is reimbursed. Medicare must respond to ALL submitted claims. The **Medicare Remittance Advice (MRA)** is sent to the physician's office. The patient receives a **Medicare Summary Notice (MSN)**. These notices outline the reimbursement of each claim submitted. The MRA sent to the physician may include multiple patients and dates of service. The MSN or EOB sent to the patient will have only claims for that patient. However, it can include multiple dates of service (Figure 6-6). Both notices will look different but have the same information included on the documents for that patient.

Medicare Summary Notice

CUSTOMER SERVICE INFORMATION

BENEFICIARY NAME
STREET ADDRESS
CITY, STATE   ZIP CODE

Your Medicare Number 111-11-1111A

If you have questions, write or call:
  Medicare (#12345) 555 Medicare Blvd., Suite 200
  Medicare Building Medicare, US XXXXX-XXXX

BE INFORMED: Beware of telemarketers offering free or discounted medicare items or services.

Call: 1-800-MEDICARE (1-800-633-4227)
Ask for Doctor Services
TTY for Hearing Impaired: 1-877-486-2048

This is a summary of claims processed from 05/10/20XX through 08/10/20XX.

PART B MEDICAL INSURANCE - ASSIGNED CLAIMS

Dates of Service Provided	Services	Amount Charged	Medicare Approved	Medicare Paid Provider	You May Be Billed	See Notes Section
Claim Number: 12435-84956-84556						
Paul Jones, M.D., 123 West Street, Jacksonville, FL 33231-0024						a
Referred by: Scott Wilson, M.D.						
04/19/06	1 Influenza immunization (90724)	**$ 5.00**	**$ 3.88**	**$ 3.88**	**$0.00**	b
04/19/06	1 Admin, flu vac (G0008)	5.00	3.43	3.43	0.00	b
	Claim Total	$10.00	$ 7.31	$ 7.31	$0.00	
Claim Number: 12435-84956-84557						
ABC Ambulance, P.O. Box 2149, Jacksonville, FL 33231						a
04/25/06	**1 Ambulance, base rate (A0020)**	**$289.00**	**$249.78**	**$199.82**	**$49.96**	
04/25/06	1 Ambulance, per mile (A0021)	21.00	16.96	13.57	3.39	
	Claim Total	$310.00	$266.74	$213.39	$53.35	

PART B MEDICAL INSURANCE-UNASSIGNED CLAIMS

Dates of Service Provided	Services	Amount Charged	Medicare Approved	Medicare Paid Provider	You May Be Billed	See Notes Section
Claim Number: 12435-84956-84558						
William Newman, M.D., 362 North Street Jacksonville, FL 33231-0024						a
03/10/06	1 Office/Outpatient Visit, ES (99213)	$47.00	$33.93	$27.15	$27.15	c

THIS IS NOT A BILL - Keep this notice for your records.

Figure 6-6. Medicare Summary Notice

The reimbursement notices will include the patient's name, Medicare number, date of service, the physician's name, claim number, and service provided (Figure 6-7). The CPT, ICD-9 codes billed, and the amounts billed are shown. Medicare will present the approved amount, amount paid to the provider, and the amount the patient will be responsible for. The reimbursement notice will indicate the amount of any deductible, any adjustment that must be made, and any denial or rejection on each claim.

The reimbursement specialist must check each MRA for correct reimbursement and denials. Denial codes will help the reimbursement specialist understand why a claim was not paid. Any corrections must be made quickly and resubmitted or appealed. Assistance is available by calling Medicare's claim status telephone line. Many Medicare carriers have a resubmission time limit on Medicare denials.

Medicare Carrier   Medicare Remittance Notice
111 Union Ave
Century, NC 37777
1-888-888-8888

Medicare Provider   Provider # 1111111111
222 Smith Street   Page #   1 of 1
Smith, NC 37777   Date: 10/01/20XX
                                                                    Check/EFT #   000231456

Medicare Part B Standard Paper Remittance

Perf Prov	Serv Date	Pos	Nos	Proc	Mods	Billed	Allowed	Deduct	Coins	Grp/Rc	Amt	Prov Pd
Name:Smith, Ronald	HIC 1234567891	Acnt:Smitro	ICN 123456789123 ASG Y								MOA	
123456ABC 0922	0922XX	11	1	99213		66.00	49.83	0.34	9.97	PR-96	16.17	39.52
Pt Resp 10.31	Claim Totals					66.00	49.83	0.34	9.97		16.17	39.52
										Net	39.52	

Perf Prov	Serv Date	Pos	Nos	Proc	Mods	Billed	Allowed	Deduct	Coins	Grp/Rc	Amt	Prov Pd
Name:Hurst, John	HIC 1234567892	Acnt:Hursjo	ICN 124565789845 ASG Y MOA									
123456ABC 0925	0925XX	11	1			66.00	49.83	0.00	9.97	PR-95	16.17	39.86
123456ABC 0925	0925XX	11	1			10.00	4.37	0.00	0.00	CO-42	5.63	4.37
Pt Resp 9.97	Claim Totals					76.00	54.20	0.00	9.97		22.30	44.23
									Net	44.23		

Claim information forwarded to: North Carolina Medicaid

Totals:	# of Claims	Billed amt	Allowed amt	Deduct	Coins	Prov Pd	Prov adj	Check amt
	2	142.00	104.03	0.34	19.94	83.75	37.97	83.75

Figure 6-7. Sample Medicare Remittance Advice

STOP AND PRACTICE

Exercise 6-4

Short answer: Answer each question with a short statement.

1. List some excluded benefits with Medicare Part B.

   _____

   _____

   _____

2. Explain in detail the ABN.

   _____

   _____

   _____

3. Describe what the Corrective Coding Initiative Manual explains.

   _____

   _____

   _____

4. Why is it so important to know how to use the local and regional determination lists?

   _____

   _____

   _____

5. What is the difference between the MRA and the MSN and what information is listed on these documents?

   _____

   _____

   _____

Figure 6-8. Sample of completed CMS-1500 billing form for Medicare

---

(1500) HEALTH INSURANCE CLAIM FORM

APPROVED BY NATIONAL UNIFORM CLAIM COMMITTEE 08/05

PICA | | | PICA | | |

1. MEDICARE [X] (Medicare #) MEDICAID ☐ (Medicaid #) TRICARE CHAMPUS ☐ (Sponsor's SSN) CHAMPVA ☐ (Member ID#) GROUP HEALTH PLAN ☐ (SSN or ID) FECA BLK LUNG ☐ (SSN) OTHER ☐ (ID)

1a. INSURED'S I.D. NUMBER (For Program in Item 1): 001223344A

2. PATIENT'S NAME (Last Name, First Name, Middle Initial): PHELPS, JASON, D

3. PATIENT'S BIRTH DATE: 05 12 1932 SEX: M [X] F ☐

4. INSURED'S NAME (Last Name, First Name, Middle Initial): SAME

5. PATIENT'S ADDRESS (No., Street): 12 DOGWOOD LANE
CITY: CENTURY STATE: NC
ZIP CODE: 37777 TELEPHONE (Include Area Code): (335) 9294545

6. PATIENT'S RELATIONSHIP TO INSURED: Self [X] Spouse ☐ Child ☐ Other ☐

7. INSURED'S ADDRESS (No., Street): SAME
CITY: STATE:
ZIP CODE: TELEPHONE (Include Area Code): ( )

8. PATIENT STATUS: Single ☐ Married [X] Other ☐
Employed ☐ Full-Time Student ☐ Part-Time Student ☐

9. OTHER INSURED'S NAME (Last Name, First Name, Middle Initial):
a. OTHER INSURED'S POLICY OR GROUP NUMBER:
b. OTHER INSURED'S DATE OF BIRTH: MM DD YY SEX: M ☐ F ☐
c. EMPLOYER'S NAME OR SCHOOL NAME:
d. INSURANCE PLAN NAME OR PROGRAM NAME:

10. IS PATIENT'S CONDITION RELATED TO:
a. EMPLOYMENT? (Current or Previous): YES ☐ NO [X]
b. AUTO ACCIDENT? PLACE (State): YES ☐ NO [X]
c. OTHER ACCIDENT?: YES ☐ NO [X]
10d. RESERVED FOR LOCAL USE:

11. INSURED'S POLICY GROUP OR FECA NUMBER:
a. INSURED'S DATE OF BIRTH: MM DD YY SEX: M ☐ F ☐
b. EMPLOYER'S NAME OR SCHOOL NAME: RETIRED
c. INSURANCE PLAN NAME OR PROGRAM NAME: MEDICARE B
d. IS THERE ANOTHER HEALTH BENEFIT PLAN?: YES ☐ NO [X] If yes, return to and complete item 9 a-d.

READ BACK OF FORM BEFORE COMPLETING & SIGNING THIS FORM.

12. PATIENT'S OR AUTHORIZED PERSON'S SIGNATURE I authorize the release of any medical or other information necessary to process this claim. I also request payment of government benefits either to myself or to the party who accepts assignment below.
SIGNED: SOF DATE: 031620XX

13. INSURED'S OR AUTHORIZED PERSON'S SIGNATURE I authorize payment of medical benefits to the undersigned physcian or supplier for services described below.
SIGNED: SOF

14. DATE OF CURRENT: ILLNESS (First symptom) OR INJURY (Accident) OR PREGNANCY (LMP): MM DD YY

15. IF PATIENT HAS HAD SAME OR SIMILAR ILLNESS, GIVE FIRST DATE: MM DD YY

16. DATES PATIENT UNABLE TO WORK IN CURRENT OCCUPATION: FROM MM DD YY TO MM DD YY

17. NAME OF REFERRING PROVIDER OR OTHER SOURCE: JOHN BERRY MD
17a.
17b. NPI: 1234567891

18. HOSPITALIZATION DATES RELATED TO CURRENT SERVICES: FROM MM DD YY TO MM DD YY

19. RESERVED FOR LOCAL USE:

20. OUTSIDE LAB?: YES ☐ NO [X] $ CHARGES

21. DIAGNOSIS OR NATURE OF ILLNESS OR INJURY (Relate Items 1, 2, 3 or 4 to Item 24E by Line):
1. 250 00
2.
3.
4.

22. MEDICAID RESUBMISSION CODE ORIGINAL REF. NO.

23. PRIOR AUTHORIZATION NUMBER

24. A. DATE(S) OF SERVICE From / To (MM DD YY)	B. PLACE OF SERVICE	C. EMG	D. PROCEDURES, SERVICES, OR SUPPLIES CPT/HCPCS / MODIFIER	E. DIAGNOSIS POINTER	F. $ CHARGES	G. DAYS OR UNITS	H. EPSDT Family Plan	I. ID. QUAL.	J. RENDERING PROVIDER ID. #
1 03 16 20XX	11		99203	1	90 00			NPI	1234567891
2								NPI	
3								NPI	
4								NPI	
5								NPI	
6								NPI	

25. FEDERAL TAX I.D. NUMBER SSN [ ] EIN [X]: 111223456

26. PATIENT'S ACCOUNT NO.: CHASEMA

27. ACCEPT ASSIGNMENT? (For govt. claims, see back): YES [X] NO ☐

28. TOTAL CHARGE: $ 90 00

29. AMOUNT PAID: $

30. BALANCE DUE: $ 90 00

31. SIGNATURE OF PHYSICIAN OR SUPPLIER INCLUDING DEGREES OR CREDENTIALS (I certify that the statements on the reverse apply to this bill and are made a part thereof.)
JOHN BERRY MD
SIGNED DATE: 031620XX

32. SERVICE FACILITY LOCATION INFORMATION:
a. NPI b.

33. BILLING PROVIDER INFO & PH # ( ):
JOHN BERRY MD
3 PARK STREET
CENTURY NC 37777
a. NPI b. 1234567891

NUCC Instruction Manual available at: www.nucc.org

NOT APPROVED FOR USE FORM CMS-1500 (08/05)

BILLING MEDICARE ON THE CMS-1500 FORM

It is important to understand what information Medicare requires on the CMS-1500 form (a completed form is shown in Figure 6-8). This information can be different from other insurance companies' requirements. If a clean claim is not submitted, a rejection will occur, delaying reimbursement. Medicare requires that all providers submit a claim for Medicare beneficiaries.

These fields are different for Medicare than for all other insurance companies.

- Block 4: Enter "SAME" — the patient is always the insured.
- Block 6: Leave blank — the patient is always the insured.
- Blocks 9-9d: Use for Medigap information.
- Block 10: Use to enter the Medicaid crossover ID number (MCD111111111).
- Block 11: Enter "NONE."
- Block 11b: Enter "RETIRED."
- Block 15: Leave blank.
- Block 17: Enter the name and credentials for the provider who referred the patient or ordered health care services or supplies.
- Block 17a: Enter the NPI for provider listed in block 17.
- Block 24j: Enter the NPI for the provider of care.

CHAPTER SUMMARY

- President Lyndon Johnson signed Medicare into law in 1965.
- The Centers for Medicare and Medicaid set the rules and regulations for Medicare (formerly administered by HCFA).
- President George W. Bush signed into law the Medicare prescription benefit.
- To be eligible for Medicare, an individual must be 65 years of age or older, have a long-term disability, or have end-stage renal disease.
- Local or Regional Carriers process the Medicare claims for CMS.
- The Medicare Program includes Plans A—hospital coverage, Plan B—outpatient physician coverage, diagnostic studies, Plan C—Medicare managed care plan, and Plan D—outpatient prescription benefit.
- Participating physicians with Medicare accept assignment with Medicare and receive higher reimbursement than non-participating physicians.
- Medicare reimburses according to a fee schedule, a predetermined amount of money determined using an RVU system.

- Medicare will automatically crossover claim information to secondary insurances called Medigap policies and Medicaid beneficiaries.

- Medicare is usually the primary payer for beneficiaries. It can be a secondary payer if the patient is covered by workers' compensation or has a liability claim. If the patient is still working, has a group health plan, or the spouse is working and has group health plan coverage, Medicare will be secondary.

- Medicare's rules and regulations can change quickly. A reimbursement specialist must keep abreast of these.

REVIEW QUESTIONS

Define the following key terms.

1. Medicare

2. Medigap

3. ABN

4. CMS

5. DME

Short answer: Answer each question with a short statement.

6.   Explain upcoding.

_____

_____

_____

_____

_____

7.   Explain how a reimbursement specialist can ensure reimbursement for a possible non-covered service.

_____

_____

_____

_____

_____

8.   Explain what is contained in the Corrective Coding Initiative Manual.

_____

_____

_____

_____

_____

9.   List the reasons why Medicare would be a secondary payer.

_____

_____

_____

_____

_____

10. Calculate the reimbursement for a participating and non-participating physician for the service listed below; also calculate the amount the patient will owe.

Charge $75.00

Medicare allowed amount (fee schedule) $50.00

PAR

Charge	Allowed	Medicare pays	Patient pays	Physician adjustment
$75.00	$50.00	_____	_____	_____

NON PAR

Charge	Allowed	Limiting amount	Medicare pays	Patient pays	Adjust
$75.00	$47.50	_____	_____	_____	_____

11. Explain the difference between fraud and abuse.

_____

_____

_____

_____

_____

12. What is RVU and what is it used for?

_____

_____

_____

_____

_____

PRACTICAL APPLICATION

Log on to the Medicare Web site, http://www.medicare.gov, and go to the provider section. Learning to navigate around this site is very helpful. Find the Outreach and Education section, which is the Medicare Learning network. Go to the Web-based training modules and pick a topic. Example: World of Medicare. Summarize what you have learned and present this information to the class.

Chapter 7

Blue Cross Blue Shield, Medicaid, TRICARE, Commercial, and Workers' Compensation Insurances

OBJECTIVES

Upon completion of this chapter, the student should be able to:

- Outline the basics of Blue Cross Blue Shield insurance.
- Outline the basics of Medicaid insurance.
- Outline the basics of TRICARE insurance.
- Outline the basics of commercial insurance.
- Outline the basics of Workers' Compensation insurance.

KEY TERMS

Accept assignment

Blue Cross Blue Shield

CHAMPVA

Commercial insurance

Defense Enrollment Eligibility Reporting System (DEERS)

First report of injury

Group policies

Medicaid

Payer of last resort

Primary care manager (PCM)

INTRODUCTION

Knowledge of the major insurance programs will be invaluable to the reimbursement specialist. A physician's office will see a large variety of these insurance programs.

Understanding the different insurance plans within these programs will be essential to collecting the correct reimbursement. This chapter will outline the basics of Blue Cross Blue Shield, Medicaid, TRICARE, commercial, and workers' compensation insurances.

BLUE CROSS BLUE SHIELD

The **Blue Cross Blue Shield** Association (BCBS) was started in the 1930s to provide health care coverage at an affordable cost. This insurance company is the oldest form of health insurance in the country. One in three Americans are Blue Cross Blue Shield enrollees. There are 39 plans in the United States and Puerto Rico. It is a national organization but is administered by locally owned companies. Each independent BCBS company processes its own claims. Ninety percent of physicians participate with Blue Cross Blue Shield.

History of Blue Cross Blue Shield

In 1929, the prototype hospital plan (Blue Cross) was offered at Baylor University in Dallas, Texas. The premium for 21 days of hospitalization cost an amazing $6.00. The Blue Cross symbol was first used in 1934. Blue Shield was developed in 1938, its symbol was introduced in 1939. Blue Cross covered hospital services and Blue Shield covered physician services.

In 1977, the Blue Cross and Blue Shield national associations combined personnel under one leadership. In 1982, they became BlueCross BlueShield Association. Today, Blue Cross Blue Shield processes the majority of Medicare claims and enrollment reaches over 99 million people. The Blue Cross Blue Shield Association is located in Chicago, Illinois, and helps the locally owned companies by:

- Establishing standards for the plans and programs
- Assisting in national advertising, education, and research
- Coordinating the nationwide BCBS plans

Blue Cross Blue Shield Plans

The majority of BCBS plans are managed care plans, which include HMO, PPO, and POS. These plans offer quality care for lower costs by managing all aspects of the patient's health care. Other plans include fee-for-service (their traditional coverage), indemnity, Healthcare Anywhere (Blue Card), a federal employee program, and Medicare supplemental Medigap plans.

Fee-for-Service

The traditional coverage for BCBS is the fee-for-service plan. Most of these plans are currently being phased out. The coverage was basic + major medical benefits. The basic coverage included hospital services, surgical fees, diagnostic lab, and x-ray. The major medical coverage included office visits, outpatient services, durable medical equipment, physical and occupational therapy, and prescription drugs.

Indemnity

Indemnity plans are similar to the fee-for-service coverage. The enrollee does not have a primary care physician, and can see the provider of their choice without a referral. The participant can choose different co-insurance options.

Managed Care

Blue Cross Blue Shield managed care provides a variety of plan options. These plans include a network of physicians and hospitals. The managed care plans offered include EPO, HMO, PPO, and POS. The Exclusive Provider Organization (EPO) has a network of physicians, hospitals, and other providers of health care. Subscribers do not need a primary care physician or referrals but must stay within the network of health care providers. The Health Maintenance Organization (HMO) is an all-inclusive plan providing health care services for a fixed, predetermined reimbursement. A primary care physician (PCP) is chosen and referrals are required for services beyond the PCP.

The point-of-service (POS) plan provides a network of providers, but the subscriber may chose to see any health care provider. The subscriber does choose a primary care physician. Higher co-pays result if the subscriber goes out of network.

The Preferred Provider Organization (PPO) is a plan that includes a network of health care providers, with a chosen primary care physician. If the subscriber receives care outside the network, a referral must be obtained.

Federal Employee Program

The Blue Cross Blue Shield Federal Employee Program is offered to federal employees and was established by Congress in 1959. The enrollee's card will indicate it is a Government-Wide Service Benefit Plan and the identification number will always begin with an "R." Each individual can choose an option plan, and it will be written on their insurance card. Code 101 is individual high option, 102 is family high option, 104 is individual low option, and 105 is family low option plan. The federal BCBS also offers a managed care plan. It is a POS that requires a primary care physician.

Healthcare Anywhere

The Healthcare Anywhere plan allows enrollees to access health care anywhere in the United States and around the world. If they are traveling or living outside their home plan area, benefits will be the same as the home plan. The BCBS insurance card will display a suitcase with the logo of the home plan. Figure 7-1 shows an example of a Blue Cross Blue Shield card.

Figure 7-1. Blue Cross Blue Shield card

Medicare Medigap

Blue Cross Blue Shield also offers Medicare Medigap supplemental plans. These Medigap policies will pay the co-payments and deductibles not covered by Medicare.

Medigap will be printed on the enrollee's insurance card.

Physician Participation

A physician has a choice whether he will participate with Blue Cross Blue Shield or not. If the physician chooses not to participate, payment in full is expected from the patient. If the physician participates with BCBS, reimbursement will be according to a predetermined fee schedule. Participating physicians receive reimbursement directly from BCBS. They receive training, newsletters, and a billing representative to help with any billing problems from the Blue Cross Blue Shield Association.

A participating physician must submit claims for all Blue Cross Blue Shield enrollees. They also agree to **accept assignment**, the reimbursement set up by the fee schedule, charging the patient only for the assigned co-pays and deductibles.

Most BCBS plans require pre-certification for elective surgeries and some diagnostic procedures. The participating physician must accept all plan members, and make referrals only to other participating physicians.

The subscriber's card should list the plan name, type of plan, subscriber's name, identification number, deductibles, co-pays, and claim submission address and telephone number. The reimbursement specialist must carefully examine each patients' Blue Cross Blue Shield card for pertinent information regarding their plan benefits.

The CMS-1500 insurance billing form must be submitted within one year of the date of service. Some plans require second surgical opinions and pre-authorizations and, all participating providers must accept assignment on the claim. The CMS-1500 form (see Figure 7-2) should be completed as explained in Chapter 4.

1500

HEALTH INSURANCE CLAIM FORM

NOT APPROVED FOR USE

| | PICA | | | | | | | PICA | | |

| 1. MEDICARE (Medicare #) | MEDICAID (Medicaid #) | TRICARE CHAMPUS (Sponsor's SSN) | CHAMPVA (Member ID#) | GROUP HEALTH PLAN (SSN or ID) | FECA BLK LUNG (SSN) [X] | OTHER (ID) | 1a. INSURED'S I.D. NUMBER (For Program in Item 1) |
| YYM1234569501 |

| 2. PATIENT'S NAME (Last Name, First Name, Middle Initial) | 3. PATIENT'S BIRTH DATE / SEX | 4. INSURED'S NAME (Last Name, First Name, Middle Initial) |
| CHASE, MARY, D | MM 04 DD 21 YY 1965 M [ ] F [X] | SAME |

| 5. PATIENT'S ADDRESS (No., Street) | 6. PATIENT'S RELATIONSHIP TO INSURED | 7. INSURED'S ADDRESS (No., Street) |
| 3 PINE OAKS | Self [X] Spouse [ ] Child [ ] Other [ ] | SAME |

| CITY | STATE | 8. PATIENT STATUS | CITY | STATE |
| CENTURY | NC | Single [X] Married [ ] Other [ ] | | |

| ZIP CODE | TELEPHONE (Include Area Code) | | ZIP CODE | TELEPHONE (Include Area Code) |
| 37777 | (335) 2629898 | Employed [X] Full-Time Student [ ] Part-Time Student [ ] | | ( ) |

9. OTHER INSURED'S NAME (Last Name, First Name, Middle Initial)

10. IS PATIENT'S CONDITION RELATED TO:

11. INSURED'S POLICY GROUP OR FECA NUMBER
00232000

a. OTHER INSURED'S POLICY OR GROUP NUMBER

a. EMPLOYMENT? (Current or Previous) YES [ ] NO [X]

a. INSURED'S DATE OF BIRTH MM DD YY M [ ] F [ ]

b. OTHER INSURED'S DATE OF BIRTH MM DD YY SEX M [ ] F [ ]

b. AUTO ACCIDENT? PLACE (State) YES [ ] NO [X]

b. EMPLOYER'S NAME OR SCHOOL NAME
JAMES COMPANY

c. EMPLOYER'S NAME OR SCHOOL NAME

c. OTHER ACCIDENT? YES [ ] NO [X]

c. INSURANCE PLAN NAME OR PROGRAM NAME
BCBS

d. INSURANCE PLAN NAME OR PROGRAM NAME

10d. RESERVED FOR LOCAL USE

d. IS THERE ANOTHER HEALTH BENEFIT PLAN? YES [ ] NO [X] If yes, return to and complete item 9 a-d.

READ BACK OF FORM BEFORE COMPLETING & SIGNING THIS FORM.

12. PATIENT'S OR AUTHORIZED PERSON'S SIGNATURE I authorize the release of any medical or other information necessary to process this claim. I also request payment of government benefits either to myself or to the party who accepts assignment below.

SIGNED SOF DATE 120520XX

13. INSURED'S OR AUTHORIZED PERSON'S SIGNATURE I authorize payment of medical benefits to the undersigned physcian or supplier for services described below.

SIGNED SOF

| 14. DATE OF CURRENT: MM DD YY ◄ ILLNESS (First symptom) OR INJURY (Accident) OR PREGNANCY (LMP) | 15. IF PATIENT HAS HAD SAME OR SIMILAR ILLNESS. GIVE FIRST DATE MM DD YY | 16. DATES PATIENT UNABLE TO WORK IN CURRENT OCCUPATION MM DD YY FROM TO MM DD YY |

| 17. NAME OF REFERRING PROVIDER OR OTHER SOURCE | 17a. | 18. HOSPITALIZATION DATES RELATED TO CURRENT SERVICES MM DD YY FROM TO MM DD YY |
| JOHN BERRY MD | 17b. NPI 1234567891 | |

| 19. RESERVED FOR LOCAL USE | 20. OUTSIDE LAB? YES [ ] NO [X] $ CHARGES |

21. DIAGNOSIS OR NATURE OF ILLNESS OR INJURY (Relate Items 1, 2, 3 or 4 to Item 24E by Line)

1. 485 ⌐ 3. ⌐

2. ⌐ 4. ⌐

22. MEDICAID RESUBMISSION CODE ORIGINAL REF. NO.

23. PRIOR AUTHORIZATION NUMBER

24. A. DATE(S) OF SERVICE From MM DD YY To MM DD YY	B. PLACE OF SERVICE	C. EMG	D. PROCEDURES, SERVICES, OR SUPPLIES (Explain Unusual Circumstances) CPT/HCPCS MODIFIER	E. DIAGNOSIS POINTER	F. $ CHARGES	G. DAYS OR UNITS	H. EPSDT Family Plan	I. ID. QUAL.	J. RENDERING PROVIDER ID. #
1	12 05 20XX		11		99203	1	90 00			NPI	1234567891
2										NPI	
3										NPI	
4										NPI	
5										NPI	
6										NPI	

| 25. FEDERAL TAX I.D. NUMBER SSN EIN | 26. PATIENT'S ACCOUNT NO. | 27. ACCEPT ASSIGNMENT? (For govt. claims, see back) | 28. TOTAL CHARGE | 29. AMOUNT PAID | 30. BALANCE DUE |
| 111223456 [X] | CHASEMA | [X] YES [ ] NO | $ 90 00 | $ | $ 90 00 |

31. SIGNATURE OF PHYSICIAN OR SUPPLIER INCLUDING DEGREES OR CREDENTIALS (I certify that the statements on the reverse apply to this bill and are made a part thereof.)	32. SERVICE FACILITY LOCATION INFORMATION	33. BILLING PROVIDER INFO & PH # ( )
JOHN BERRY MD		JOHN BERRY MD 3 PARK STREET
SIGNED DATE 120220XX	a. NPI b.	a. NPI b. 1234567891

NUCC Instruction Manual available at: www.nucc.org

NOT APPROVED FOR USE FORM CMS-1500 (08/05)

Figure 7-2. Sample of completed CMS-1500 billing form for Blue Cross Blue Shield

STOP AND PRACTICE

Exercise 7-1

Fill in the blanks for each statement.

1. Blue Cross Blue Shield is a national organization but is administered by _____ companies.

2. The deadline for the submission of BCBS is _____ from the _____.

3. The majority of BCBS plans are _____.

4. BCBS has a/an _____ to supplement Medicare.

5. The participating physician with BCBS must accept a/an _____ and _____ to other participating physicians.

Short answer: Answer each question with a short statement.

6. Define EPO.

   _____

   _____

   _____

7. Explain the pros to participating with Blue Cross Blue Shield.

   _____

   _____

   _____

MEDICAID

The **Medicaid** health care program was established on July 30, 1965, authorized by the Social Security Act. This program was set up to reimburse physicians for the treatment of patients with low income, few resources, and disabilities. The Medicaid program is funded by both the federal and state governments.

Individuals must apply for coverage in the Medicaid program and meet strict income requirements. These requirements vary from state to state. The federal government sets some standards for the Medicaid program, but the states' government will set the specific requirements and programs. The regulations in each state may be different. Coverage in one state does not ensure the individual will qualify in another state. The plans within the Medicaid program include fee-for-service and managed care programs.

Medicaid Eligibility

Eligibility in the Medicaid program can be confusing. The major groups are: limited-income families in the Temporary Assistance for Needy Families program, SSI recipients, infants born to Medicaid-eligible mothers, children under six and pregnant women with family income at or below 133 % of the federal poverty level, foster care and adoption assisted, and some Medicare recipients. Some states have **spend down** programs for individuals who are medically needy but are slightly above the Medicaid eligibility. These individuals are asked to spend a certain amount of money on their health care before Medicaid will start reimbursement.

It is important for the reimbursement specialist to know the rules and regulations of the Medicaid program in their state. Medicaid verification is extremely important in the billing process. The patient must produce their Medicaid identification card at each appointment. Verification should be done before the patient sees the physician. This can be accomplished online, by phone, or electronically.

Covered Services

Covered services can vary by state but due to federal funding, certain services are mandated.

Covered services for all states due to the federal funds include:

- **Hospital services**
- **Physician services**
- **Emergency services**
- **Lab and x-ray services**
- **Prenatal care**
- **Early and periodic screening**
- **Skilled nursing services**
- **Home health care**
- **Vaccines for children**
- **Rural health clinic services**
- **Family planning**
- **Midwife services**

Some states include:

- **Diagnostic services**
- **Prescription drugs**
- **Vision care**
- **Physical therapy services**
- **Prosthetic devices**

Excluded services are cosmetic procedures, experimental or investigative procedures, and services that are deemed not medically necessary. Each state has specific preauthorization requirements that are essential to remember in the physician's office. The Medicaid insurance program should always be billed last if the patient has multiple health care policies. This is called the **payer of last resort**. Many Medicare patients qualify for Medicaid coverage as well. These claims are sent to Medicare as the primary insurance. Medicare will automatically cross-over the claim to Medicaid for automatic secondary payment. It is imperative to include the Medicaid identification numbers on all Medicare claims.

Medicaid Claim Submission

All physicians who treat a Medicaid patient must accept assignment on the claim. The claim submission deadline will vary from state to state. Claims are reimbursed on a predetermined fee schedule. Because Medicaid is the payer of last resort, a primary insurance remittance advice must be attached to the Medicaid claim. The only exception to this is automatic crossover claims (for example, Medicare).

TRICARE

TRICARE is the health care coverage for active military personnel and their families. These military forces include the Army, Navy, Air Force, Marine Corps, Coast Guard, Public Health Service, and National Oceanic and Atmospheric Administration. TRICARE replaced the Civilian Health and Medical Program of the Uniformed Services (CHAMPUS).

The History of TRICARE Insurance

In July of 1775, Congress established a medical department to care for military members, and in 1818, the Secretary of War established a permanent medical department. In 1956, the Dependents Medical Care Act created what was to be CHAMPUS. CHAMPUS was a cost-sharing program providing

Exercise 7-2

Short answer: Answer each question with a short statement.

1. Explain Medicaid.

    _____

    _____

    _____

2. Why is Medicaid called the payer of last resort?

    _____

    _____

    _____

3. Explain what a spend down is.

    _____

    _____

    _____

4. Why is it important to verify Medicaid benefits and how is this accomplished?

    _____

    _____

    _____

active-duty family members inpatient and outpatient care. This program ran from 1965–1993. In 1993, the Department of Defense and Congress established TRICARE insurance.

TRICARE Plans

There are four TRICARE regions: three in the United States and one overseas. These regions are managed by a Lead Agent and staff. The regions are North, South, West, and overseas. The subscriber, or military service member, is called the **sponsor**.

It is very important for the reimbursement specialist to copy the TRICARE identification card, front and back. TRICARE will honor a submitted claim, even if benefits have stopped, when a copy of the card can be submitted. Eligibility can be verified by the sponsor through TRICARE's Internet Web site. It can be found on the **Defense Enrollment Eligibility Reporting System (DEERS)**.

TRICARE uses a network of military physicians and hospitals. There are also certain civilian providers that are eligible to treat the military families, but any services must be authorized. Civilian physicians can choose to participate or not. The fee schedules and reimbursement is driven by the same fee schedule Medicare uses.

The most common TRICARE plans are TRICARE Standard, TRICARE Prime, TRICARE Extra, and TRICARE for Life.

- *TRICARE Standard:* A fee-for-service program; treatment is done at a military facility. A civilian provider can be used if a military facility is not available. A deductible and co-insurance amount is required.

- *TRICARE Prime:* A managed care plan similar to an HMO. The patient must have a **primary care manager (PCM)**. There are no deductibles but some co-pays are required if a civilian provider is used.

- *TRICARE Extra:* An alternatively managed care plan that uses civilian providers. Deductibles are required for this plan.

- *TRICARE for Life:* A health care program for eligible Medicare retirees. Benefits are similar to a Medicare HMO.

Claims are submitted to TRICARE's regional contractors (insurance companies), according to the patient's home address, not where the treatment was rendered. Verification of the regional address and regional contractor is needed before a health claim is filed. Knowledge of covered services is important in the billing process.

Some of TRICARE's covered services are:

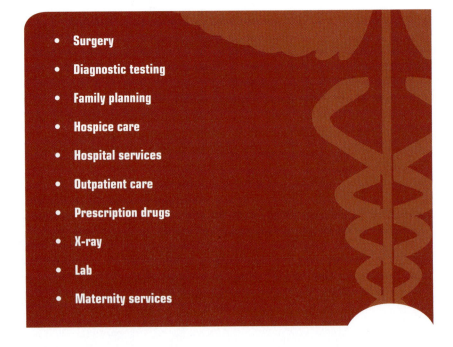

- **Surgery**
- **Diagnostic testing**
- **Family planning**
- **Hospice care**
- **Hospital services**
- **Outpatient care**
- **Prescription drugs**
- **X-ray**
- **Lab**
- **Maternity services**

Non-covered services include:

- **Cosmetic services**
- **Custodial care**
- **Routine physicals**

TRICARE Billing

The physician can choose to accept assignment or not on TRICARE claims. It would be important to check with the patient regarding transfers. Many active-duty personnel move frequently. Accepting assignment would be the easiest in these cases. Always check on any necessary reauthorizations for non-emergency treatment.

Contact the sponsor's regional contractor (insurance company) if reimbursement has not been received within 45 days. If you do not know the regional contractor, call the closest military facility; they will know the current address of the insurance company or contractor assigned to your region. Billing is done on the standard CMS-1500 billing form.

CHAMPVA

CHAMPVA is the governmental and civilian medical health program for the department of veteran affairs. This is health coverage for veterans with a 100% service-related disability and their families.

STOP AND PRACTICE

Exercise 7-3

True or False: Choose the correct answer to each question.

_____ 1. TRICARE is a health care program for veterans with 100% service-related disability.

_____ 2. Eligibility can be verified by the sponsor using DEERS.

_____ 3. The patient must have their health care administered by a PCP.

_____ 4. The TRICARE sponsor is the subscriber or military service member.

Short answer: Answer the question with a short statement.

5. Explain the different plans offered in TRICARE.

_____

_____

_____

COMMERCIAL INSURANCES

There are many, many **commercial insurances**, also called private payers. Some examples of commercial insurances include: United Healthcare, Aetna, Prudential, Mail Handlers, Cigna, and many more. There are different policies offered within each commercial insurance system. The policies could be managed care programs, fee-for-service, indemnity plans, and cafeteria plans, to name a few.

Most of these commercial insurance plans are offered through a patient's employer.

Policies that are offered to a large number of employees are called **group policies**. Employees and employers share the premium cost and receive quality health care coverage. Each employer will negotiate the policy benefits and price of the plan. The combinations of benefits are endless.

Some commercial insurance companies offer individual private policies. These policies are for individuals who are not employed or are self-employed. The individual receives benefits depending on the premium price.

**HealthCare
Commercial Insurance**   PPO

Rx # 111111
Medix Rx Group: HCI

Subscriber/Group Number   Smith Nurseries

James / 222222   Certificate ID # 994506837
                                     Enrollment date: 07/20XX

Name: Payer ID # 85265
James Smith
999 Jones Road
Century, NC 37777   OV copay-$20
                                     Specialist copay-$30
                                     Surgical prior authorization required

---

Claim Submission address: HealthCare Commercial Insurance
                                     1 Insurance Avenue
                                     Jonestown, CA 21547

Member Services: 1-800-123-4567

Precertification: 1-800-123-7893

Provider information: 258-365-7894

healthcarecommercialinsurance.com

Figure 7-3. Commercial insurance card

The reimbursement specialist must verify all insurance policies and benefits. Claim submission can be different for each commercial insurance and group policy. This is why the patient's identification card is an important source of information as well as verifying eligibility for all services performed. If there is any doubt, the insurance company must be contacted for rules and regulations. The commercial insurance companies are not under the same regulations as the governmental insurances, but many copy Medicare's rules. An example of a commercial insurance card in Figure 7-3 will show where to locate pertinent information.

STOP AND PRACTICE

Exercise 7-4

Short answer: Answer each question with a short statement.

1. List some commercial insurance companies.

_____

_____

_____

_____

2. Explain employer group policies.

_____

_____

_____

_____

3. What kind of plans are offered by the commercial insurances?

_____

_____

_____

_____

4. Why is the patient's insurance card so important with commercial insurances?

_____

_____

_____

_____

WORKERS' COMPENSATION

Workers' Compensation (W/C) is a program that covers individuals for the treatment of work-related injuries and illnesses. This program pays the employee's medical expenses and also compensates them for lost wages. All employers are required to carry workers' compensation coverage for their employees. Workers' compensation coverage is for injuries that occur only when an employee is injured within the scope of their job description, or by a job required by the employer. The injury can be compensated even if the employee is not on the employer's property, as long as it happens while performing their required job.

History of Workers' Compensation Insurance

Workers' compensation began in Wisconsin in 1911 and other states followed along.

W/C is a major cost to employers today. Businesses are seeking to limit the cost of workers' compensation coverage and unions are looking to increase the benefits for workers.

Workers' compensation coverage is provided under many commercial insurance companies. The premiums are high but, in turn, do not produce much of a profit for these commercial insurance companies. There are many complaints with this coverage. Employers feel the premiums are driven higher by fraudulent claims and workers complain that the W/C insurance companies are not in compliance with the laws.

The workers' compensation laws in the US do protect the employer by limiting the monetary awards and eliminating liability for any negligence on the part of the employer or other workers.

Federal Workers' Compensation Programs

There are both federal and state workers' compensation programs. The federal W/C programs are:

- The Energy Employees Occupational Illness Compensation Program
- The Federal Black Lung Program
- The Federal Employee's Compensation Act (FECA) Program
- The Longshore and Harbor Workers' Compensation Program
- Mine Safety and Health Administration (MSHA)
- Occupational Safety and Health Administration (OSHA)
- Federal Employment Liability Act (FELA)
- Merchant Marine Act (Jones Act)

The United States Department of Labor administers these programs. They provide medical reimbursement, lost wage benefits, and vocational rehabilitation for federal workers. These benefits can be for those injured at work or for work-related diseases.

OSHA and MSHA are programs relating to the prevention of work-related injuries.

OSHA training in the medical office is very important, dealing with many important safety issues including airborne, blood-borne, and infectious diseases. Many chemical and hazardous materials in the medical office must be listed on Material Safety Data Sheets (MSDS), giving all employees information regarding the safe handling of these substances.

State Workers' Compensation Programs

State W/C programs pay workers for lost wages, reimbursement for medical treatment, and pay dependants if the worker dies from an employment-related injury.

Each state has a Workers' Compensation Board that oversees the workers' compensation laws for that state. They also deal with any denials from the W/C insurance companies, and decide on the outcome of any appeals made by the employee. Each state sets its own workers' compensation rules and regulations and they may vary from state to state.

The employer pays the premium for the workers' compensation coverage. They may choose a state-funded W/C plan, a private commercial W/C insurance plan, or choose a self-funded W/C coverage plan.

Office Procedures

The reimbursement specialist must have knowledge of the rules and regulations in the state he or she is working. The medical office must remember that the claim must be filed as soon as possible to the proper insurance carrier. The information that must be collected at the first visit to the medical office is:

1. **Employer name, address, and telephone number**

2. **Employee's direct supervisor's name**

3. **Date and time of injury, description of injury or illness**

4. **Workers' compensation insurance carrier, address, telephone number, and file case number, if assigned**

If any of the above information is not available, the employer should be called for the exact information.

The medical office should keep the billing and clinical information for a workers' compensation claim separate from any other medical information the patient may have in the office. This ensures the patient's privacy rights are secured. Care should be taken to correctly submit a claim, as well as submit any specialized reports that must be filed. The **first report of injury** must be filed when the patient first visits the office with a work-related injury. Many states have special report formats that must be filed with the following groups:

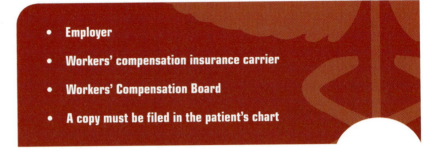

- **Employer**
- **Workers' compensation insurance carrier**
- **Workers' Compensation Board**
- **A copy must be filed in the patient's chart**

The information required is the patient's name, address, employer, date and time of injury, description of injury, physician's name and address, diagnosis, treatment plan, prognosis, description of any follow-up planned, and work status.

Figure 7-4 shows an example of a first report of injury form.

A progress report should be filed with all the parties involved at any follow-up visits. Most workers' compensation insurance carriers require a copy of the office notes attached to the CMS-1500 form when submitted.

Reimbursement for a workers' compensation claim is based on a fee schedule set up by each state's Workers Compensation Board. Physicians are required to accept assignment and accept this fee schedule amount as payment in full. Many workers' compensation insurance companies offer managed care coverage. This type of health care coverage for the injured worker keeps health care costs down while providing coordinated quality care. There are no deductibles or co-pays involved in the W/C reimbursement, and all physicians must accept assignment on these claims. Billing is done on the CMS-1500 form and no patient signature is required for blocks 12 and 13.

Workers' compensation claims may be denied and reimbursement may be delayed for long periods of time. Some of the workers' compensation patients will enlist the help of attorneys to appeal these denials. Caution should be taken when attorneys are involved in these cases. Before any information is released to an attorney, a specific release of information must be obtained from the patient. The release must be obtained before any information can be released.

INSTRUCTIONS

1. Type answers to ALL questions and file original with the Worker's Compensation Commission within 72 hours after first treatment.
2. DO NOT FAIL to forward to the Worker's Compensation Commission PROGRESS REPORTS and FINAL REPORT upon discharge of patient.

WORKERS' COMPENSATION COMMISSION
6 NORTH LIBERTY STREET, BALTIMORE, MD 21201-3785
SURGEON'S REPORT

This is First Report ☐   Progress Report ☐   Final Report ☐

DO NOT WRITE IN THIS SPACE

WCC CLAIM #

EMPLOYER'S REPORT   Yes ☐   No ☐

1. Name of Injured Person:	Soc.Sec.No.	D.O.B.	Sex M ☐ F ☐
2. Address: (No. and Street)	(City or Town)	(State)	(Zip Code)

3. Name and Address of Employer:

4. Date of Accident or Onset of Disease:	Hour: A.M. ☐ P.M. ☐	5. Date Disability Began:

6. Patient's Description of Accident or Cause of Disease:

7. Medical Description of Injury or Disease:

8. Will injury result in:
   (a) Permanent defect?   Yes ☐   No ☐   If so, what?   (b) Disfigurement?   Yes ☐   No ☐

9. Causes, other than injury, contributing to patient's condition:

10. Is patient suffering from any disease of the heart, lungs, brain, kidneys, blood, vascular system or any other disabling condition not due to this accident? Give particulars.

11. Is there any history or evidence present of previous accident or disease? Give particulars.

12. Has normal recovery been delayed for any reason? Give particulars.

13. Date of first treatment:	Who engaged your services?

14. Describe treatment given by you:

15. Were X-rays taken? Yes ☐ No ☐	By whom? – (Name and Address)	Date:

16. X-rays Diagnosis:

17. Was patient treated by anyone else? Yes ☐ No ☐	By whom? – (Name and Address)	Date:
18. Was patient hospitalized? Yes ☐ No ☐	Name and Address of Hospital	Date of Admission: Date of Discharge:
19. Is further treatment needed? Yes ☐ No ☐	For how long?	20. Patient was ☐ will be ☐ able resume regular work on: Patient was ☐ will be ☐ able resume light work on:
21. If death ensued give date:	22. Remarks: (Give any information of value not included above.)	
23. I am a qualified specialist in:	I am a duly licensed Physician in the State of:	I graduated from Medical School: (Name) Year:

Date of this report: (Signed)

(This report must be signed PERSONALLY by Physician.)

Address: Phone:

EVERY QUESTION MUST BE ANSWERED AND FORM SIGNED

Figure 7-4. Sample of a first report of injury form for workers' compensation

STOP AND PRACTICE

Exercise 7-5

Define the following key terms.

1. Workers' compensation

    _____

    _____

    _____

    _____

2. The first report of injury

    _____

    _____

    _____

    _____

3. Release of information

    _____

    _____

    _____

    _____

Short answer: Answer each question with a short statement.

4. Explain the advantages of the workers' compensation program for both the employee and the employer.

    _____

    _____

    _____

    _____

5. List who should receive copies of the first report of injury.

    _____

    _____

    _____

    _____

INSURANCE SUMMARY

The reimbursement specialist should remember each insurance company will have its own set of rules and regulations. Understanding these rules and regulations will come with experience. Billing departments understand that the training process for expertise in these extensive rules is ongoing. It is important to keep current on the regulations, as they can change quickly. A well-managed billing office will have interdepartmental training as well as periodic seminar training. Communication and continual learning is a large part of the medical profession.

CHAPTER SUMMARY

- Knowledge of insurances and their rules and regulations will ensure the correct reimbursement.
- Physicians can choose to participate or not with insurance companies.
- The major insurance programs are Medicare, Medicaid, BlueCross BlueShield, commercial insurances, TRICARE, and workers' compensation.
- The type of plans offered by insurance companies are managed care, indemnity, fee-for-service, and governmental plans.
- Blue Cross Blue Shield policies are mainly managed care plans.
- BCBS-participating physicians must accept all Blue Cross Blue Shield members and refer to other participating physicians.
- Participating physicians must accept assignment and accept BCBS payment in full.
- Medicaid is a federally and state-funded health care program for individuals with low income and resources.
- Medicaid benefits are developed by each state and can vary from state to state.
- Medicaid is the payer of last resort.
- Medicaid benefits should always be verified before the patient is treated.
- Commercial insurance companies are private payers.
- Many commercial insurance companies cover employer-based group plans.
- Commercial insurance companies also offer private policies to the unemployed and self-employed.

- TRICARE health care policies cover active military personnel and their families.
- The different plans offered by TRICARE include TRICARE Standard, TRICARE Prime, TRICARE Extra, and TRICARE for Life.
- TRICARE eligibility can be verified thru their Web site DEERS.
- Workers' compensation is employer-purchased health care coverage for employees injured on the job, within the scope of their employment.
- Workers' compensation health insurance protects the employee for on-the-job injuries and illnesses by reimbursing health care costs and lost wages.
- Workers' compensation health insurance protects the employer from claims submitted for injuries sustained by employee negligence and caps high claim awards.

REVIEW QUESTIONS

Define the following key terms.

1. PPO

_____

_____

_____

2. POS

_____

_____

_____

3. HMO

_____

_____

_____

4. Sponsor

_____

_____

5. Accept assignment

_____

_____

_____

6. Managed care

_____

_____

_____

True or False: Choose the correct answer for each question.

_____ 7. Medicaid health coverage is available to any individual who signs up and pays the premium.

_____ 8. Blue Cross Blue Shield provides a representative to help with claim problems if the physician is participating.

_____ 9. Medicaid is the payer of last resort and is a supplemental insurance to Medicare.

_____ 10. Commercial insurances are governmental plans set up for patients with Medicare.

_____ 11. The premium for workers' compensation insurance is paid by the employee.

Short answer: Answer each question with a short statement.

12. Explain the eligibility for Medicaid.

_____

_____

_____

13. List the covered services in all states for Medicaid.

_____

_____

_____

14. Why should the reimbursement specialist make a copy of a patient's TRICARE insurance card, front and back?

_____

_____

_____

15. Why should the medical office keep a workers' compensation medical record separate from any other record the patient may have?

_____

_____

_____

16. Explain what information should be collected from a patient on workers' compensation.

_____

_____

_____

17. Explain the problems that may arise when billing a workers' compensation claim.

_____

_____

_____

18. What kind of ongoing education can be useful to the reimbursement specialist?

_____

_____

_____

PRACTICAL APPLICATION

Research and prepare a classroom presentation on your state's Medicaid or workers' compensation insurance. Areas of interest would be eligibility, covered services, information for a patient (e.g., office address, contact information), and claim submission information.

Chapter 8

Coding Overview of CPT and ICD-9-CM Coding

OBJECTIVES

Upon completion of this chapter, the student should be able to:

- Outline the history of CPT and ICD-9-CM codes.
- Select an appropriate ICD-9-CM diagnosis code.
- Select an appropriate CPT procedural code.
- Select the appropriate HCPCS National Level II code.
- Practice how to use the ICD-9-CM, CPT, and HCPCS manuals.

KEY TERMS

Add on codes

American Health Information Management Association (AHIMA)

Conventions

Current Procedural Terminology (CPT)

E codes

Evaluation and management codes (E&M)

Healthcare Common Procedure Coding System (HCPCS)

Indented code

International Classification of Diseases (ICD)

Modifier

INTRODUCTION

Medical coding is one of the most important steps in collecting the correct reimbursement. A correct CPT code should best describe the services and procedures performed. It will be linked with an ICD-9-CM code for medical necessity. This combination will result in a clean claim. The clean claim will save the reimbursement specialist time and effort. The physician will receive the correct and highest payment for his work. Choosing these codes can be very complicated. Many reimbursement specialists will go on to specialize in this area. In many physicians' offices, the reimbursement specialists will collect the patient demographic information, assign medical codes, and audit the physician's claims. They are required to submit the health claim, follow up on the insurance claims, and oversee the collections process. The reimbursement specialist should strive to be an expert in all phases of this process.

ICD-9-CM CODING

The International Classification of Diseases, ninth revision manual (ICD-9-CM), is used to select the illness, injury, disease, condition, or symptom of a patient every time treatment is rendered.

One essential job for the reimbursement specialist is to verify diagnosis codes (ICD-9-CM) from a number of different sources in the physician's office. They may be listed on the encounter form by the physician himself, or extracted from the medical records dictated by the physician. Knowledge of medical terminology, anatomy and physiology, and the medical diagnosis coding guidelines is a necessity for the reimbursement specialist.

History of ICD-9-CM Coding

Diagnostic coding is important for many reasons. This is an important step in obtaining the correct reimbursement from the insurance companies for every claim submitted. But diagnostic coding was not originally developed for this purpose. Researchers wanted to better understand the process of **morbidity** (illness) and **mortality** (cause of death). Tracking diseases and mortality rates helped measure the quality of health care. Collection of this kind of data was difficult to obtain from different sources, such as the physician and hospitals. Everyone described a condition in different terms. A more standardized method of recording the diseases and conditions was developed by the **World Health Organization (WHO)**. These standardized terms were developed into codes based on the **International Classification of Disease (ICD)**. ICD-9-CM codes are three five-digit codes that reference standard descriptions of diseases, conditions, and injuries. This system of coding diagnoses has been revised numerous times. The current system is the ICD-9-CM, the ninth revision, clinical modification. This system was published in 1979 and is still in use. ICD-10 is currently in the process of development. Medicare mandated the use of ICD-9-CM codes in 1988 for their claims. All insurance companies use this system for medical health claims today.

The collection of data from physicians, hospitals, and surveys from the **National Center for Health Statistics** has helped researchers track the diseases and causes of death in the United States. This information is used not only by the researchers and medical reimbursement, but also by the news media. The diagnostic codes selected by medical coders and reimbursement specialists must be completely accurate for these reasons.

ICD-9-CM Updates

Four different parties are responsible for the update of ICD-9-CM codes on a yearly basis. The changes are effective October 1. These parties are the American Hospital Association (AHA), the **American Health Information Management Association (AHIMA)**, the Centers for Medicare and Medicaid Services (CMS), and the National Center for Health Statistics (NCHS).

Knowledge of the rules and regulations regarding the reporting of the ICD-9-CM codes is very important for the reimbursement specialist. The yearly updates of the diagnostic codes are essential, otherwise claims will be rejected. Keeping up-to-date on the code changes ensures a clean claim and correct reimbursement. It is also important to train other office personnel in coding updates.

ICD-10

ICD-10 is currently being developed. This update has taken a long time due to the nature of the changes being implemented. This large undertaking is being developed under contract with CMS.

The objectives of ICD-10 are to improve the quality of measurement of diseases, improve public health and bio-terrorism monitoring, limit the NOS and NEC classifications, improve expandability, and provide more accurate reimbursement and reporting.

According to AHIMA, the 21st century needs a more stable and flexible classification system. They state ICD-9-CM is obsolete. The current international Statistical Classification of Diseases and Related Health Problems, 10th Revision, Version for 2007, shows the diagnostic codes as seven-character alphanumeric codes, using numbers 0–9 and letters A–Z. Figure 8-1 is a list of chapters in the new ICD-10.

Preparing for the conversion is a great task. Some associations are indicating it will take up to three years to complete this conversion, but everyone agrees it will be necessary.

ICD-10 CODING SYSTEM CHAPTER TITLES

Chapter	Block	Title
I	A00-B99	Certain infectious and parasitic diseases
II	C00-D48	Neoplasms
III	D50-D89	Diseases of the blood and blood-forming organs, certain disorders involving the immune mechanism
IV	E00-E90	Endocrine, nutritional and metabolic diseases
V	F00-F99	Mental and behavioral disorders
VI	G00-G99	Diseases of the nervous system
VII	H00-H59	Diseases of the eye and adnexa
VIII	H60-H95	Diseases of the ear and mastoid process
IX	I00-I99	Diseases of the circulatory system
X	J00-J99	Diseases of the respiratory system
XI	K00-K93	Diseases of the digestive system
XII	L00-L99	Diseases of the skin and subcutaneous tissue
XIII	M00-M99	Diseases of the musculoskeletal system and connective tissue
XIV	N00-N99	Diseases of the genitourinary system
XV	O00-O99	Pregnancy, childbirth and the puerperium
XVI	P00-P96	Certain conditions originating in the perinatal period
XVII	Q00-Q99	Congenital malformations, deformations and chromosomal abnormalities
XVIII	R00-R99	Symptoms, signs and abnormal clinical and laboratory findings, not elsewhere classified
XIX	S00-T98	Injury, poisoning and certain other consequences of external causes
XX	V01-Y98	External causes of morbidity and mortality
XXI	Z00-Z99	Factors influencing health status and contact with health services
XXII	U00-U99	Codes for special purposes

Figure 8-1. ICD-10: New chapter headings

The ICD-9-CM codes are published in a manual. Having the expertise in using the manual is crucial. Understanding the manual's organization will help the reimbursement specialist choose correct codes. Knowing how to use the manual, where to find the correct information, and what kind of information is listed in the manual is extremely important. There is a wealth of knowledge contained in the ICD-9-CM manual. The accuracy in choosing the correct diagnosis codes will also depend on the knowledge of the diagnosis guidelines.

The ICD-9-CM manual contains three volumes. Volume 1 is the tabular list of diseases and injuries, Volume 2 is the alphabetic index of disease descriptions, index of drugs and chemicals, and an index of external causes of injury. Volume 3 is the tabular and index of hospital procedures. Our discussion will be of Volume 1 and 2 only in this textbook.

Steps to Coding

The steps to correct coding are:

1. Look up the main term of the disease in the alphabetic index of the ICD-9-CM manual.

2. Check the sub-terms and any cross-references, which are listed in the index under the main diagnosis. These are words that will direct the specialist to the correct diagnosis.

3. Look up the code, listed in the index, in the tabular list of codes.

4. Read the description *carefully* and check all conventions and prompts.

5. Check the coding guidelines for appropriate primary and secondary diagnoses placement.

6. *Never* code from just the alphabetic index of the ICD-9-CM manual.

Volume 2: Index and Tabular Listings

Figure 8-2 shows some samples of both the ICD-9-CM index and tabular listings.

ICD-9-CM Index

Croup, croupous (acute) (angina) (catarrhal) (infective) (inflammatory) (laryngeal) (membranous) (nondiphthertic) (pseudomembranous) 464.4
    asthmatic (see also Asthma) 493.9
    bronchial 466.0
    diphtheritic (membranous) 032.3
    false 478.75
    spasmodic 478.75
        diphtheritic 032.3
    stridulous 478.75
        diphtheritic 032.3
Crouzon's disease (craniofacial dysostosis) 756.0
Crowding, teeth 524.31
CRST syndrome (cutaneous systemic sclerosis) 710.1

ICD-9-CM Tabular List

5th   464.3   Acute epiglottis
                Viral epiglottis
        Excludes: epiglottis, chronic (476.1)
              464.30   Without mention of obstruction
              464.31   With obstruction

        464.4   Croup
                Croup syndrome
              DEF: Acute laryngeal obstruction due to allergy, foreign body or infection: symptoms include barking cough, hoarseness and harsh, persistent high-pitched respiratory sound.

5th   464.5   Supraglottitis, unspecified
              DEF: A rapidly advancing generalized upper respiratory infection of the lingual tonsillar area, epiglottic folds, false vocal cords, and the epiglottis, seen most commonly in children, but can affect people of any age.
              464.50   Without mention of obstruction
              464.51   With obstruction

Figure 8-2. Samples of the ICD-9-CM index and tabular listings

The alphabetic index (Volume 2) is located first in the ICD-9-CM manual. The main term of the disease or injury is listed in bold lettering, alphabetically. The sub-terms, or types of the main term, are listed (indented) under the main term. The ICD-9-CM diagnosis code is listed after the term. Many of these diagnosis codes listed in the index will have a black box with a check mark. This indicates that a fourth or fifth digit must be selected.

Once the diagnosis to be coded has been determined, decide which word in the diagnosis will be the main term. The main term should be looked up in the alphabetic index. If it cannot be found, another term can be tried until the correct main term is found. Many times, both words of a diagnosis will be found in the index of the manual. Coders are searching for a condition, disease, or injury, not a body part. For example, if you are looking for foot pain, the main term will be *pain*, not foot.

There are some diagnosis codes that are listed in chart form within the index section of the manual. They include hypertension and neoplasms. Also listed separately is a chart of drugs and chemicals. Section 2 of Volume 2 is the alphabetic index for poisoning and external causes of adverse effects of drugs and other chemical substances. Section 3 of Volume 2 is the alphabetic index to external causes of injury and poisoning. These special lists will be discussed later in this chapter.

ICD-9-CM Conventions

The ICD-9-CM manual is set up much like a dictionary. The word or ICD-9-CM code is on the top of the page. The bottom of each page will have a list of conventions used on those pages. Conventions are symbols designed to help the coder gain more information about the codes.

The conventions are listed throughout the manual. Understanding these symbols is essential to accurately choosing the correct diagnosis code.

Common conventions are as follows:

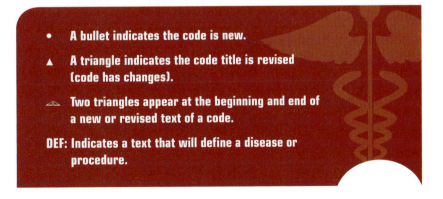

- • A bullet indicates the code is new.
- ▲ A triangle indicates the code title is revised (code has changes).
- ◁▷ Two triangles appear at the beginning and end of a new or revised text of a code.
- DEF: Indicates a text that will define a disease or procedure.

These definitions are excellent learning tools, and should not be ignored. It is important to stop and read. Symbols are seen to designate sex (male or female) related codes. There are codes related to specific age groups of the patient. Color-coding may be used to alert the coder to classifications of codes.

The most important conventions used in the ICD-9-CM manual will alert the coder to code the disease to the highest specificity. The manual will show a box with a check mark indicating that a fourth or fifth digit is required.

Some other conventions include:

- *NEC*, or not elsewhere classifiable, signifies that ICD-9-CM does not provide a code specific for the patient's condition.

- *NOS*, or not otherwise specified, signifies no other code is available. This code is used only when the coder lacks the information necessary to code more specifically.

- [ ] Brackets enclose synonyms, which are alternative terminology or explanatory phrases.

- *[ ]* Slanted brackets in the alphabetic index will indicate a mandatory multiple coding situation. Both codes must be assigned to fully describe the condition in the listed sequence.

- ( ) Parentheses signify enclosed supplementary words or nonessential modifiers.

- : Colons are used in the tabular list. It is used after an incomplete term that needs one or more of modifiers listed to be the correct assigned code.

- [ ] Braces are used to enclose a series of terms. Each term is modified by a single statement.

ICD-9-CM Instructions and Notes

Instructions and notes used in the manual are essential to choosing the correct diagnosis code.

Knowledge of all the conventions, instructional notes, footnotes, and directions in the ICD-9-CM manual will make coding quick and easy. They will be listed in the beginning of any manual.

Some instructions are:

- **Includes:** Indicates a note that further defines or clarifies a diagnosis.

- **Excludes:** Indicates a note that is not classified by that specific code.

- **Use additional code:** Indicates that a coder should use an additional code to completely describe a diagnosis. Some conditions require two codes. One code is for the etiology and the second is for the manifestation (sign or symptom).

- **Code first underlying disease:** Indicates that another code needs to be coded primary to the selected code to completely describe a condition.

- **See cross-references:** Guides the coder to other more specific codes or descriptions. Example: flu – see influenza.

Volume 1: Tabular List of Diseases

The tabular list of diseases, conditions, and injuries is organized by number from 001 through 999.9. There is a section of V codes and E codes, which will be discussed later in the chapter.

These diseases/illnesses are organized into chapters according to body systems, or etiology. Each chapter is then divided into sections according to related types of diseases and conditions.

The chapter categories are the nervous system, circulatory system, respiratory systems, digestive system, and genitourinary system. Chapters are also divided into infectious diseases, neoplasms, endocrine, blood, mental disorders, complications of pregnancy and child birth, musculoskeletal, congenital anomalies, conditions in the perinatal period, symptoms, signs and ill-defined conditions, injury, and poisoning. These categories show why the reimbursement specialist needs to be an expert in anatomy and physiology.

Once the main term is located in the index, the coder checks the sub-term. This locates the code. At this point, the coder checks the code in the tabular list. This is Volume 1 in the ICD-9-CM manual. The coder should then read all the conventions and notes before deciding if that code is the correct code for the condition. It is crucial to code the condition to the highest specificity, three digits, four digits, or five digits.

E Codes

Other types of diagnostic ICD-9-CM codes found in the manual are **E codes** and **V codes**. E codes are used to describe the external causes, environmental events, circumstances, and conditions of the patient's injury. It covers poisoning and other adverse effects. The index for the E codes is separate from the main index of the ICD-9-CM manual. This E code index is located in Volume 2, Section 3. The tabular listing of the E codes is found in Volume 1 after the V code listings. The E codes can be challenging and practice is the best approach to be proficient at assigning these codes. E codes are used in addition to a primary diagnosis code. They should never be used as a primary code.

Included in the ICD-9-CM manual is a table that helps choose the poisoning, external causes, and adverse effects of drugs and other chemical substances. It is located in Volume 2, Section 2, of the manual. Each code is assigned a poisoning code and a choice of adverse effect codes from the poisoning columns: accidental, therapeutic, suicide, assault, and undetermined.

V Codes

V codes can be found in the main index of the ICD-9-CM manual. The tabular codes are found in Volume 1 after the numeric codes. Care must be used in assigning these codes. Some can be primary diagnoses, while some cannot. It is important to read the notes and conventions carefully.

V codes describe patient encounters other than illness or injury:

- **When a patient is not currently sick but must follow-up with a physician.**
- **When a patient has a resolving illness/injury.**
- **Health status needs to be described.**

Common main terms to look up in the index for the V codes are:

- **History**
- **Admission**
- **Contraception**
- **Check-up**
- **Encounter**
- **Pregnancy**
- **Supervision**
- **Examination**

For correct reimbursement, all diagnosis codes must be listed correctly in order of importance to the encounter of the patient.

ICD-9-CM Guidelines

The ICD-9-CM official guidelines for coding were developed by the American Hospital Association, American Health Information Association, CMS, and the National Center for Health Statistics.

These guidelines should be followed for the correct reimbursement. Reading these guidelines can be a challenge but it is essential for the reimbursement specialist to be an expert in the assignment of diagnosis codes. These ICD-9-CM guidelines can be found in most ICD-9-CM manuals.

The most important aspect of coding diagnoses is to understand what the doctor is treating the patient for and *knowing how to use the ICD-9-CM manual*. It is essential to read, read, read, and practice, practice, practice.

STOP AND PRACTICE

Exercise 8-1

Define the following key terms.

1. ICD-9-CM

   _____

   _____

2. V codes

   _____

   _____

3. E codes

   _____

   _____

Short Answer: Answer each question with a short statement.

4. Describe the steps to correct ICD-9-CM coding.

   _____

   _____

   _____

(continues)

STOP AND PRACTICE

Exercise 8-1 (*continued*)

_____

_____

5. Why were ICD-9-CM codes developed?

    _____

    _____

6. Name the four parties responsible for the updates to ICD-9-CM.

    _____

    _____

Identify the main term for the following diseases/conditions.

7. Joint effusion _____

8. Hand pain _____

9. Otitis Media _____

10. Brain cyst _____

Identify the ICD-9-CM code for the following diseases/conditions.

11. Family history of breast cancer _____

12. Systemic lupus erythematosis _____

13. Open transcervical fracture of the femur _____

14. Malignant neoplasm of the male breast (primary) _____

15. Diabetes mellitus type II without complications _____

16. Eating disorder, unspecified _____

17. Acute pneumonia _____

18. Screening for cardiovascular disease _____

19. Alcohol poisoning, accidental _____

20. Thrombocytopenia _____

Current Procedural Terminology (CPT) manual is a set of codes used to describe procedures and services performed by the physician and other health professionals.

The American Medical Association publishes the CPT codes. They were first published in 1966 with the current five-digit codes adopted in 1970. In 1983, the **Healthcare Common Procedure Coding System (HCPCS)** was adopted for reporting Medicare services. All other insurance companies followed suit in the use of these codes. Level I codes and National Level II codes are now in use. The CPT codes were developed to standardize and simplify the descriptions of procedures and services performed by physicians everywhere.

It is much easier to report a code of 50951 instead of the description of the procedure: Ureteral endoscopy through established ureterostomy, with or without irrigation, instillation, or ureteropyelography, exclusive of radiologic services. With the introduction of the common billing form, CMS-1500, the use of numeric and alphanumeric codes was essential. Reimbursement is also standardized by the use of the CPT codes. As with the ICD-9-CM manual, extensive knowledge of anatomy and physiology is essential to choose the correct CPT code.

The CPT Manual

The official title of the CPT manual is *Current Procedural Terminology (CPT®),* Fourth Edition. The AMA updates this manual yearly, in the fall, and it is important to keep a current manual on hand, as codes can change from year to year. There is a tremendous amount of information included in the CPT manual.

The reimbursement specialist must be knowledgeable in the use of this manual. No one is expected to memorize all of the codes in the manual, but coders must know how to use the manual correctly. It is important to know the billing regulations and how to choose the correct procedural code.

Most patient encounters require multiple CPT codes to best describe the treatment by the physician. Many times the encounter will require a Level I code, a National Level II code, and possibly a modifier attached to a CPT code. A **modifier** is a two-digit code used with a five-digit CPT code. It gives the insurance company more information about that procedure. We will discuss modifiers later in this chapter.

The CPT Level I codes are listed in six sections:

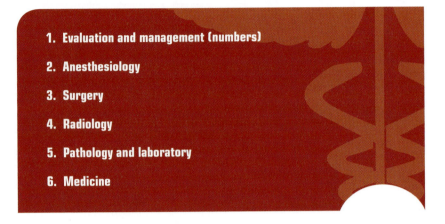

1. **Evaluation and management (numbers)**

2. **Anesthesiology**

3. **Surgery**

4. **Radiology**

5. **Pathology and laboratory**

6. **Medicine**

The manual is color-coded and is set up like a dictionary with the first and last code listed at the top of each page. The index is listed in the back of the manual and the tabular listings are in the front. **Evaluation and management codes (E&M)** are listed first (99201-99499), then codes from 00100-99602. These are codes used for physician office and hospital visit codes.

CPT Manual Format

The symbols next to the codes are important in the understanding of the code chosen. The format of terminology in the CPT manual is important to learn. The publishers have saved time and space by developing stand-alone codes and indented codes. The **stand-alone code** is a code with a full description of the procedure. The **indented code** is a code with a description that refers back to a common stand-alone code with a slightly different description. The stand-alone code will include the full description with a semicolon, after which sub-terms may be added. The indented code will refer back to the description before the semicolon, with a different description listed after the semicolon (the sub-terms).

See the example of these stand-alone and indented codes:

10080 is a stand-alone code: Incision and drainage of pilonidal cyst: simple

10081 complicated

So the expanded description of the indented code is Incision and drainage of pilonidal cyst: complicated. But to save space it is only listed as: 10081 complicated.

Some procedures are performed in addition to primary procedures. These additional procedures are listed as **add on codes**. They cannot be coded as a primary procedure, and these codes are indicated in the manual by a large bold "plus" sign (+).

CPT Modifiers

Modifiers are used with a CPT code to indicate a specific, special circumstance that will alter the reimbursement of the procedure. The modifier will give the insurance company more information on which to base the reimbursement for the physician.

Possible reasons to use a modifier are:

- Indicates either the professional or technical component of the procedure.

- Procedure was performed by more than one physician or in more than one location.

- Procedure was reduced or increased.

- A bilateral procedure was performed (bilateral left and right, both sides).

- A procedure was performed more than once.

- Unusual events occurred during the procedure.

A list of common modifiers is usually listed on the front cover of the CPT manual for quick reference. By practicing the use of the modifier, the reimbursement specialist is able to obtain correct reimbursement for every procedure. Not all procedures need a modifier, but the reimbursement specialist must always be aware of possible modifiers.

Commonly used modifiers used are:

- Prolonged evaluation and management services - 21

- Unusual procedural service - 22

- Significant, separately identifiable evaluation and management service by the same physician on the same day of the procedure or other service - 25

- Bilateral procedure - 50

- Multiple procedures - 51

- Distinct procedural service - 59

- Repeat procedure by the same physician - 76

- Repeat procedure by another physician - 77

CPT Unlisted Codes

Sections of the CPT manual will also include unlisted service codes. Some services are not listed because they are not performed enough to be listed or they are a new service or procedure. The CPT manual allows for the reimbursement of these services by using the unlisted procedure codes within the coding sections the procedure is related to. For correct reimbursement of these unlisted codes, a special report must be attached to the billing form. The insurance company will not pay for a service unless the description is attached. The special report must include a description of the service or procedure, and the nature and extent of the procedure. It must describe the time, effort, and equipment necessary for the procedure. Also included might be symptoms, final diagnosis, physical findings, and follow-up care. These reports must be dictated by the physician and in layman's terms for the insurance company.

Additional Information in the CPT Manual

Many informational illustrations, charts, and descriptions are included in the CPT manual. The coder must remember to always read these to continually learn new concepts.

Also included in the manual are the Appendixes. These are:

- Appendix A is a full description of all modifiers.
- Appendix B is a summary of additions, deletions, and revisions.
- Appendix C is a list of some clinical examples for E&M codes.
- Appendix D is a summary of CPT add on codes.
- Appendix E is a summary of CPT codes that do not need the modifier 51 (multiple procedure modifier).
- Appendix F is a summary of CPT codes that do not need modifier 3 (procedures performed on infants).
- Appendix G is a summary of CPT codes that include moderate (conscious) sedation, (sedation administered by the surgeon). Moderate sedation cannot be billed separately.
- Appendix M is a crosswalk to deleted CPT codes.

The important key to CPT coding is learning to use the index. Knowledge of the index will allow the coder to look up any service or procedure.

Coding with the CPT Manual

As with the ICD-9-CM manual, the coders must first choose the main term of the procedure or service they wish to code. After reading the report/surgical note, a main term must be chosen and that term found in the index. The coder must check under that main term for any sub-terms, or a more specific procedure.

Main terms are listed in four ways:

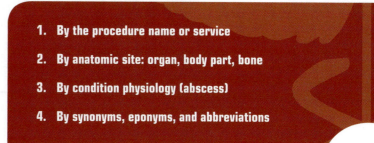

1. **By the procedure name or service**

2. **By anatomic site: organ, body part, bone**

3. **By condition physiology (abscess)**

4. **By synonyms, eponyms, and abbreviations**

It is important to remember, many codes can be found in different ways. If a main term is chosen and the correct code cannot be found, the coder must keep looking, using another method.

A coder must *never* code from the index. The code must always be checked in the tabular listing. Always *read* the full description before deciding on a CPT code. If the description is not correct, the coder must keep looking. When checking the index of the CPT manual, multiple codes can be listed; always check the tabular listing for a complete description before choosing the correct code. Practice, practice, practice.

Any physician can code from any section of the CPT manual, but many times the reimbursement specialist will code from only certain areas of the CPT manual. It will depend on the practice specialty. Knowledge of how to use the CPT manual will enable the reimbursement specialist to code from any section. Each section of the CPT manual will contain an introduction with a few pages outlining the guidelines for each section. These guidelines will include invaluable information on how to choose a correct code from that section.

HCPCS NATIONAL LEVEL II CODES

The National Level II codes are five-digit alphanumeric codes. These codes can be a challenge to look up in the HCPCS manual. The same techniques learned in finding CPT and ICD-9-CM codes must be used. They are listed in their own manual, with an index and a tabular section. Many of the National Level II codes are insurance-specific (i.e., Medicare, Medicaid). Dental codes are listed in this manual and are maintained by the American Dental Association. The Level II codes begin with a letter and are followed by four numbers.

HCPCS National Level II codes include:

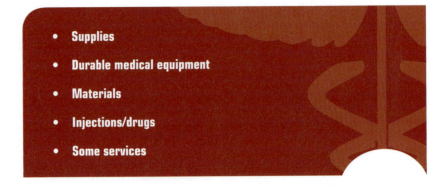

- **Supplies**
- **Durable medical equipment**
- **Materials**
- **Injections/drugs**
- **Some services**

For the reimbursement specialist, medical coding may be a large part of his or her job description, or a small part. Many physicians' offices employ a certified professional coder. The reimbursement specialist in any office, however, will need to be knowledgeable in coding as well. Many of the insurance company denials will be for coding errors or problems. Correct reimbursement is the main goal of the billing office and correct code selection will be worth your time and effort. Coding seminars are always available for the reimbursement specialist and coders to better understand the important regulations regarding ICD-9-CM and CPT coding. It is always important to keep up-to-date regarding this important part of reimbursement.

STOP AND PRACTICE

Exercise 8-2

Define the following key terms.

1. CPT

_____

_____

_____

2. HCPCS

_____

_____

_____

3. Add on code

_____

_____

_____

(continues)

STOP AND PRACTICE

Exercise 8-2 (continued)

Short answer: Answer each question with a short statement.

4. Describe how and why CPT was developed.

_____

_____

_____

5. List the six sections of the CPT manual.

_____

_____

_____

6. Name the main terms for looking up CPT codes.

_____

_____

_____

7. Describe stand-alone codes and indented codes.

_____

_____

_____

8. What is a modifier used for and describe four modifiers.

_____

_____

_____

9. Describe the HCPCS National Level II codes.

_____

_____

_____

CHAPTER SUMMARY

- Medical codes are essential to the submission of a clean claim, resulting in correct reimbursement.

- ICD-9-CM (International Classification of Diseases, ninth revision, clinical modification) describes diagnoses for diseases and conditions.

- The ICD-9-CM manual includes an index and a tabular listing of diseases.

- When assigning an ICD-9-CM code, look up the main term first, then any sub-term.

- Never code only from the ICD-9-CM index; check each code in the tabular listing and read all conventions and notes.

- Knowledge of the ICD-9-CM guidelines is essential in choosing the correct diagnosis.

- E codes are special ICD-9-CM codes that describe external causes, environmental events, circumstances, and causes of a patient's injury.

- V codes are special ICD-9-CM codes that describe treatment circumstances other than illness or injury.

- HCPCS is the Healthcare Common Procedure Coding System, which includes CPT Level I codes and National Level II codes.

- CPT (Current Procedural Terminology) codes describe services and procedures.

- It is easier to report a five-digit numeric CPT code than to submit a full description of the service or procedure.

- The CPT manual is divided into six sections: Evaluation and Management, Anesthesia, Surgery, Radiology, Lab and Pathology, and Medicine.

- A two-digit modifier can be added to the CPT code to describe unusual circumstances to the insurance company, for correct reimbursement.

- National Level II codes describe dental codes, supplies, durable medical equipment, materials, and injections/drugs.

REVIEW QUESTIONS

Code the following ICD-9-CM diseases/conditions.

1. Nodular tuberculosis of the lung _____

2. Malignant neoplasm of the eyeball _____

3. Nontoxic multinodular goiter _____

4. Unspecified anemia _____

5. Acute alcoholic intoxication _____

6. Vascular myelopathies _____

7. Pulmonary valve disorders _____

8. Abscess of lung _____

9. Acute gastric ulcer with perforation _____

Code the following CPT services/procedures.

10. Biopsy of the soft tissue (lower arm): superficial _____

11. Removal of a blood clot, anterior segment of eye _____

12. Repair and division of plantar fascia and muscle of the foot _____

13. X-ray of the sinuses, less than three views _____

14. X-ray chest, single view, frontal _____

15. Lab, basic metabolic panel _____

16. Complete blood count (CBC) automated _____

17. Electrocardiogram, with at least 12 leads, interpretation and report _____

18. Office visit, established patient level 1 _____

19. Office consultation, level 2 _____

20. EEG during sleep _____

PRACTICAL APPLICATION

Pick 10 ICD-9-CM codes and 10 CPT codes. Record the codes and their descriptions. Take turns writing the descriptions of the chosen code in front of the class. All other learners should try to look up the code. The first learner to find the correct code wins a point. At the end of the exercise, the learner with the most points wins. Or research the development of ICD-10, report the changes to the class, and discuss the pros and cons of this new diagnosis coding system.

Chapter 9

Charge Entry

OBJECTIVES

Upon completion of this chapter, the student should be able to:

- Define an encounter form and why it is used in the charge entry process.
- Recognize what information is found on the encounter form.
- Outline the normal patient flow through the medical office.
- Define the auditing process.

KEY TERMS

Abuse

Ancillary charges

Audits

Charge entry

Chief complaint

Compliance

Encounter form

Evaluation and management (E&M)

Exam

Fraud

History

In-house audit

Medical decision-making (MDM)

Router

Superbill

The information to be billed is now correct and it is now time to manually enter it into the medical billing software. This is an easy process as long as attention to detail is used and the keyboarding skills of the reimbursement specialist are accurate. The charges and diagnoses are mainly numerical, so 10-key skills are very important. The medical code numbers can easily be confused, especially when keyboarding a high volume of encounter forms. Care *must* be taken in correct entry of all the information. The importance of correct charge entry cannot be stressed enough. These codes represent patients and important confidential personal information. The medical claim will become a part of the patient's legal record, both in the office and at the insurance company. It must be entered correctly.

The information is now documented on the computer in the billing software. The process of producing the CMS-1500 form can now be done. This process was discussed in detail in Chapter 5. The reimbursement specialist can be sure their hard work will produce a clean claim and correct reimbursement.

STOP AND PRACTICE

Exercise 9-2

Short answer: Answer each question with a short statement.

1. Explain the patient flow through the medical office.

   _____

   _____

   _____

   _____

2. Explain an in-house audit.

   _____

   _____

   _____

   _____

3. Why is it so important to double-check patient information so many times during the billing process?

   _____

   _____

   _____

   _____

PATIENT FLOW IN THE MEDICAL OFFICE

A patient is checked into the office at the receptionist's desk, where the patient's chart and encounter form are set up for the clinical area. The nurse will check the patient into the clinical area where treatment is performed. The job of the billing office is to check the patient out at the end of their visit, collecting the encounter form. During the checkout process, the reimbursement specialist should double-check all of the information on the encounter form. This extra step can make a difference to produce a clean claim and correct reimbursement.

At the end of the day, the billing office should check the clinical check-in list against the encounter forms collected at checkout. If any encounter forms are missing, the information on the missing encounter form can be recreated by the staff involved with the patient care that day. It is much easier to recreate this information at the time of service rather than days later. The more efficient the office is in this process, the quicker the charges are entered, and the faster the reimbursement is received.

Once all encounter forms are collected, the process of double-checking the information is again an important step in producing the important clean claim. Many offices may skip these steps in double-checking information, but it does save time in the long run. The patient demographic information should be verified against the information already listed in the computer. New patient information should be entered for the first time. Most physicians' encounter forms have CPT codes listed on them.

Many encounter forms also have common ICD-9-CM or diagnosis codes the physician can check off for each encounter. Because of space, not every medical code can be listed on this document. If the physician documents a procedure and the diagnosis not listed on the encounter form, the reimbursement specialist (or CPC) must find the ICD-9-CM code for that diagnosis. Medical coding was discussed in Chapter 6 of this textbook. Even if the reimbursement specialist does not code the patient's services (a CPC may be employed), he or she should be familiar with these codes. This is a very important double-check for the billing process as many insurance company denials pertain to incorrect coding.

At this point, the reimbursement specialist should be very confident that all the information is correct. Many physicians' offices perform an **in-house audit** on the medical codes selected. In-house audits of the medical codes are an important process that will be done at this point. An audit is the process of checking the patient's medical records against the medical code selected to be billed to the insurance company.

The physician must document what was performed on each patient, information that is kept in his or her medical record file in the office. This documentation must match what was billed to the insurance company for that patient. The in-house audit is important to ensure against any fraudulent billing. The auditing process will be discussed in depth later in this chapter.

The information to be billed is now correct and it is now time to manually enter it into the medical billing software. This is an easy process as long as attention to detail is used and the keyboarding skills of the reimbursement specialist are accurate. The charges and diagnoses are mainly numerical, so 10-key skills are very important. The medical code numbers can easily be confused, especially when keyboarding a high volume of encounter forms. Care *must* be taken in correct entry of all the information. The importance of correct charge entry cannot be stressed enough. These codes represent patients and important confidential personal information. The medical claim will become a part of the patient's legal record, both in the office and at the insurance company. It must be entered correctly.

The information is now documented on the computer in the billing software. The process of producing the CMS-1500 form can now be done. This process was discussed in detail in Chapter 5. The reimbursement specialist can be sure their hard work will produce a clean claim and correct reimbursement.

STOP AND PRACTICE

Exercise 9-2

Short answer: Answer each question with a short statement.

1. Explain the patient flow through the medical office.

    _____

    _____

    _____

    _____

2. Explain an in-house audit.

    _____

    _____

    _____

    _____

3. Why is it so important to double-check patient information so many times during the billing process?

    _____

    _____

    _____

    _____

Outpatient Encounter Form

Patient Information	
Patient ID number	
Patient name	
Address	
City/State	
Social Security number	
Phone number	
Date of birth	
Age	

Payment Method	
Primary	
Primary ID number	
Primary group number	
Secondary	
Secondary ID number	
Secondary group no.	
Cash/credit card	
Other billing	

Visit Information	
Visit date	
Visit number	
Rendering physician	
Referring physician	
Reason for visit	

E/M Modifiers
24 — Unrelated E/M service during postop.
25 — Significant, separately identifiable E/M
57 — Decision for surgery

Procedure Modifiers
22 — Unusual, excessive procedure
50 — Bilateral procedure
51 — Multiple surgical procedures in same day
52 — Reduced/incomplete procedure
55 — Postop. management only
59 — Distinct multiple procedures

Other Modifiers

CATEGORY	CODE	MOD	FEE	CATEGORY	CODE	MOD	FEE
Office Visit — New Patient				**Wound Care**			
Minimal office visit	99201			Debride partial thick burn	11040		
20 minutes	99202			Debride full thickness burn	11041		
30 minutes	99203			Debride wound, not a burn	11000		
45 minutes	99204			Unna boot application	29580		
60 minutes	99205			Unna boot removal	29700		
Other				Other			
Office Visit — Established				**Supplies**			
Minimal office visit	99211			Ace bandage, 2"	A6448		
10 minutes	99212			Ace bandage, 3"–4"	A6449		
15 minutes	99213			Ace bandage, 6"	A6450		
25 minutes	99214			Cast, fiberglass	A4590		
40 minutes	99215			Coban wrap	A6454		
Other				Foley catheter	A4338		
General Procedures				Immobilizer	L3670		
Anascopy	46600			Kerlix roll	A6220		
Audiometry	92551			Oxygen mask/cannula	A4620		
Breast aspiration	19000			Sleeve, elbow	E0191		
Cerumen removal	69210			Sling	A4565		
Circumcision	54150			Splint, ready-made	A4570		
DDST	96110			Splint, wrist	S8451		
Flex sigmoidoscopy	45330			Sterile packing	A6407		
Flex sig. w/biopsy	45331			Surgical tray	A4550		
Foreign body removal—foot	28190			Other			
Nail removal	11730			**OB Care**			
Nail removal/phenol	11750			Routine OB care	59400		
Trigger point injection	20552			OB call	59422		
Tympanometry	92567			Ante partum 4–6 visits	59425		
Visual acuity	99173			Ante partum 7 or more visits	59426		
Other				Other			

Vitals:
B/P _____
Pulse _____
Temp. _____
Height _____
Weight _____

Other Visit Information:
Lab Work to Order: _____
Referral to: _____
Provider Signature: _____
Next Appointment: _____

Fees:
Total Charges: $_____
Copay Received: $_____
Other Payment: $_____
Total Due: $_____

Company Name, Street Address, City, State ZIP Code, phone number

Figure 9-1. Sample of an outpatient encounter form

Date of service

A list of services/procedures common for that office (both description and CPT code)

A list of common diagnoses for the office

A release of information statement for the patient to sign

A space for the physician's signature

A space for remarks (return visit date, etc.)

The reimbursement specialist overseeing the charge entry billing process must be sure every patient seen has checked out of the office and the encounter form collected from the patient. This is important for the correct collection of all reimbursement for every patient seen daily by the physician. If a patient inadvertently takes that encounter form home, or it becomes lost, the physician will lose revenue.

STOP AND PRACTICE

Exercise 9-1

Short answer: Answer each question with a short statement.

1. Explain the process of charge entry.

_____

_____

_____

2. List the information included on an encounter form.

_____

_____

_____

3. Why is it important for the reimbursement specialist to collect all encounter forms?

_____

_____

_____

Chapter 9

Charge Entry

OBJECTIVES

Upon completion of this chapter, the student should be able to:

- Define an encounter form and why it is used in the charge entry process.
- Recognize what information is found on the encounter form.
- Outline the normal patient flow through the medical office.
- Define the auditing process.

KEY TERMS

Abuse

Ancillary charges

Audits

Charge entry

Chief complaint

Compliance

Encounter form

Evaluation and management (E&M)

Exam

Fraud

History

In-house audit

Medical decision-making (MDM)

Router

Superbill

INTRODUCTION

In this chapter on charge entry, we will discuss what is involved in the charge entry process. It is important to the billing process to correctly take the data collected at the time of service and input that data into the computer to produce a clean claim. Correct reimbursement is the primary goal in the physician's office and attention to detail is an important job requirement.

ENCOUNTER FORMS

A reimbursement specialist will need to be proficient in the charge entry process. This step in the billing process must be done with extreme care. The information regarding the procedures, services, and diagnoses for every patient determines the reimbursement or payment collected for the medical office. Knowledge of what the physician provides for each patient, correct medical coding, and attention to detail when collecting this data are all important to the billing office. All of the data collected must then be entered into the billing software on the computer. The billing software inserts all of the data onto the CMS-1500 form and sends it to the insurance company. Correct data inputted into the computer produces a clean claim for the insurance company. Attention to detail in this initial step saves time for the reimbursement specialist as well as insures a correct reimbursement.

The information for each patient that is seen in the physician's office is recorded into the computer. Both new patients and established patients must have their records documented and an encounter form must be printed for each of their dates of service (or treatment dates). An encounter form is a document that defines the services and procedures performed for a patient at each visit. It is produced by the billing software program. Some physicians' offices call these forms encounter forms, superbills, or routers. Regardless of the name, most encounter forms will look basically the same. Different offices may design their own, or a basic form may be purchased. Figure 9-1 is an example of an encounter form.

Some important information listed on the encounter form includes:

- **Office name, address, phone number**

- **Physician's name and the federal tax identification numbers**

- **Patient's name, address, phone number, and insurance numbers**

- **Patient's account number assigned by the medical office**

- **Patient's demographic information (sex, Social Security number, dob, date of injury)**

AUDITING

In-house auditing, as explained earlier in this chapter, is a must for every physician's office. Auditing is the process of checking the documentation of a patient's visit against the billed charges, for compliance reasons. Medicare, as well as many other insurances, will conduct **audits** on physicians' records to ensure correct billing and coding. Compliance with all insurance company regulations should be the goal of all medical billing offices. Fraudulent medical billing is a problem for everyone: the insurance company, the patient, and the physician. Correct reimbursement saves money for everyone.

Compliance auditing before the claim goes out of the office can be done by an experienced reimbursement specialist, medical coder, or an outside firm. Auditing can be done at different times during the medical billing process, but the ideal time to audit and code a patient's records is before the charge leaves the office. Audit time can depend on the office dynamics and how quickly the physician documents his charges. Some offices can see delays in charge entry of up to a week. Many offices prefer to send their charges out the next day, trusting their physicians are accurate in their documentation. This choice will be made by the physician and administrative team. Either way, the audit process is the same. **Ancillary charges** are usually easier to audit or check than the charges for **evaluation and management (E&M)** charges. Ancillary charges include laboratory, radiology, minor surgical procedures, and diagnostic testing.

E&M codes include the charges for the physician services. This includes the patient history, the physical exam, and the medical decision-making or physician management of the patient's problem.

Documentation

When Medicare or any other payer audits your claim, they will ask for certain documents from the patient's records. When the reimbursement specialist audits in the office, the same documents should be checked.

They are:

- **Chart note for the date of service in question**

- **Any previous notes referenced**

- **Supporting information; history form, patient's registration form, medication list, ancillary charges**

- **The claim form**

None of these forms should be changed. If the physician needs to add any information, the physician must dictate an addendum.

An audit form is a template and should have checklists that include:

- **Chief Complaint**: the reason a patient is seeing the physician in his or her own words.

- **History**: HPI: history of present illness, ROS: review of systems, and PFSH: past medical, family, social history.

- **Exam**: general multi-system exam or specialty exam.

- **Medical decision-making (MDM)**: number of diagnoses or treatments, amount and/or complexity of data to be reviewed, and risk of complications and/or morbidity or mortality. Other factors on the auditing template will include time spent with the patient, counseling, coordinating care, nature of presenting problem.

The elements of the above items will determine the level of the CPT code for the E&M charge billed. Reading the patient's record will allow you to determine if the documentation from the physician supports the level (code) billed to the insurance company. This checklist will enable the reimbursement specialist to report to the physician whether or not he has been compliant in choosing the correct E&M code for the billing process. This is an invaluable tool to train the physician and staff about documentation, thus allowing the billing office to collect a correct reimbursement. **Compliance** in the rules and regulations of the insurance companies is of high importance. Compliance is the conforming to these rules and regulations. The physician could be fined for any fraudulent billing practices. See the audit check sheet in Figure 9-2.

Auditing medical records can be complex, requiring much practice and experience in the coding profession. When in doubt, always check with the treating physician on any questions regarding the patient's treatment. It is also very important to remember this simple rule: If it wasn't documented, it didn't happen, and it cannot be billed. Be sure the physician has documented every encounter with a patient.

The charge entry process is complete and the claim is ready to be sent. The specialist is confident the claim is clean and is compliant with all the insurance regulations.

Fraud vs. Abuse

Medical fraud verses abuse; there is a difference. A good reimbursement specialist should remember the results of either are the same. Medical **fraud** is knowingly billing incorrectly to inflate reimbursement. Medical **abuse** is unknowingly billing incorrectly. It is the reimbursement specialist's job to have

AUDIT FORM

Patient Name _____ MRN No. _____ new pt _____ est pt _____

Date of service _____ Physician _____

Level billed _____ outpt _____ inpt _____ observ _____ other _____

Chief complaint _____ Final Diagnosis _____

_____

HISTORY

History of Present Illness (HPI)

No. of elements _____ Brief (1-3) _____ Extended (4-8) _____

Location _____   Symptom _____

Quality (sharp, dull) _____   Timing (time of day) _____

Severity (mild, moderate) _____   Context (with meal, exercise) _____

Duration _____   Modifing factors (relief with rest) _____

Past, Family, Social History (PFSH)

# of elements _____ None _____ Pertinent (1) _____ Extended (2-9) _____

Comprehensive (10 or more) _____

Past history (illness, operations, injuries, treatments, Rx, allergies, drug reactions) _____

Family history (heritable diseases, associated risk) _____

Social history (job, habits, marital status, sexual preference) _____

Review of Systems (ROS) for history

# of elements _____ None _____ Pertinent (1 system) Extended (2-9 syst) _____

Comprehensive (10 or more syst) _____

Constitutional _____   Endo _____   Skin/Breast _____

Gastrointestinal _____   Ears, nose, mouth, throat _____   Allergic/Immun. _____

Psychiatiric _____   Musculoskeletal _____   Respiratory _____

Eyes _____   Hemo/lymph _____   Neurological _____

Genitourinary _____   Cardio/vascular _____   All others negative _____

Figure 9-2. Sample audit form *(continues)*

HISTORY SUMMARY:

HPI   Brief (1-3) _____ Extended (4 or more) _____

PFSH   None _____ Pertinent (1) _____ Complete (2-3) _____

ROS   None _____ Pertinent (1) _____ Extended (2-9) _____ Comp (10 or more) _____

Problem focused _____ Expanded problem focused _____ Detailed _____ Comprehensive _____

If no column has 3 elements, check the column furthest to the left to identify the History Level.

_____

EXAM

<u>Body Area:</u>

Head _____ Neck _____ Chest (breast & axillae) _____

Genitalia, groin, buttocks _____ Abdomen _____ Each extremity _____

Back, including spine _____

<u>Organ System:</u>

Constitutional _____ Eyes _____ Ears, nose, mouth, throat _____ Car/Vasc. _____

Respiratory _____ Gastrointestinal _____ Genitourinary _____ Musculoskeletal _____

Skin/breast _____ Neurological _____ Psychiatric _____ Hemo/lymph/immune. _____

# of elements _____

Problem focused (1 BA or OS) Expanded problem focused (2-4) Detailed (5-7)

Comprehensive (8 or more)

EXAM SUMMARY:

Problem focused _____ Expanded problem focused _____ Detailed _____ Compr _____

_____

MEDICAL DECISION MAKING (MDM)

<u>Amount and complexity of data obtained/analyzed/reviewed:</u>

Order and/or review of reports (lab, pathology, X-ray, medical records) 1 or more _____ 1 point

Discuss results (lab, X-ray, diagnostic test _____ 1 point

Evaluating the appropriateness of obtaining old records _____ 1 point

Review old records and/or obtaining additional history from family _____ 2 points

Direct visualization and independent evaluation of specimen or image _____ 2 points
    from another physician

Figure 9-2. Sample audit form (*continued*)

Total of Points _____ minimal/low (0-1) _____ limited (2) _____ moderate (3) _____

extensive (4 or more)_____

Number of diagnoses:

Self-limited or minor (stable, improved or worsening) _____ 1 point each

Established problem (stable, improved) _____ 1 point each

Established problem (worsening) _____ 1 point each

New problem (no additional work-up) _____ 1 point each

New problem (additional work-up planned) _____ 1 point each

Total points _____

Minimal (0-1) _____ Limited (2) _____ Multiple (3) _____ Extensive (4 or more) _____

Associated Risks:

Level	Presenting Problem	Diagnostic Procedure	Medical Management
Minimal	1 self-limiting or minor problem	lab, X-ray, EKG/EEG	rest, superficial bandage
Low	2 or more self-limiting problems—1 stable chronic or 1 uncomplicated subacute	skin biopsies, non-card imaging, lab	minor surgery, over the counter drugs, PT, OT, IV fluids with no additives
Moderate	1 or more chronic illness with mild progression, undiagnosed new problem with uncertain prognosis, acute illness with systemic symptoms, acute complicated injury	Dx endoscopies, deep biopsy, cardio imaging, obtain fluid from body	minor surgery with risks, elective surgery with no risks, Rx, closed fx or dislocation w/o manipulation
High	1 or more chronic illness with severe progression, acute or chronic illness or injuries that pose a threat, an abrupt neurologic change	cardi/vas imaging with associated risks, diagnostic tests with associated risks	elective major surgery, emergency major surgery, decision not to resuscitate due to poor prognosis

Minimal (0-1) _____ Limited/Low (2) _____ Moderate/Multiple (3) _____

Extensive/High (4 or more) _____

Figure 9-2. Sample audit form (*continues*)

Summary of MDM:

Complexity of data _____

Management options _____

Associated Risks _____

Level: Straightforward _____ Low _____ Moderate _____ High _____

After determining each level of data, management, and risk, choose the overall level by finding the lowest value.

E&M SUMMARY

PF- problem focused

EPF- expanded problem focused

D- detailed

C- comprehensive

SF- straight-forward

H- high complexity

L- low

LEVEL OF CODING		OUT PT	NEW PT	or EST PT	
	1	2	3	4	5
History	PF	EPF	D	C	C
Exam	PF	EPF	D	C	C
MDM	SF	SF	L	M	H

Check the levels in the CPT manual for specific codes.

Figure 9-2. Sample audit form (*continued*)

the knowledge of billing and coding regulations, so incorrect billing should not be an option. Insurance companies will fine the physician for either fraud or abuse. These fines can be substantial. Fraud and abuse can easily take place in a physician's office; untrained personnel can choose wrong codes, bill for services not performed, and bill for incorrect services.

STOP AND PRACTICE

Exercise 9-3

Define the following key terms.

1. Audit

   _____

   _____

2. Chief Complaint

   _____

   _____

3. History

   _____

   _____

4. Exam

   _____

   _____

5. MDM

   _____

   _____

Short answer: Answer each question with a short statement.

6. What documents should be checked for an audit?

   _____

   _____

   _____

7. What is the difference between fraud and abuse?

   _____

   _____

   _____

COMPLIANCE TRAINING

Knowledge of the insurance regulations should prevent any problems in the billing process. Training the reimbursement specialist, staff, and physician is important.

The physician must learn to document the patient's records correctly. He must choose correct codes to coincide with the documentation of every treatment and have a compliance process in place for the medical office. The compliance process is a system implemented within the medical office to ensure all billing meets the insurance company's rules and regulations for claim submission. Auditing is a large part of the compliance process. Every staff member must have the knowledge of documentation, and correct collection of patient information. The billing office should be up-to-date in this knowledge and be prepared to train the rest of the office in insurance regulations, documentation, and correct medical coding. Keeping current with these insurance regulations is a must. The insurance industry is always changing, and the reimbursement specialist must continually monitor these changes. They must pass this information on to the physician and staff.

STOP AND PRACTICE

Exercise 9-4

Short answer: Answer each question with a short statement.

1. Explain why a compliance process is important in the medical office.

   _____

   _____

   _____

2. Who should be trained for the compliance process?

   _____

   _____

   _____

3. When should the auditing of claims be done?

   _____

   _____

   _____

Auditing is so important to the physician's office it has become a subspecialty to the reimbursement specialist's job description. Many thousands of books, articles, and seminars have been produced regarding auditing. Becoming a great auditor will be a huge career opportunity for any reimbursement specialist. Studying and understanding the auditing process, as well as the experience in auditing patient records, is worth the effort. Compliance in any medical offices has become high priority.

CHAPTER SUMMARY

- Charge entry requires attention to detail, keyboarding skills, and knowledge of insurance companies' rules and regulations.

- The encounter form is essential to the charge entry process because it is a statement of the treatment rendered to the patient at each date of service.

- A clean claim is the result of the correct collection of patient information, clinical information, documentation, and appropriate medical coding.

- Audits should be conducted on claims before they are submitted to the insurance company.

- Audits ensure compliance with insurance companies' rules and regulations to prevent fraud and abuse in the billing process.

- A compliance system should be in place for all medical office personnel.

REVIEW QUESTIONS

Define the following key terms.

1. Encounter form

    _____

    _____

2. In-house audit

    _____

    _____

3. Compliance

    _____

    _____

4. E&M charges

    _____

    _____

5. Ancillary charges

    _____

    _____

True or False: Choose the correct answer for each question.

_____ 6. The reimbursement specialist should be proficient in the 10-key keyboarding skills.

_____ 7. Physician documentation of a patient's encounter should be written on the encounter form.

_____ 8. A clean claim is submitted to the insurance company after the reimbursement specialist checks the patient's billing information, checks the medical codes, and audits the physician's documentation for the patient's visit.

_____ 9. It is only important for the billing department to keep updated on insurance companies' rules and regulations.

_____ 10. The reimbursement specialist should never submit charges to the insurance company if the physician has not documented the patient's treatment.

Short Answer: Answer each question with a short statement.

11. What is the primary goal of the reimbursement specialist in the physician's office?

    _____

    _____

    _____

    _____

    _____

12. Explain how the reimbursement specialist checks that all encounter forms for the day have been collected.

_____

_____

_____

_____

_____

13. What are some other names for the encounter form?

_____

_____

_____

_____

_____

14. How would fraud and abuse take place in a physician's office?

_____

_____

_____

_____

_____

15. What should be done to the physician's documentation if, during an audit, a mistake has been found?

_____

_____

_____

_____

_____

PRACTICAL APPLICATION

Research compliance programs in the medical office. Prepare a classroom presentation regarding what important steps should be included in the compliance mission for the medical office and why this is so important.

Chapter 10

Payment Entry

OBJECTIVES

Upon completion of this chapter, the student should be able to:

- Define what is involved in the payment entry process.
- Outline what an explanation of benefits is and what information is included on the EOB.
- Define what payment posting involves.
- Outline claim denials and rejections.

KEY TERMS

Adjustment

Appeal

Batch proof

Contractual payments

Coordination of benefits (COB)

Denied claim

Electronic fund transfer (EFT)

Explanation of benefits (EOB)

Payment entry

Payment posting

Rejected claim

Remittance advice

Write-off

INTRODUCTION

Payment entry is an integral part of the billing process. The hard work spent producing and sending a clean claim to the insurance company will pay off in the ease and speed in which the insurance company will reimburse the physician. **Payment entry** is the accounting process of entering reimbursement payments to the patient's account. The important part of payment entry will be discussed, which is the explanation of benefits (EOB), contracted payments, denials, and rejections.

PAYMENT ENTRY

A clean claim has been submitted to the insurance company and the processing of the claim begins. Each insurance company has its own individual regulations regarding the processing of this claim. The reimbursement specialist must know each of the major insurance companies the medical office contracts with. Having a contract with an insurance company determines what kind of reimbursement, or **contractual payment**, the physician will expect for his or her services, procedures, and diagnostic testing. This special contract with the insurance company will also determine what billing regulations the medical office will need to understand.

Understanding the regulations and the reimbursement expected from different insurance companies will make the payment entry process more efficient. Entering the payment from the insurance company for each claim sent can be a daunting task. Depending on the volume of patients in the medical office, the number of payments to be entered on each patient's account in the computer can be an enormous job. Knowing what payment is expected can make the process quicker.

STOP AND PRACTICE

Exercise 10-1

True or False: Choose the correct answer for each question.

_____ 1. Reimbursement from insurance companies only depends on the patient's policy benefits.

_____ 2. Insurance companies have different rules and regulations set up regarding the processing of health claims.

_____ 3. A contractual payment explains what the physician's reimbursement will be.

_____ 4. The processing of a health claim begins when any claim is received at the insurance company.

_____ 5. The reimbursement specialist is only concerned with the patient's policy benefits.

EXPLANATION OF BENEFITS

Payments can be in the form of paper checks or **electronic fund transfer (EFT)**. The electronic fund transfer is much faster and the reimbursement is directly deposited into the physician's bank account. Whether reimbursement is done by paper check or EFT, an **explanation of benefits (EOB)** is necessary for the payment entry to be accomplished. The EOB is a statement from the insurance company explaining how they reimbursed each claim. Insurance companies may have different names for these documents: EOB, **remittance advice**, Medicare remittance notice, or provider claim summary. Many reimbursement experts state: the EOB goes to the patient, and a remittance advice document goes to the physician's office. However, medical billing offices will use these terms interchangeably.

The information found on the EOB will include:

- The insurance company name, address, phone number
- The patient's name
- Medical office account number
- Patient certificate number
- Policyholder's name
- Policy group name
- Physician's name, identification number, address
- Date of remittance
- Check number
- Date of service
- Place of service
- Claim number
- CPT code and ICD-9-CM code, any modifier
- Claim-billed amount
- Allowed amount
- Deductible
- Co-insurance (co-pay) amount

- **Adjusted amount**
- **Amount paid to the provider**
- **Secondary insurance information**
- **Denials or rejections**
- **Remark codes**

Medicare Carrier
111 Union Ave.
Century, NC 37777
1-888-888-8888

Medicare Remittance Notice

Medicare Provider
222 Smith Street
Smith, NC 37777

Provider # 1111111111
Page #   1 of 1
Date: 10/01/20XX
Check/EFT #   000231456

Medicare Part B Standard Paper Remittance

Perf Prov	Serv Date	Pos	Nos	Proc	Mods	Billed	Allowed	Deduct	Coins	Grp/Rc	Amt	Prov Pd

---

Name:Smith, Ronald   HIC 1234567891   Acnt:Smitro   ICN 123456789123 ASG   Y   MOA

Perf Prov	Serv Date	Pos	Nos	Proc	Mods	Billed	Allowed	Deduct	Coins	Grp/Rc	Amt	Prov Pd
123456ABC	0922 0922XX	11	1	99213		66.00	49.83	0.34	9.97	PR-96	16.17	39.52
Pt Resp 10.31	Claim Totals					66.00	49.83	0.34	9.97		16.17	39.52
										Net		39.52

Name:Hurst, John   HIC 1234567892   Acnt:Hursjo ICN 124565789845 ASG Y MOA

Perf Prov	Serv Date	Pos	Nos	Proc	Mods	Billed	Allowed	Deduct	Coins	Grp/Rc	Amt	Prov Pd
123456ABC	0925 0925XX	11	1	99213		66.00	49.83	0.00	9.97	PR-95	16.17	39.86
123456ABC	0925 0925XX	11	1	82962		10.00	4.37	0.00	0.00	CO-42	5.63	4.37
Pt Resp 9.97	Claim Totals					76.00	54.20	0.00	9.97		22.30	44.23
										Net		44.23

Claim information forwarded to: North Carolina Medicaid

Totals:	# of Claims	Billed amt	Allowed amt	Deduct	Coins	Prov Pd	Prov adj	Check amt
	2	142.00	104.03	0.34	19.94	83.75	37.97	83.75

Figure 10-1. Sample Medicare EOB

Each insurance company's remittance advice (RA) will look different, so understanding what is documented on the RA is very important. Insurance companies may send a separate RA for each claim, each patient, or an RA with multiple patients and claims on one document. Medicare, Medicaid, Anthem Blue Cross, and many others will send very large RAs, which require great attention to detail when entering the payments correctly. Figures 10-1 through 10-4 show examples of RAs; make special note of the difference in some formats, see if you can locate all the information required.

Care4Kids REMITTANCE ADVICE | SAMPLE FORM

1234 Silas Deane Hwy

Rocky Hill, CT 0000-0000

1-888-555-KIDS (5437)

For services provided during: Provider ID:
Invoice number: Provider SSN/FEIN:
Check Number: Phone number:
Check Amount: $
Check Date:

NAME of CENTER
Mailing Address
City, State   Zip

Child				Payment Calculation							
Child Name	Certificate Number	Family ID Number	Child with Special Needs?	Care 4 Kids Basic Rate per Month	Payments from Other Sources	Additional Hours Supplement	Supplemental Special Needs Payment (+)	Family Fee	Adjustment (+)	Net State Payment for Child	Incentive Payment to Provider
										1	
										2	
										3	
										4	

Sub Totals: $ **A.**

A. Total payments for children in care: $
Quality Bonus and Reimbursement for Underpayments (+) $
Deductions (e.g., liens, recoupment due to provider error, etc.) (-) $
B. Total other provider payment adjustment (if applicable): $
C. NET PAYMENT: $

[1]If applicable, payments from other sources are outside funds paid to the provider for the care of the child (e.g. child support payments).

[2]If applicable, these are supplemental special needs payments to provide services for the child. These may be ongoing or for this month only.

[3]If applicable, this includes child-related adjustments due to overpayments/underpayments. These adjustments apply to the child for a previous month of care.

[4]If applicable, includes incentive payments per child for providers that are accredited with NAEYC, NSACCA, NAFCC, CASFC.

SPACE for PRINTING of CHECK

Figure 10-2. Sample Medicaid EOB

Blue Cross Blue Shield

January 5, 20XX
Page 1 of 1
Need Help? Call 1-888-888-8888

THIS IS NOT A BILL

Contract Holder Name: Kelsey Corner
Member ID: 222222336000
Group Name: Franklin Franks
Claim Activity for: Kelsey Corner
Claim Number: 00832100000

Explanation at a Glance
  Date of Service: 01/07/20XX
  We sent payment to: Robert Rabbitt, MD

  Claim amount: $215.90
  Provider may bill you $20.00

Provider Date of Service Type of Service Service Code (Number of Services)	Providers charge	Plan allowance	Co-pay	Plan pays Provider
Robert Rabbitt MD 01/07/20XX Office/Outpatient visit 99204 (1)	321.00	235.90	20.00	215.90
Total	321.00	235.90	20.00	215.90

Patient: Kelsey Corner
Benefit Period: 01/01/20XX–12/31/20XX

$0.00 has been applied to your $500.00 in-network, out-of-pocket amount.
$0.00 has been applied to your $1000.00 individual out-of-network, out-of-pocket amount
out-of-pocket amount Please refer to your benefit booklet or agreement for further information. Amount(s)
shown may include totals that claims that are still being processed and for which you have not
been notified.

Figure 10-3. Sample Blue Cross Blue Shield EOB

DELAWARE

Delaware Physicians Care, Incorporated
100 Chapman Road, Suite 200
Newark, DE 19702

Forwarding Service Requested

PROVIDER/FACILITY NAME
123 E. MAIN St,
PO BOX 1234,
NEWARK, DE 19702

**If you have any questions,
please contact the Claims Department at**
(866) 555-2167. option 2 **then** option 1

Remit Date:	**01/31/2006**
Beginning Balance:	**-232.10**
Processed Amount:	**1,422.38**
Discount/Penalty:	**-15.39**
Net Amount:	**1,406.99**
Refund Amount:	**116.50**
Amount Recouped:	**-232.10**
Amount Paid:	**1,291.39**
Ending Balance:	**0.00**
Check*:	**1234567**
Check Amount:	**1,291.39**

SAMPLE

PROVIDER NAME

TIN: 123456789
Benefit Plan: Delaware Medicaid

Patient: MEMBER NAME A   Patient Acct #: 5555555555555   Claim Status: PAID   Member ID: 222222222
Authorization ID: Claim #: 06001777777777   Date of Birth: 03/26/1978
Provider: PROVIDER NAME   Refund Amount:

Line #	Dates of Service (From - Thru)	Serv Code	Mod Code	Rev Code	FFS/ CAP	Units	Billed Amount	Disallowed	Allowable Amount	Co-Pay	COB Paid	Processed Amount	Discount / Penalty	Net Amount
1	01/05/06	95810		740	FFS	1	1,603.00	0.00	1,538.88	0.00	0.00	1,538.88	-15.39	1,523.49
	Claim Totals						1,603.00	0.00	1,538.88	0.00	0.00	1,538.88	-15.39	1,523.49

Patient: MEMBER NAME B   Patient Acct #: 5555555555555   Claim Status: REVERSED   Member ID: 333333333
Authorization ID: Claim #: 0600388888888   Date of Birth: 06/30/1992
Provider: PROVIDER NAME   Refund Amount:116.50

Line #	Dates of Service (From - Thru)	Serv Code	Mod Code	Rev Code	FFS/ CAP	Units	BiUed Amount	Disallowed	Allowable Amount	Co-Pay	COB Paid	Processed Amount	Discount / Penalty	Net Amount
1	12/10/05	99285			FFS	-1	-388.00	0.00	-116.50	0.00	0.00	-116.50	0.00	-116.50
	Claim Totals						-388.00	0.00	-116.50	0.00	0.00	-116.50	0.00	-116.50

Code/Description
Reversal of Claim # 033012345678
123 - Payer refund due to overpayment

Patient: MEMBER NAME C   Patient Acct #: 555555555555   Claim Status:DENIED   Member ID:666666666
Authorization ID: Claim #: 0536099999999   Date of Birth:05/20/1962
Provider: PROVIDER NAME   Refund Amount:

Line #	Dates of Service (From - Thru)	Serv Code	Mod Code	Rev Code	FFS/ CAP	Units	Billed Amount	Disallowed	Allowable Amount	Co-Pay	COB Paid	Processed Amount	Discount / Penalty	Net Amount
1	12/16/05	71010	26		FFS	0	43.00	0.00	0.00	0.00	0.00	0.00	0.00	0.00
	Claim Totals						43.00	0.00	0.00	0.00	0.00	0.00	0.00	0.00

Code/Description
Line 1   M86 - Service denied because payment already made for similar procedure within set timeframe. Service denied per finding of a Review Organization

Remit Totals

Billed Amount	Disallowed	Allowable Amount	Co-Pay	COB Paid	Processed Amount	Discount / Penalty	Net Amount
1,258.00	**0.00**	**1,422.38**	**0.00**	**0.00**	**1,422.38**	**-15.39**	**1,406.99**

SAMPLE

Figure 10-4. Sample Commercial insurance EOB

STOP AND PRACTICE

Exercise 10-2

Define the following key terms.

1. Electronic fund transfer

    _____

    _____

    _____

2. EOB

    _____

    _____

    _____

3. Remittance advice

    _____

    _____

    _____

Short answer: Answer each question with a short statement.

4. Explain the difference between the explanation of benefits and the remittance advice.

    _____

    _____

    _____

5. List the information included on the explanation of benefits.

    _____

    _____

    _____

PAYMENT POSTING

Posting reimbursement payments to the patient's account is called **payment posting**. This also includes posting **adjustments** according to the contract set up with the physician. An adjustment, or **write-off**, is a contractual percentage of the charge taken off a patient's account. The more information a payment poster can document on a patient's account, the easier it is to follow up on any problem account. A clean claim sent to an insurance company should be processed and reimbursed within 30 days to 2 weeks. Unpaid claims past this time should be immediately followed up on. Chapters 12 and 13 will discuss this process in detail.

If the physician is a participating doctor, or has a specific contract with the insurance company, certain adjustments are made to the billed amount. For more information regarding these contracts, refer to Chapter 5, Health Insurance. It is imperative that the reimbursement specialist has good 10-key and keyboarding skills for the payment entry process.

As in any accounting program, the medical billing software requires that the posted amounts equal the amount of the checks the payment poster receive for deposit. Many payment posters enter all checks to prove (reconcile) their accounting process. Some billing software programs allow the payment poster to calculate the amount of the checks to be entered in a batch and enter that amount into a **batch proof**. As the reimbursement specialist enters the payments, the computer will track these payments and reconcile the amounts at the end of entering the batched checks on the patient's account. Accuracy is important. If multiple checks and accounts are posted, it is difficult to find a small error.

When a payment is posted to the patient's account, the date the payment is posted will be recorded, not the date of the check. This is important for record-keeping purposes. All EOBs must be kept by the physician's office. Many offices file the original EOB in files for five to seven years, or electronically scan them into a computer program for easy access. These original EOBs are filed by the posting date; it makes retrieval much easier using the same date that the payment was posted to the patient's account.

The payment poster can also make insurance follow-up easier by:

1. Making copies of the original EOB for any denial follow-up
2. Making copies of the original EOB for any secondary claim submissions
3. Making copies of the original EOB for any rejected claims

Medical reimbursement specialists may be required to make the office deposit. Knowledge of banking procedures is important. The deposits very often will include the checks posted to the computer accounts and the co-pay money collected from patients at checkout.

STOP AND PRACTICE

Exercise 10-3

Define the following key terms.

1. Batch proof

   _____

   _____

   _____

2. Payment posting

   _____

   _____

   _____

3. Adjustment

   _____

   _____

   _____

4. Write-off

   _____

   _____

   _____

Short answer: Answer each question with a short statement.

5. What skills are important to develop for the payment poster?

   _____

   _____

   _____

6. Explain what the payment poster should do to help in the claim follow-up phase.

   _____

   _____

   _____

DENIALS AND REJECTIONS

Do not assume the insurance company is correct in their reimbursement. Everyone makes mistakes and tracking what the correct reimbursement for your office is is very important. The billing specialist is the employee responsible for the reimbursement for the medical office. He or she must be sure the payments and adjustments are correct. A **rejected claim** is denied reimbursement because of a technical error on a claim (not a clean claim), whereas a **denied claim** is not reimbursed for a coverage issue.

Some reasons for a rejected claim:

- Missing information (such as patient's, physician's, or codes)

- Incorrect CPT or ICD-9-CM codes

- Incorrect place of service codes

- CMS-1500 form not filled in correctly

- Typographical errors

Some reasons for a denied claim:

- Insurance coverage non-effective or terminated, or other insurance is primary

- Incorrect patient or policyholder information

- Diagnosis does not support procedure coverage

- Non-covered benefit

- No prior authorization obtained

- Filing deadline not met

It is also important to remember that the reimbursement is not just determined by the contract the physician has with the insurance company but also with what kind of policy the patient has with the insurance company. The patient or policy holder has entered into a contract with the insurance company. This contract will also determine what services, procedures, and ancillary charges are reimbursed by the insurance company for that particular patient. It is difficult to know what each policy covers or doesn't cover, but the patient should have some knowledge of his or her policy. If there is a question on any particular service, calling the insurance company before the service and getting pre-authorization can be very helpful. Many governmental insurance policies will publish their covered services online.

Any type of claim denial will be coded by the insurance company and listed on the EOB. Each individual insurance company will use different denial codes. Knowledge of each insurance and what its denial codes mean is important for any follow up to the denial. Many medical billing software programs will have a standardized denial code system. It will be the job of the payment poster to understand the insurance company's codes and convert them to the computer program denial codes. Posting these denial codes will be important to the reimbursement specialist who will be following up on unpaid claims. It is much easier to check the computer accounts than to pull each individual EOB to check the denial. Some denials are correct and are either adjusted off the patient's account, appealed by the billing office with the insurance company, or billed to the patient. An **appeal** is a written request to the insurance company to research the health claim and reverse the previous denial on that claim. All supporting documentation should be submitted with the appeal. Discussion of denials and appeals will be covered in depth in Chapter 11 of this text.

STOP AND PRACTICE

Exercise 10-4

Define the following key terms.

1. Denied claim

   _____

   _____

2. Rejected claim

   _____

   _____

3. Appeal

   _____

   _____

Short answer: Answer each question with a short statement.

4. What are some reasons for a denied claim?

   _____

   _____

5. What are some reasons for a rejected claim?

   _____

   _____

SECONDARY INSURANCES

Many patients now have health care coverage with more than one insurance company. One insurance is always considered primary to the other insurance. The determination of the order in which the insurance companies pay was discussed in Chapter 5 of this text. During the payment posting process, an EOB will list any secondary insurance information if known. Some insurance companies will send the primary payment information directly to the secondary insurance, but more often the medical billing office will need to submit any balance on the claim to the secondary payer. Secondary insurance coverage requires a copy of the primary EOB before any reimbursement is made. This is required so that **coordination of benefits (COB)** is accurate. When a patient is covered by more than one insurance, the two (or three) insurances will not pay more than 100% of the amount billed on the claim.

If the primary insurance automatically sends this payment information (EOB), no further claim submission is needed by the reimbursement specialist. It is important to track the secondary payment, however. If this secondary claim must be submitted by the billing department, a copy of the original EOB from the primary insurance must be attached to the patient's claim and sent to the secondary insurance. Completing the secondary insurance submission is important to the collection of all reimbursement due the physician. As with all insurance companies, a time limit for submission of claims must be carefully adhered to. Many dollars are lost to the physician if the billing office is not well managed. The reimbursement specialist as a payment poster has a tremendous job in the correct posting of reimbursement for the medical office.

STOP AND PRACTICE

Exercise 10-5

True or False: Choose the correct answer for each question.

_____ 1. Coordination of benefits happens when the physician coordinates his services with the patient's policy benefits.

_____ 2. A secondary insurance will pay the portion of the charge that was not paid by the primary insurance.

_____ 3. The billing department is responsible for submitting all secondary insurance claims.

_____ 4. Secondary insurance companies require a copy of the primary insurance's EOB.

_____ 5. It is not always necessary to collect the secondary insurance reimbursement.

CHAPTER SUMMARY

- Each insurance company processes the clean claim according to its rules and regulations, according to the contract set up with the physician, and according to the patient's individual policy.

- The physician's reimbursement is sent to the medical office either by paper check or electronic fund transfer.

- All reimbursement sent to the physician is accompanied by a remittance advice and the patient receives an explanation of benefits.

- The remittance advice includes the insurance company's name, address, and phone number, patient's name, office account number, certificate number, policy holder's name, group name, physician's name and address, date of remittance, check number, date of service, place of service, claim number, CPT codes, ICD-9-CM codes, modifiers, claim-billed amount, claim-adjusted amount, amount paid to the provider, deductible amounts, co-pay and co-insurance amounts, secondary insurance information, denials, and remark codes.

- Payment posting is the recording of payment and adjustments to the patient's account.

- The reimbursement specialist must employ correct accounting practices by accurate posting of all money.

- Claim denials and rejections must be accurately posted for quick and efficient claim follow-up.

- Claim denials may happen because insurance coverage is non-effective or terminated, other insurance is primary, incorrect patient or policy holder information, the diagnosis does not support the procedure, a service is not a covered benefit, prior authorization was not obtained, or the filing deadline was not met.

- Claim rejection may happen because of missing information, incorrect CPT and ICD-9-CM codes, incorrect place of service code, CMS-1500 form incorrectly filled in, or for typographical errors.

- Secondary insurance information must be listed for correct coordination of benefits.

- Secondary insurance claims must be accompanied by the primary insurance remittance advice.

REVIEW QUESTIONS

Fill in the blank for each statement.

1. Once a/an _____ claim is submitted, the _____ of the claim begins.

2. Reimbursement is determined by the insurance company's _____ with the physician, the patient's _____, and the _____ and regulations set by the insurance company.

3. Knowledge of the correct reimbursement from each insurance company makes the payment posting process more _____.

4. The _____ is the direct transfer of funds from the insurance company to the physician's bank account.

5. The explanation of benefits may be called a/an _____, or a/an _____.

True or False: Choose the correct answer for each question.

_____ 6. The secondary insurance information will be listed on the electronic fund transfer.

_____ 7. Medicare, Medicaid, and Blue Cross remittance advices will look the same.

_____ 8. Posting is the process of entering payments and adjustments to the patient's account.

_____ 9. It is the job of the reimbursement specialist to collect the correct reimbursement for the medical office.

_____ 10. Most commercial insurance companies publish their covered services online.

Short answer: Answer each question with a short statement.

11. Why must a payment poster be knowledgeable with denial and rejection codes listed on the remittance advice?

_____

_____

_____

_____

_____

_____

_____

12. What reasons would cause an insurance company to reject a claim?

_____

_____

_____

_____

_____

_____

_____

13. What reasons would cause an insurance company to deny a claim?

_____

_____

_____

_____

_____

_____

_____

14. Explain coordination of benefits.

_____

_____

_____

_____

_____

_____

_____

15. Why should the secondary insurance information be included on the primary health insurance claim form?

_____

_____

_____

_____

_____

_____

_____

PRACTICAL APPLICATION

Form a team and examine one of the explanations of benefits in Figures 10-1 through 10-4. Each team should research the insurance company belonging to the EOB they are examining. Do a presentation on the explanation of benefits (where each piece of information is located on their EOB).

Chapter **11**

Problem Solving

OBJECTIVES

Upon completion of this chapter, the student should be able to:

- Define the difference between denials and rejections of claims.
- Examine the basics of medical reimbursement problems and how to solve them.
- Summarize how to appeal a problem claim.
- Summarize how to follow-up on problem claims.
- Recognize how to talk with insurance companies.

KEY TERMS

Appeal

Clearinghouse

Co-insurance

Co-pay

Coverage termination

Deductible

Follow-up

Prior-authorization

Resubmitted

Supporting documentation

Time limit

INTRODUCTION

Knowledge of when and how to deal with denials, rejections, and appeals is a very important part of the reimbursement specialist's job. Reimbursement can be lost due to incorrect payment **follow-up**. Knowing how to follow-up a claim and how to talk with insurance companies will help in collecting the full reimbursement due to the physician.

UNDERSTANDING REIMBURSEMENT PROBLEMS

In Chapter 10 of this textbook, the difference between denials and rejections was discussed. A rejected claim due to technical errors can be stopped at the clearinghouse, or rejected by the insurance company itself. A **clearinghouse** is a service that receives electronically submitted claims from the physicians' offices, checks the claims for technical errors, and sends the claims on to the correct insurance company in the correct electronic format. This kind of rejection is usually easy to rectify but will delay reimbursement and cause more work for the reimbursement specialist. The earlier discussion regarding clean claims and the double-checks set in place should limit these kinds of rejections. Human errors can happen, but remember, a clean claim will save the billing office time and money. Rejected claims can be corrected and **resubmitted**. Resubmitting a claim is resending the claim after correction. The first step is determining the cause of the rejection. Rejection and denial codes found on the explanation of benefits will help in this process. Remember, if a claim has been rejected, and the error has been corrected, always check the remaining information on the claim. Do not assume the one error rejected is the only problem on the claim.

A denied claim is a much bigger problem. These claims can be denied for many different reasons. All insurance companies will send an EOB for every claim submitted. If a particular claim is denied, the insurance company will notate a denial code. This denial code must be recorded on the patient's account and resolved as soon as possible. Most insurance companies have a time limit for the resolution of these denials. The **time limit** gives the billing office a very specific amount of time to resolve the denial. One of the easiest denials to resolve is for a non-covered benefit. This type of denial indicates the patient's policy does not cover a particular service or procedure. If the physician does not have a contract with the insurance company involved (non-participating), the claim balance can be billed directly to the patient. If the physician, however, is a participating doctor, the physician must adjust off either part of or the entire billed amount. It is important that the reimbursement specialist knows what services are non-covered. Many times, a billing office can call the insurance company for a **prior-authorization**. The prior-authorization is the insurance company's permission to proceed with a specific service and receive reimbursement.

Another important role for the reimbursement specialist is to educate the patients on their own policies. Inform patients about non-covered procedures and allow them to make a knowledgeable decision on whether to have the procedure or not. If a physician is a participating doctor, many insurance companies require a document signed by the patient indicating they are aware of the non-covered service. This allows the physician to bill the patient. If the patient is not aware of this non-coverage, the physician will be required to adjust the whole amount off of the patient's account.

Other denial codes encountered might be due to the deductible not being met. The **deductible** is the patient's responsibility once a year. Denials can be seen for **co-pay** and **co-insurance** as well. These denials for deductible, co-pay, and co-insurance are predetermined amounts of the charge that the patient is responsible for before the insurance company will pay benefits on a charge. They are simply billed to the patient if the amounts were not collected at the time of service.

Insurance **coverage termination** will be a denial seen on the remittance advice and should be resolved with the patient. Coverage termination indicates the patient no longer has a policy with the insurance company. A possible cause of this kind of denial is misinformation from the patient at the time of registration at the medical office. If this denial is not resolved with the patient (i.e., new insurance information received to be submitted), the entire charged amount can be billed to the patient. The denial for "past the filing date" is a denial that a billing office should not see. This indicates the insurance company has a certain time frame in which the claim must be sent, usually within a year of the date of service. If the claim was sent but the insurance company indicates it did not receive the claim, proof must be sent showing the original submission date.

A very common denial seen on the admittance advice is "the diagnosis does not support the need for the procedure." The reimbursement specialist can check the patient's medical record for accuracy of the ICD-9-CM code. If the submitted diagnosis code is incorrect, and the physician has documented another diagnosis, this claim can be resubmitted. If the submitted ICD-9-CM code is correct, an appeal can be submitted to the insurance company.

APPEALS

An **appeal** to the insurance company is a written request for the claim processor to reexamine the claim. When sending the appeal, the reimbursement specialist must send:

- The original claim

- A letter explaining why the claim should be reprocessed

- Supporting documents

Supporting documents are proof that the claim is a correct clean claim. Examples of some supporting documents are:

- Proof of claim submission date

- Patient's medical record

- Documentation from the ICD-9-CM or CPT manual

- Special reports from the physician explaining any unusual circumstances

STOP AND PRACTICE

Exercise 11-1

Short Answer: Answer each question with a short statement.

1. What is a clearinghouse?

   _____

   _____

2. What kind of claim can be resubmitted?

   _____

   _____

3. Where can the rejections codes be found?

   _____

   _____

4. List some common denials seen on the remittance advice.

   _____

   _____

True or False: Choose the correct answer for each question.

_____ 5. A rejected claim is due to a technical billing error.

_____ 6. Rejected claims cannot be resubmitted.

_____ 7. Rejection and denial codes can be found on the encounter form.

_____ 8. The prior-authorization is permission from an insurance company to proceed with a procedure or service.

_____ 9. The "time limit" denial will allow the reimbursement specialist to limit the time it takes the insurance company to process a claim.

_____ 10. The "coverage termination" denial from the insurance company indicates that the patient will pay the charged amount on the claim.

Many appeals sent to the insurance company will be for denials regarding the ICD-9-CM, CPT codes, and modifiers submitted. Medicare and many other insurance companies will use the Corrective Coding Initiative to edit procedural (CPT) coding. Other insurance companies use their own edits when it comes to correct submission of the CPT codes. Many insurance companies bundle many codes into one code, reducing physician reimbursement. The correct use of modifiers should prevent many of these reduced reimbursements. Documentation from the CPT manual can be used in these appeal situations. The billing office should have appeal letter templates set up for common appeal situations. An example of one of these common appeal letters is seen in Figure 11-1.

If an appeal is denied, this would be the second denial for the claim, the reimbursement specialist must either adjust the claim balance off of the patient's account or call the processing representative at the insurance company.

TALKING WITH THE INSURANCE COMPANY

Talking with the processing representative at the insurance company may be helpful in understanding that particular company's policies regarding the billing process. The reimbursement specialist should remember a few rules when calling the insurance company. It is important to remain professional at all times. Working with the insurance company is always better than being argumentative. Remember, the billing office is representing the physician and his or her business. A good working relationship with an insurance company will help when calling them repeatedly. Asking for their help, instead of telling them what they must do, is always the better approach to a problem claim. It can become very frustrating to understand their policies when trying to explain why a claim should be reimbursed. If the specialist is entirely sure the claim is correct, and it cannot be resolved with an appeal or a telephone call, deal with a supervisor regarding the claim. Contacting a contract representative is another method to explore in resolving a problem claim. In the end, if the denial cannot be resolved, ask for a copy of the insurance company's internal policy in writing. Understanding each insurance company's billing policies (rules and regulations) is the best way to submit a clean claim the first time it is submitted.

Whenever any follow-up to a claim is done, be sure all attempts to resolve the claim are documented on the patient's account. Medical billing software programs will have a remarks section to document the denial, appeal, telephone calls, and resubmissions. This remarks section will allow any staff member to access the documentation and understand what is being done for the claim follow-up. This documentation will help in the collection process. Always include a simple, direct note as to what was attempted, a date, and the reimbursement specialist's name.

The reimbursement specialist's goal in working with the denials and rejections on health claims is to collect the correct reimbursement for the physician. The problem-solving process should always be done in a lawful and professional manner.

October 22, 20xx

Insurance Company Name,
12345 Street Address
City, State and ZIP

RE: Patient Name
ID#:   123-45-6789-01
DOS: 01.01.2005
Claim#:   0123456789

Dear _____ :

We received a denial on the above-referenced claim for an E&M service on the same day as a minor procedure even though we submitted the E&M code with a modifier -25. Per CPT, Modifier -25 is used when the patient's condition requires a significant, separately identifiable E&M service above and beyond the other service provided or beyond the usual preoperative and postoperative care associated with the procedure.

As you will see from the attached documentation, this patient required a detailed work-up before the procedure because _____.

It is my position that this E&M service was clearly significant and separately identifiable and the physician deserves to be reimbursed for the services she provided.

Please reconsider this denial. If payment is not released on this claim, I would appreciate a written response, including a copy of any applicable internal policy.

Sincerely,

You Name here, xxx
Your title here
(123) 456-789 ext. 1234

Figure 11-1. Sample of an appeal letter

Exercise 11-2

Short answer: Answer each question with a short statement.

1. What is an appeal?

_____

_____

_____

_____

2. List what information is sent on an appeal.

_____

_____

_____

_____

3. What would be used as supporting documentation for an appeal?

_____

_____

_____

_____

4. Why is it important to document all inquires with an insurance company on the patient's account?

_____

_____

_____

_____

CHAPTER SUMMARY

- Reimbursement can be lost if correct insurance payment follow-up is not completed in a timely manner.

- Claims sent to a clearinghouse will be edited for rejections due to technical errors.

- Rejected claims can be corrected and resubmitted.

- Denied claims must be appealed.

- Some common reasons for denials are non-covered benefit, deductible, co-pay, co-insurance, coverage termination, diagnosis not supporting procedure, and unbundling procedure codes.

- Following up on unpaid claims should be done before the time limit deadline.

- When sending an appeal to the insurance company, include the original claim, a letter from the physician, and supporting documentation.

- Supporting documentation could include proof of claim submission, copies of the patient's medical record, documentation from ICD-9-CM and CPT manuals, and special reports from the physician.

- Calling the insurance company, talking with the processing representative, contract representative, and a supervisor should be done in a follow-up to an appeal.

- Always act professionally when dealing with the insurance company.

- Always document any insurance payment follow-up done.

REVIEW QUESTIONS

Define the following key terms.

1. Appeal

   _____
   _____
   _____

2. Clearinghouse

   _____
   _____
   _____
   _____

3. Coverage termination

   _____
   _____
   _____

4. Prior authorization

   _____
   _____
   _____

5. Supporting documentation

   _____
   _____
   _____

Short answer: Answer each question with a short statement.

6. Why is professionalism so important in the insurance payment follow-up?

   _____
   _____
   _____
   _____

7. Why is it so important to resolve an unpaid claim quickly?

_____

_____

_____

_____

_____

8. What is the ultimate goal for the reimbursement specialist in insurance payment follow-up?

_____

_____

_____

_____

_____

9. What is the difference between a rejection and a denial?

_____

_____

_____

_____

_____

10. Who is responsible for the deductible, co-insurance, and co-pay?

_____

_____

_____

_____

_____

Fill in the blank for each statement.

11. One process that the clearinghouse performs is to _____ the health claim for errors.

12. The clearinghouse receives _____ submitted health claims and changes the electronic _____.

13. Rejected health claims can be corrected and _____.

14. The _____ is the insurance company's written permission to proceed with a specific service or procedure.

15. The _____ code must support the procedure billed.

True or False: Choose the correct answer for each question.

_____ 16. When an appeal is denied, the reimbursement specialist can always bill the patient for the fully billed amount on a claim.

_____ 17. Always document any insurance payment follow-up performed on a claim.

_____ 18. The reimbursement specialist's goal is to always get a correct reimbursement on a claim.

_____ 19. Supporting documentation should never include the patient's medical records.

_____ 20. Never call the insurance company when submitting an appeal.

PRACTICAL APPLICATION

Research appeal letter templates online and write an appeal letter to an insurance company. You may choose the type of appeal you wish to write. Present the appeal letter to the class. Discuss good points of each appeal letter and how to make it better.

Chapter 12

Aged Trial Balance Reports

OBJECTIVES

Upon completion of this chapter, the student should be able to:

- Define what an aged trial balance report is.
- Identify how to use an aged trial balance report in claim follow-up.
- Outline account receivable.
- Discuss the billing cycle.

KEY TERMS

Account receivable

Aged trial balance report

Assignment of benefit

Billing cycle

Claim follow-up

Claim status

Outstanding claim

INTRODUCTION

Insurance **claim follow-up** is one of the most important steps in the reimbursement process.

Once the claim has been submitted, the reimbursement specialist must track, or follow-up, claims. With the help of the follow-up, the reimbursement specialist will know the status of every billed claim. Knowing when and how to track, check, and follow-up on unpaid claims requires knowledge of insurance company policies. With this knowledge, the reimbursement specialist will save the physician hundreds of dollars. This chapter will discuss the aged trial balance report and how to efficiently use it to increase reimbursements and lower the account receivable.

ACCOUNT RECEIVABLE

Account receivable in the physician's office is monies owed to the physician from unpaid claims. The unpaid claims may be the result of monies owed by the patient or the insurance company. In either case, this unpaid claim will affect the physician's monthly account receivable report. Collecting these unpaid claims is a very large part of the job description for the reimbursement specialist.

The age of the unpaid claim needs to be controlled by insurance follow-up. Not only is this important for reducing the account receivable report, but most insurance companies have a time limit for resolving unpaid claims.

All physicians' billing departments have their specific policies and procedures regarding the follow-up of these unpaid claims. The reimbursement specialist must be knowledgeable and diligent in implementing these policies.

STOP AND PRACTICE

Exercise 12-1

Short answer: Answer each question with a short statement.

1. Define account receivable.

   _____

   _____

2. Why is insurance follow-up so important?

   _____

   _____

AGED TRIAL BALANCE REPORTS

Understanding how to work an insurance **aged trial balance report** is a very important aspect of the billing department. The aged trial balance report is produced by the medical billing software and reports all unpaid claims, the age of the unpaid claims, and what insurance company (or patient) is responsible for the balance.

All claims sent to the insurance company should be processed and reimbursed within 30 days, sometimes less. Many offices will automatically resubmit a claim after 30 days if reimbursement is not received. The billing department may make a call to the insurance company to follow-up on any unpaid claims at this point. Without a denial or rejection documented on a remittance advice, many of the unpaid claims would be lost. The reimbursement specialist *must* track these claims.

Medical billing software programs have many variations of the report designed to track and report unpaid claims. Aged trial balance reports will be sorted by the age of the unpaid claim, insurance company, and patient. The information contained on the aged trial balance report should include the following:

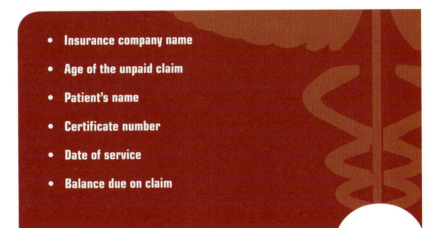

- **Insurance company name**

- **Age of the unpaid claim**

- **Patient's name**

- **Certificate number**

- **Date of service**

- **Balance due on claim**

THE BILLING CYCLE

The aged trial balance report should be generated on a specific day during the month. Follow-up on each claim should be done promptly. Knowing where each claim is in the **billing cycle** is important to claim follow-up. The billing cycle starts with collecting data for the health claim, producing a clean claim, submitting a clean claim, and collecting reimbursement for that claim. How often and at what time of the month the report is generated will be up to the physician's office policy. Most are done once or twice a month depending on the staffing of the office.

STOP AND PRACTICE

Exercise 12-2

Short answer: Answer each question with a short statement.

1. Define aged trial balance report.

   _____

   _____

   _____

   _____

2. List the information contained on the aged trial balance report.

   _____

   _____

   _____

   _____

3. How is the aged trial balance report sorted?

   _____

   _____

   _____

   _____

4. When should the medical office expect reimbursement for a clean claim?

   _____

   _____

   _____

   _____

5. Why is it important to work on an aged trial balance report?

   _____

   _____

   _____

   _____

The aged trial balance report will report the total amounts of the monies that are due. The physician will often examine these reports on a monthly basis.

It is the responsibility of the billing department to keep the account receivable below 90 days outstanding. Reimbursement beyond 90 days will restrict the cash flow for the physician's office.

Figure 12-1 is an example of an aged trial balance report.

STOP AND PRACTICE

Exercise 12-3

True or False: Choose the correct answer for each question.

_____ 1. The billing cycle starts after the insurance company sends a remittance advice.

_____ 2. The physician monitors the aged trial balance report closely.

_____ 3. The billing department should keep the account receivable below 90 days outstanding.

_____ 4. The aged trial balance report should be worked quarterly.

_____ 5. Cash flow in the medical office is restricted if unpaid claims go beyond 90 days.

IMPLEMENTATION OF THE AGED TRIAL BALANCE REPORT

The use of the aged trial balance report is the most effective way to follow-up on all unpaid claims. Checking the status of each claim is essential to maintain the lowest account receivable for the physician. The most time-effective way to check the status of each claim is to call the insurance company. Talking with a claim processor can yield more information regarding the claim.

Many insurance companies now offer an automated system to check the **claim status** online by logging on to their claims network. The claim status is the reporting of where the claim is in the insurance company's processing cycle. These systems are a quick and effective way to check the status of these unpaid claims. The disadvantage to this method is possible computer logon problems. When utilizing automated systems, the disadvantage is that it is not possible to discuss the claim with a claims processor.

18. Many billing offices will automatically resubmit a claim after _____.

19. The aged trial balance report can be sorted by _____ or by _____.

20. The status of every claim must be verified to maintain the _____ account receivable.

PRACTICAL APPLICATION

Group together in teams. Each team should set up a billing department, map out the billing cycle, decide when the aged trial balance report is worked, and the method used for unpaid claim follow-up. Explain in a classroom presentation how the billing department will keep the account receivable below 90 days.

8. Explain three ways a reimbursement specialist can follow-up on an unpaid claim.

_____

_____

_____

_____

_____

9. List what information can be found on the aged trial balance report.

_____

_____

_____

_____

_____

10. List some results found when following up on unpaid claims.

_____

_____

_____

_____

_____

True or False: Choose the correct answer for each question.

_____ 11. The billing department must collect payment from the patient if the insurance company incorrectly pays the patient instead of the physician.

_____ 12. Any unpaid claim that is not followed up on is at risk for denial due to timely filing.

_____ 13. Account receivable are the amount of reimbursement the physician's billing department has collected.

_____ 14. The aged trial balance report is the most efficient method of tracking unpaid claims.

_____ 15. The account receivable should be kept below 45 days.

Fill in the blank for each statement.

16. Reimbursement beyond 90 days will restrict the _____ for the physician's office.

17. Understanding how to work an insurance aged trial balance report is a very important aspect of the _____.

REVIEW QUESTIONS

Define the following key terms.

1. Aged trial balance report

   _____

   _____

2. Assignment of benefits

   _____

   _____

3. Billing cycle

   _____

   _____

4. Insurance follow-up

   _____

   _____

5. Account receivable

   _____

   _____

Short answer: Answer each question with a short statement.

6. Explain the importance of tracking a claim once it is submitted.

   _____

   _____

   _____

   _____

   _____

7. When should the reimbursement specialist expect payment once a claim has been submitted?

   _____

   _____

   _____

   _____

   _____

STOP AND PRACTICE

Exercise 12-5

Short answer: Answer each question with a short statement.

1. Define assignment of benefits.

   _____

   _____

2. List the common problems that may arise in the unpaid claim insurance follow-up.

   _____

   _____

3. Explain why insurance follow-up is the most important part of the reimbursement specialist's job, yet the most overlooked.

   _____

   _____

4. Why is an unchecked claim at risk for final denial?

   _____

   _____

CHAPTER SUMMARY

- Account receivable are the monies owed to the physician.
- Tracking unpaid claims is important to keep the account receivable low.
- Money can be lost if unpaid claim follow-up is not done.
- Aged trial balance reports efficiently track unpaid claims.
- Clean health claims should be paid within 30 days.
- Aged trial balance reports sort unpaid claims by age, insurance company, or by patient.
- Information listed on the aged trial balance report is insurance company name, age of unpaid claim, patient's name, certificate number, date of service, and balance due on each claim.
- Implementation of the insurance follow-up can tell the reimbursement specialist if a claim was received by the insurance company and if the claim had been processed, denied, rejected, or paid to the patient.

RESULTING REIMBURSEMENT PROBLEMS

An insurance company who directly reimburses a patient when the benefits were assigned to the physician must correct its mistake. An **assignment of benefit** indicates to the insurance company that the patient wants the reimbursement to go directly to the physician's office. It is the insurance company's responsibility to reimburse the medical office. If the benefits were not assigned to the physician, or the physician is not contracted (non-participating) with that insurance company, a bill should go to the patient.

It should be the goal of every billing department, specifically the reimbursement specialist, to complete the follow-up on every **outstanding claim** reported on the aged trial balance report. The outstanding claim is an unpaid claim. The status of every claim must be verified to maintain the lowest account receivable possible. Any unchecked claim is at risk for denial due to timely filing deadlines.

Common problems that may arise in the insurance claim follow-up include:

- **Appeals may be required for reimbursement**

- **Claim repeatedly not processed**

- **Difficulty communicating with the insurance company**

- **Insurance company may restrict the number of vclaims that can be checked at one time**

- **Time management for a large number of claims to check**

The valuable reimbursement specialist is meticulous in claim follow-up. This process is very often the most time-consuming part of the job description and the most overlooked because it is so time-consuming.

Some results of unpaid claim follow-up will include:

- **The claim was never received; the claim can be resubmitted immediately.**

- **The claim has been received and is being processed; an admittance advice can be expected soon.**

- **The claim was processed and rejected or denied; request an admittance advice copy.**

- **The claim was processed and paid to the patient.**

STOP AND PRACTICE

Exercise 12-4

Fill in the blank for each statement.

1. The use of _____ is the most effective way to follow-up on unpaid claims.

2. The reimbursement specialist should _____ the insurance company to check the _____ of unpaid claims.

3. Checking claim _____ by logging on to the insurance company's _____ is an efficient way to check the status of unpaid claims.

4. The disadvantage of electronically checking the status of unpaid claims is _____ problems and not being able to talk with a/an _____.

Short answer: Answer each question with a short statement.

5. List some results the reimbursement specialist will find on unpaid claims.

   _____

   _____

6. Explain why it is more effective to call the insurance company on an unpaid claim than to check the status of a claim electronically.

   _____

   _____

CUSTOMER NAME	LAST PAYMENT	LAST DOS	BALANCE	CURRENT	1–30	31–60	61–90	OVER 90
		PYR						
C107 Briley, Nancy	09/28/00	09/27/00	3408.37	792.35	920.94	1695.08	.00	.00
Medicaid								
Sales: 38172.60 YTD	49053.32							
		PYR						
C108 Sims, Samuel	08/10/00	09/27/00	2874.24	652.43	613.02	1608.79	.00	.00
Medicaid								
		PYR						
C109 Franc, Joy	09/12/00	09/27/00	5973.51	.00	5850.75	122.76	.00	.00
United Healthcare								
		PYR						
C110 Tinley, Chris	09/28/00	09/27/00	14076.23	1256.23	2333.78	10486.22	.00	.00
Aetna								
		PYR						
C111 Williams, Doug	09/12/00	09/30/00	2936.77	.00	359.68	1390.00	1187.09	.00
Workers Compensation		PYR						

Figure 12-1. Sample aged trial balance report

The aged trial balance report will report the total amounts of the monies that are due. The physician will often examine these reports on a monthly basis.

It is the responsibility of the billing department to keep the account receivable below 90 days outstanding. Reimbursement beyond 90 days will restrict the cash flow for the physician's office.

Figure 12-1 is an example of an aged trial balance report.

STOP AND PRACTICE

Exercise 12-3

True or False: Choose the correct answer for each question.

_____ 1. The billing cycle starts after the insurance company sends a remittance advice.

_____ 2. The physician monitors the aged trial balance report closely.

_____ 3. The billing department should keep the account receivable below 90 days outstanding.

_____ 4. The aged trial balance report should be worked quarterly.

_____ 5. Cash flow in the medical office is restricted if unpaid claims go beyond 90 days.

IMPLEMENTATION OF THE AGED TRIAL BALANCE REPORT

The use of the aged trial balance report is the most effective way to follow-up on all unpaid claims. Checking the status of each claim is essential to maintain the lowest account receivable for the physician. The most time-effective way to check the status of each claim is to call the insurance company. Talking with a claim processor can yield more information regarding the claim.

Many insurance companies now offer an automated system to check the **claim status** online by logging on to their claims network. The claim status is the reporting of where the claim is in the insurance company's processing cycle. These systems are a quick and effective way to check the status of these unpaid claims. The disadvantage to this method is possible computer logon problems. When utilizing automated systems, the disadvantage is that it is not possible to discuss the claim with a claims processor.

DATE: 11/1 7/00
USER: Orthopedic Assoc.

ARR715PAGE: 1
TIME: 5:19 PM

AGED TRIAL BALANCE

AGING DATE 11/17/00

CUSTOMER NAME	LAST PAYMENT	LAST DOS	BALANCE	CURRENT	1–30	31–60	61–90	OVER 90
C100 Abbott, Carl	09/07/00	10/10/00	22152.02	190.00	8216.16	12389.81	1356.05	.00
Medicare 7708929623								
C101 Barnes, Stacey	09/12/00	PYR 09/30/00	16793.00	1902.85	7087.67	7665.68	136.80	.00
Medicare 404-331-0988								
C102 Cilley, Joseph	09/28/00	PYR 09/27/00	6969.32	1198.30	4110.52	38.50	1622.00	.00
Medicare 404-971-0093								
C103 Davis, Charles	09/13/00	PYR 09/27/00	847.89	.00	262.12	344.09	241.68	.00
Medicare								
C104 Evans, Jean	09/07/00	PYR 09/27/00	4926.57	220.95	1564.27	3141.35	.00	.00
Medicare								
C105 Foley, Jan	09/21/00	PYR 09/27/00	8832.71	.00	7968.64	864.07	.00	.00
Blue Cross Blue Shield								
C106 Johnson, James	08/17/00	PYR 09/30/00	19662.54	1199.45	4473.07	13990.02	.00	.00
Blue Cross Blue Shield								

Figure 12-1. Sample aged trial balance report (*continues*)

Chapter 13

Collections

OBJECTIVES

Upon completion of this chapter, the student should be able to:

- Define the medical office collection process.
- Examine the importance of communication skills when collecting reimbursement.
- Examine the importance of consistent medical office collection policies.
- Define the federal and state collection laws.

INTRODUCTION

Knowledge of the medical office patient collections process can be one of the more difficult concepts for the reimbursement specialist. Each medical office will have its own policies regarding collecting unpaid balances from patients. Each state will also have its own laws regarding procedures to collect money from patients. This chapter will explain some of these policies and laws.

COLLECTIONS

The primary job of the reimbursement specialist is to collect the money due to the physician. This money may come from an insurance company or from the patient. **Patient collections** can be a difficult process. It is never easy to collect money from a patient, but it is an essential process in the medical office.

The medical profession is dedicated to the treatment of ill people, but it must be maintained as a business as well. The **overhead**, the cost of running an office, must be maintained as well as paying the physician and staff for the services rendered. The overhead would includes the cost of the facility, facility maintenance, utilities, medical equipment and maintenance, medical supplies, office supplies, and much more.

It should be the primary goal for all medical staff to keep the cost of medical care down, while maintaining quality treatment for the patient. Many medical offices have a difficult time billing the patient for co-pays, co-insurance amounts, deductibles, and any unpaid balances. Knowing that the patient may be extremely ill makes it more difficult to ask them for money.

STOP AND PRACTICE

Exercise 13-1

Short answer: Answer each question with a short statement.

1. Explain why it is important to collect all reimbursement due the physician.

   _____

   _____

   _____

2. What is the primary goal of the medical staff?

   _____

   _____

   _____

PAYMENT AT THE TIME OF SERVICE

It is important to inform the patient, on the first visit, regarding the payment policies of the office. Do not assume the patient will know or understand these policies, or his or her own insurance policies. Include the office payment policy, in writing, when sending registration forms to the patient in advance of his or her visit. Have the written payment policy posted in the reception area or in the patient waiting area of the office. Have the receptionist or check-in staff go over the payment policy with the patient.

See Figure 13-1 for a sample billing office policy.

At checkout time, explain the payment policy to the patient or responsible party (parent) again. The easiest way to collect money the patient is responsible for is by collecting at the time of service. Some strategies for this type of collection could be:

- Collect all co-pay amounts before the patient is seen by the physician.
- Offer a variety of payment methods (i.e., cash, check, credit card).
- Offer consistent payment plans for patients.

The reimbursement specialist must be knowledgeable in all aspects of insurance reimbursement to clearly explain it to the patient. Knowing the co-pay, co-insurance, and deductible rules for each insurance policy is a must. If a patient presents an unusual insurance policy, it is essential to call that company and find out the specific details.

Communication with the patient is a must. The reimbursement specialist must have excellent communication skills to explain the policy to the patient. It must be explained in uncomplicated, clear terms that the patient will understand. Treating each patient with a respectful, caring attitude will help in this process.

It is important to remember to keep each office collection policy consistent. Patients will come to understand that this collection policy does not discriminate or change.

Billing Policy

The following sets forth the general billing policy of _____. Please review this information and sign where indicated.

* I understand that it is my responsibility to provide the office of _____ with current, accurate billing information at the time of check-in and to notify GVS of any changes in this information.

* I understand that it is my responsibility to know my specialist co-pay (which can be different than my Primary Care co-payment) and to pay it prior to services being rendered. I understand that this is a contractual agreement that I have with my health plan and that the clinic also has a contractual agreement with my health plan to collect co-pays at the time of service, and they are required to report to the carrier any enrollees failing to pay the co-pay.

* I understand that if I present an insufficient funds check (NSF check) for payment on my account that I will be charged a $35 NSF fee. I further understand that to rectify my account, I will be required to pay with either cash, a money order, cashier's check, or credit card.

* I understand that there is a $20 fee to complete disability paperwork associated with my care. I will be provided a standard form free of charge; however, if additional disability forms (such as FMLA) require completion, I understand that the $20 fee (payable prior to completion) is required.

* I understand that the clinic will verify my insurance eligibility, deductible amounts, and co-insurance amounts prior to any elective surgery that I may have. I further understand that it is the policy to collect the deductible and/or co-insurance prior to scheduling my elective surgery. I further understand that THE FEE I AM QUOTED IS AN ESTIMATE based on 1) anticipated surgery to be performed and 2) current information provided to the clinic by my insurance carrier.

* I understand that I will be billed for any amounts due by me (co-payments/co-insurance amounts/deductibles) and that I have a financial responsibility to pay these amounts. I understand that I will be provided with two (2) statements for any balance due after insurance payment. I further understand that if I have not made payment prior to the second statement being mailed, that the second statement will be marked as "Final Notice" and may be sent to an outside collection service if I do not fulfill my financial obligations. I also understand that I will be responsible for any collection, interest, or legal expenses associated with the collection efforts.

* I understand that the clinic will obtain the necessary authorizations prior to rendering treatment. I further understand that prior authorization is not a guarantee of payment, and that I am responsible for any bills not paid by my insurance carrier.

* I understand that the clinic may also take a verbal request to use my listed credit card for payment on my account or it may also use the same listed credit card on my account should my account become delinquent, or to cover an NSF check.

My signature below confirms that I have read these billing policies and my financial obligation as pertains to the physicians of _____

Legal Signature _____   Date _____

Relationship to Patient _____

Figure 13-1. Sample billing policy

STOP AND PRACTICE

Exercise 13-2

Short answer: Answer each question with a short statement.

1. Why is it important to explain the medical office payment policy?

    _____

    _____

    _____

2. When and where should the office payment policy be presented?

    _____

    _____

    _____

3. Why is communication important to the reimbursement specialist?

    _____

    _____

    _____

    _____

4. Why is it important to keep the medical office payment policy consistent?

    _____

    _____

    _____

    _____

OUTSTANDING BALANCES

A statement is sent to the patient by mail when an **outstanding balance** is a patient's responsibility after an insurance company reimburses the physician's office. This statement is sent if the outstanding balance was not collected at the time of service.

Figure 13-2 is an example of a common statement.

Family Care Center
29 Smith Avenue
Smith, NC 27777
333-321-1234
fax 333-321-1235

— Visa	MasterCard		
Card Number			Amount
Signature			Expiration Date
Statement Date Pay This		Amount	**Account #**
Billing Dept. Jane Smith			Amount Paid

Addressee
Sandberg, Bobby
1345 Main Street
Pawtucket, RI 34658

Remit To
Family Care Center
29 Smith Avenue
Smith, NC 27777

Pt Date		Provider	Description	Charges	Credits	Balance	
8/16/20XX		Dr. Amy Lee	Octoplasty	$3,998.00	$4,000.00	$0.00	$0.00
8/16/20XX	*	Dr. Steven Scott	Anethesia-	$245.33	$817.81		
8/20/20XX		Dr. Amy Lee	General Injection	$33.26			
8/16/20XX		Dr. Amy Lee	Hospital Fee	$56.24			
8/16/20XX	*	Dr. Amy Lee	Finance Charge	$22.11			
8/16/20XX		Dr. Steven Scott	Ploxyglobin	$462.87			
8/16/20XX		Dr. Amy Lee	Patient Payment				
9/1/20XX		Dr. Amy Lee	Insurance				
			Adjustment				

Patient Aged Receivable					Due From Patient	$0.00
0-30 Days	30-60 Days	60-90 Days	90 + Days		Insurance Pending	$0.00
$0.00	$0.00	$0.00	$0.00		Account Balance	$0.00

Next Appointment:	None Scheduled

Figure 13-2. Sample patient statement

A **statement** is an **invoice** or bill explaining the money that is owed to the physician. Statements are commonly sent to patients on a monthly basis. This can be a very demanding time for the reimbursement specialist. Many patients will call the office for an explanation of their bill. The reimbursement specialist needs to be prepared for this. All calls must be handled in a professional and caring manner. It can be a difficult time for patients when discussing financial matters, especially when they are ill and worried about money.

Statements should be reviewed before they are mailed for any errors or problems. Personal notes written on the statement can be helpful to alert the patient to the importance of the statement. Collection labels are often used to bring attention to the age of the bill, or the reason for the statement. An example is "Your insurance has paid, and the balance is due by you." A return envelope should be included with the statement.

Each medical office will have its own policy regarding how many statements will be sent to the patient before the next collection step is taken. Often it takes a telephone call to the patient to alert them to the unpaid bill. It is important to remember the patient confidentiality rules when calling any patient. The collection calls should be made after 8am and before 9pm. An office employee must never leave a detailed message regarding a bill on an answering machine. When leaving a message, it is important to always leave a name and telephone number and ask for a return call. When talking with a patient, an effective reimbursement specialist will never appear threatening or harassing. He or she will listen to what the patient is saying and respond in a caring but firm manner.

One common question a patient will ask during a collection call is, "Why didn't my insurance company pay this bill?" If the balance went to the patient's deductible or co-insurance amount, the reimbursement specialist can explain these concepts to the patient. However, if the unpaid balance is due to an insurance policy issue, the specialist must direct the patient to call their insurance company.

If the billing statement or collection call does not result in a payment from the patient, many medical offices will send a series of collection letters. These letters will progressively become stronger. All unpaid accounts must follow the same procedure to keep the collection process consistent and fair. Figure 13-3 is a sample collection letter.

City Medical Office
1 City Drive
Century, NC 27777

June 3, 20XX

Dear Patient,

You currently have a balance of $_____ with Dr. Goodnow.
Our office policy requires all balances to be paid in full within 60 days of
the treatment. Please remit payment for the overdue balance on your account.

If you disagree with the payment made by your insurance company, please
contact it directly to discuss those concerns. Let us know if we can be of
any help.

We understand that many of our patients experience financial difficulties. If
this is the case, please let us know so we can assist you in making a budget
arrangement. If you would like to discuss your account, please do not hesitate
to contact us at 333-222-1111, between 8:00 a.m. and 5:00 p.m. daily.

We look forward to receiving your payment or response within 10 days of this
letter. Your prompt attention is appreciated.

Sincerely,
Jane, reimbursement specialist

Figure 13-3. Sample of a collection letter

Exercise 13-3

Define the following key terms.

1. Statement

_____

_____

2. Outstanding balance

_____

_____

True or False: Choose the correct answer for each question.

_____ 3. A billing statement is given to the patient after each office visit.

_____ 4. Collection labels are often used to bring attention to the age of the bill.

_____ 5. When leaving a message for a patient regarding an unpaid bill, always leave your name, telephone number, and amount owed on the bill.

_____ 6. When discussing an unpaid bill with a patient, be caring but firm.

WRITE-OFFS

Most offices have a policy in place for patients who cannot afford the cost of medical bills. The reimbursement specialist must be familiar with these policies and keep them consistent. Some offices will allow the patient to set up payment plans enabling them to pay on a monthly basis. Many offices will have a policy in place to write off the balances of the patients with very low incomes. A **write-off** is an adjustment made to the patient's account, releasing them from the debt. A standard income documentation form prepared for this purpose keeps this adjustment simple and consistent.

Depending on each office policy, the physician can choose to write off a balance if the patient is deceased, the patient is **indigent** (no income available), or if the patient cannot be located. There are certain reasons a balance should be written off immediately by the medical office. These reasons are:

- Errors made in the billing process by the billing staff (an example is for untimely filing).
- When balance billing is restricted.

STOP AND PRACTICE

Exercise 13-4

Define the following key terms.

1. Write-off

   _____

   _____

2. Balance billing

   _____

   _____

Short answer: Answer each question with a short statement.

3. What kind of help can the reimbursement specialist give to patients who have an outstanding bill?

   _____

   _____

   _____

   _____

4. What circumstances would allow the reimbursement specialist to adjust off an outstanding patient's account?

   _____

   _____

   _____

   _____

Balance billing is the billing of an unpaid balance to the patient when the physician has a contract with the patient's insurance company. The physician is a participating doctor, and this contract will not allow any balance to be billed to the patient above the contracted fee schedule amount. The patient is only responsible for the co-pay.

COLLECTION AGENCIES

When all of the **soft collection** methods (normal statement billing and calls) have been exhausted, some medical offices will employ the services of an outside collection agency. A collection agency can be contracted to collect any outstanding money due the physician from the patient.

Collection agencies have different means to collect payments. Depending on the contract, the medical office will either pay the agency for the work performed or the agency will receive a percentage of the monies collected.

FEDERAL AND STATE COLLECTION LAWS

Collections from patients are called **consumer collections** and are regulated by federal and state laws. The Fair Debt Collection Practices Act was passed in 1977. The Telephone Consumer Protection Act was passed in 1991. These laws outline the guidelines for consumer collections. These guidelines include:

- Collection employees must call patients after 8:00 a.m. and before 9:00 p.m.
- Threatening or profane language is prohibited.
- Confidentiality rules must be respected.
- Deceptions or threats of violence are prohibited.

It is necessary to always check the state's specific collection laws. There are also state laws regulating reimbursements due by insurance companies. Most states regulate how quickly the physician's office can expect reimbursement. A clean claim should be paid or denied by law anywhere from 10–60 days. Knowledge of the state laws will help in the collection process of unpaid claims from all insurance companies.

If the medical billing office cannot resolve claim issues through normal communication with the insurance company, each state has an **insurance commissioner**. The insurance commissioner is with the Department of Insurance. The commissioner handles complaints that are filed with the Department of Insurance. A complaint is usually in the form of a letter explaining the reimbursement problem. The reimbursement specialist must include all documentation regarding a problem claim when asking the insurance commissioner for help. The problem will then be researched and hopefully resolved.

Collecting the correct reimbursement for the physician is always an ongoing process. The success of this process depends on the policies set by the physician's office, knowledgeable reimbursement specialists, and the teamwork of the entire medical office staff.

STOP AND PRACTICE

Exercise 13-5

Define the following key terms.

1. Soft collection

_____

_____

2. Consumer collections

_____

_____

3. Insurance commissioner

_____

_____

Short answer: Answer each question with a short statement.

4. Name two federal acts that deal with consumer collections.

_____

_____

_____

5. Explain some guidelines for consumer collections.

_____

_____

_____

_____

_____

_____

CHAPTER SUMMARY

- Individual medical offices can have their own policies for debt collection.
- The primary goal for the reimbursement specialist is to collect payment from insurance companies and patients.
- The medical office is dedicated to the treatment of ill patients but must be maintained as a business.
- The medical staff should keep medical costs low while maintaining quality care.
- Collecting the patient's portion of the payment at the time of service is the best policy.
- Communicating the medical office payment policy to the patient is essential.
- Keeping the medical office payment policy consistent is important.
- Statements are sent to the patient monthly, explaining the outstanding balance due by the patient.
- Write-offs or adjustments to the patient's balance must be consistent with the office payment policy.
- A participating physician is prohibited from balance billing the patient any amount above the fee schedule.
- After all soft collection methods are attempted, a collection agency can be employed to collect any unpaid balance from a patient.
- Consumer collections are regulated by federal and state laws.
- Each state has a Department of Insurance, set up to regulate medical insurances and resolve complaints.

REVIEW QUESTIONS

Fill in the blank for each statement.

1. The _____ costs of running a medical office must be maintained; the reimbursement specialist must collect the correct _____ for the physician.

2. It should be the _____ of the medical staff to keep _____ low, while keeping the _____ of care high.

3. _____ is very important in explaining payment policies to patients.

4. A/An _____ is a monthly invoice send to patients.

5. Statements should be reviewed before mailing; _____ and _____ can be added to alert the patient.

6. When calling a patient regarding an outstanding balance, always remember _____ rules.

7. Medical offices have policies in place to adjust patient's balances if they have _____.

8. Many medical offices can adjust off all balances if the patient is _____, _____, or _____.

9. Statements should not be sent to a patient if _____ is restricted.

10. _____ can be hired to collect unpaid balances.

True or False: Choose the correct answer for each question.

_____ 11. The Fair Debt Collection Practices Act was passed in 1991.

_____ 12. Consumer collections are regulated only by state agencies.

_____ 13. One of the guidelines outlined in the Fair Debt Collection Practices Act and The Telephone Consumer Protection Act indicates deceptions or threats of violence are prohibited.

_____ 14. Collection rules and regulations can vary from state to state.

_____ 15. If the medical office has a dispute with an insurance company, the state consumer department can help resolve the problem.

Short answer: Answer each question with a short statement.

16. Explain why communication skills are important to the reimbursement specialist in the collections process.

_____

_____

_____

_____

17. Explain soft collection methods.

_____

_____

_____

_____

18. What are the federal guidelines set up for consumer collections?

_____

_____

_____

19. The success of the collection process will depend on what circumstances?

_____

_____

_____

20. Why is the process of patient collections so difficult for the reimbursement specialist?

_____

_____

_____

_____

_____

PRACTICAL APPLICATION

Form groups of two. Set up payment policies for a medical office. Once the policies are developed, have one learner represent the reimbursement specialist and the other learner represent a patient. Set up a scenario to present to the class, showing how a well-managed office presents the collection process to the patient.

Chapter 14

Résumés and Interviews

OBJECTIVES

Upon completion of this chapter, the student should be able to:

- Outline how to develop a professional résumé.
- Prepare a cover letter.
- Prepare a thank you letter and define why it is important.
- Prepare for an interview.

KEY TERMS

Action verb

Contact information

Cover letter

Font

Headings

Interview

Objective

Résumé

Reverse chronological order

Soft skills

Spell-check

Summary of qualifications

Thank you letter

INTRODUCTION

Once the learning process of Medical Reimbursement is accomplished, it is time to move on to the job market. How will the prospective employer make the decision to hire? How does a prospective employee stand out to the employer? The first step is to develop a professional résumé. The second step is to write a cover letter that will catch the employer's attention. The last step in the process is to be comfortable at the interview and prepare a thank you letter. This chapter will explain the progression of developing the cover letter, résumé, and thank you letter. It will also describe proper interview skills.

THE RÉSUMÉ

The **résumé** is a document that outlines an applicant's skills and experiences at a glance. This document must be specific to the job that is being applied for. Developing a résumé that is flexible enough to modify and still meets the needs for that specific job is important. One size does not fit all.

There are many avenues for résumé advice available today. There are books, classes, résumé experts, and online information. Opinions differ on the content of a great résumé. With a little research and some basic steps, writing a great résumé is not difficult.

Talking with and knowing what employers want in a résumé is most important. With a new career as a reimbursement specialist, it is not likely that there will be a large amount of pertinent experience to list on the résumé. Employers will know this. They will look for other aspects of knowledge. The most important task is presenting a professional résumé. Employers will want to know what can be contributed to their work place. The new reimbursement specialist will be able to demonstrate that with classroom work, grades, and any other work experience.

Résumé Basics

The first step in developing a résumé is to explore the job title, job description, and who to address the résumé to. Research the physician's office. It is important to know the name, address, and physician's name. Knowledge of the physician's specialty, the office manager's name, and the billing manager's name is also essential. Any knowledge regarding the office can be helpful. Any questions regarding the job description should be cleared up before sending the résumé, cover letter, and having the interview.

Presentation

Now it is time to actually write the résumé. How the résumé is presented will make a first impression on the employer. It is crucial to watch for typing and grammatical errors. It is an easy step to proofread, but if it is not done, the employer will immediately put the résumé aside. If the prospective employee does not take the effort to present a perfect résumé, he or she will not be the detail-oriented reimbursement specialist the office is looking for. It is not wise to depend completely on the computer spell-check.

Spell-check is a dictionary that is built into the computer. It will alert the user of a misspelled word. Unfortunately, the computer feature will not recognize all words. It cannot determine the difference between similar words, such as your and you're. Many times the writer can read his own résumé and not recognize a problem. It may be helpful to have a family member, friend, or teacher proofread what is written. This small step could be the difference between landing a perfect job or losing it. The easy route is not the best route.

A good résumé must be visually attractive. Using the same **font**, which is the style of letters used on a computer, and type size is appropriate. The letter style should be simple and easy to read. By using a stylish, fancy font, the résumé may be difficult to read and the employer will choose not to read it at all. A second, honest opinion is always helpful.

A résumé must contain the correct information. Correct contact information is a must. Most importantly, a résumé must reflect true experiences. Dishonesty on a résumé will be detected and any job will be at risk.

Length

The length of a résumé is important. Many experts believe a résumé should be one page long, but if the important information requires two pages, it must not be cut short. Employers do not want to read a lengthy résumé. They do want to read the important experiences that may apply to the prospective position. Most employers want to read important accomplishments and previous duties. It is important not leave out any important information.

Experience

When writing a résumé, it is key to be specific regarding experiences and accomplishments. It is not enough to just list responsibilities at a previous job. It is necessary to explain exactly how they were accomplished.

Examples of this concept could include:

- Wrong - Worked in a child day care.
- Right - Worked with children, ages 4–6, with their daily activities, art projects, play groups, and story time.

It is important to remember to use **action verbs** in a résumé. The action verb will indicate a motivated applicant. A list of possible action verbs would be:

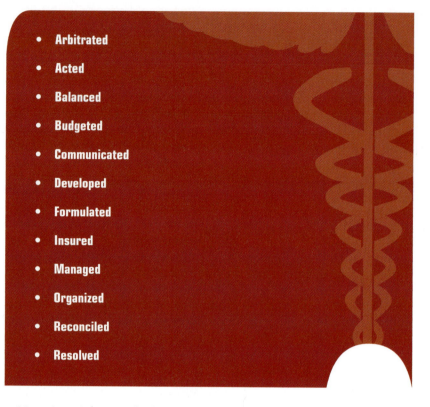

- Arbitrated
- Acted
- Balanced
- Budgeted
- Communicated
- Developed
- Formulated
- Insured
- Managed
- Organized
- Reconciled
- Resolved

Most résumés have multiple **headings**. By using these headings as a template, they can be applied to the reimbursement specialist's situation. Common heading include: contact information, objective, summary of qualifications, education, skills, and experience.

We will look at these one by one.

Contact Information

The **contact information**, as we discussed earlier, is very important. This should include a full name, a permanent address, pertinent telephone numbers, and e-mail addresses. This information should be centered at the top of the résumé.

Objective

The **objective** is a very controversial heading. It is a short statement stating the goal of the applicant in applying for a specific job. Some experts state the objective is not needed and is outdated. Others believe the applicant should write a statement regarding the specific job applied for. This statement or objective *must* be specific. To use a generic statement is not correct. As we have stated earlier, one size does not fit all jobs. This statement should be short and to the point. The applicant should avoid the "canned" statements such as: Objective: To seek a job in the health care profession.

Include in the statement any goals for the specific job listing.

Summary of Qualifications

The **summary of qualifications** is often a heading for experienced professionals. Though a novice may not have the experience in the field of reimbursement, a narrative statement is still helpful. It should motivate the employer to call for an interview.

Education

The education heading should contain a list of schools attended. These schools should relate to the position being applied for. It should include the name of the school, the address, and GPA (optional). This is an appropriate place to list the job-related classes that have been accomplished. A list could include medical reimbursement, medical coding (CPT and ICD-9-CM), CMS-1500 forms, medical insurances, multiple computer courses, and any English and math courses.

Skills

The skills heading may be more difficult for those without experience. By using action verbs, the novice can describe the skills mastered at other jobs. Many of these skills are significant to the current position being applied for. The applicant should include customer service skills, telephone skills, accounting skills, and computer skills. These are called **soft skills**. Employers will take notice. Awards and accomplishments can also be important.

Experience

The experience heading is a list of previous employment. Employment should be listed in **reverse chronological order**, with the most recent first. This list includes the names of the employers and their addresses. The direct supervisor's name, phone number, and years of employment (e.g., 1999–2001) should also be included. Accuracy is important in this section as the possible employer might be contacting these companies.

See Figure 14-1 for an example of a professional résumé.

It is vital at this point to remind learners that honesty is a must when developing a résumé. If the information is not accurate, it cannot be listed. It is also important for the applicant not to undermine himself or herself. Be sure to list *all* accomplishments. Many employers have related that they want the prospective employee to sell his or her strong points.

Joanne Q Graduate

123 Main Street
Green, NC 27722
336-555-1234
JoanneQ@gmail.com

Objective: To find a medical reimbursement specialist job in the medical
                billing field in the Triad area.

Summary: More than two years of progressive accounting experience.
                Internship in North Carolina University.
                Proficient with MS Office, Quicken, Peachtree and the Internet.

Education: Graduate of Medical Reimbursement, Sept. 20XX
                North Carolina University
                Graduated with a GPA of 3.6 on a 4.0 scale

Courses taken include:

    Medical Reimbursement   Medical Coding

    Medical Billing Software   Medical Terminology

    Accounting   MS Office

Experience: **Auditor Internship, May 20XX to Sept. 20XX**
                North Carolina University, 22 University Drive
                John Doe, supervisor 336-555-1233
                Participated in auditing hospital medical records.
                Participated in auditing physician records.
                Developed Excel spreadsheets, reducing record errors.
                Received employee of the month award in June 20XX.

                Accounts Payable Clerk, Jan. 20XX to May 20XX
                Johnson Billing Company, 88 Lotus Drive
                Bill Johnson, supervisor 336-555-1222
                Assisted in payroll, taxes, and account collections.
                Developed monthly sales collection system.
                Customer service help-desk representative.

Figure 14-1. Sample résumé

STOP AND PRACTICE

Exercise 14-1

Short answer: Answer each question with a short statement.

1. Explain an objective.

   _____

   _____

2. List the different headings on a résumé.

   _____

   _____

   _____

   _____

   _____

3. Why is the font important in a professional résumé?

   _____

   _____

   _____

4. What are action verbs and why are they important in a résumé?

   _____

   _____

   _____

   _____

5. Explain soft skills and why they are important to include on a résumé.

   _____

   _____

   _____

   _____

THE COVER LETTER

A **cover letter** is a personalized, written document that is intended to introduce a résumé to a prospective employer. This letter is a key tool to obtain the perfect job. A cover letter is meant to grab the attention of the employer and should never be sent without an enclosed résumé. An enthusiastic applicant can reveal his attitude with a cover letter. It can reflect motivation and enthusiasm for the job listed.

A cover letter should not be lengthy. The information that is stated in the attached résumé does not need to be repeated in the cover letter. The intent is to motivate the employer to read the résumé. As with the résumé, the cover letter must be written specifically for the job listed. Writing a generic cover letter for multiple jobs is ineffective. The employer will recognize this non-specific cover letter and be less likely to read the résumé.

Certain information should be included in the cover letter. The specific company's name and address is needed. The contact person's name and title should personalize the letter.

The writer must explain the purpose for correspondence. The letter must be specific and include the job title and job description. Include an explanation of how the job opening was discovered. If there is not a specific job opening, a cover letter expressing interest in the office can be written. Professionalism, motivation, and enthusiasm should be apparent to the reader. The cover letter must sell the respective employee.

By calling attention to professional background, schooling, and experience, an applicant can appear to be invaluable to the work place. This should be done briefly so as not to repeat all of the information in the résumé.

The applicant must specify a follow-up date. This communicates to the employer that the applicant will be checking on the status of position at a specific date. An example might be stating, "I will be calling about the job opening next Tuesday at 10:00 am." The writer should remind the reader that a résumé is enclosed and end the letter with personal contact information. This contact information will include name, address, phone numbers, and e-mail. A cover letter should be no more than one page. If it is more than one page, it will overwhelm the employer.

Figure 14-2 displays an example of a cover letter.

Your Name
Your Address
Your City, State, Zip Code
Your Phone Number
Your Cell Phone Number
Your E-mail

Date
James Hopper, Billing Manager
Southern Orthopedic Assoc.
55 Hopkins Road
Green, NC 27255

Dear James Hopper,

I was excited to read about the Medical Reimbursement job opening at Southern Orthopedics. I have several years of experience in a variety of fields, including insurance and finance.

In addition to my extensive office experience, I have strong communication, customer service, and administrative skills. My broad background makes me an excellent candidate for this position. Please see my enclosed resume.

Thank you for your consideration. I look forward to hearing from you to arrange an interview. I would like to follow-up with you on the application process on Tuesday, September 10, 20XX.

Sincerely,

Signature

Your Typed Name

Figure 14-2. Sample cover letter

STOP AND PRACTICE

Exercise 14-2

True or False: Choose the correct answer for each question.

_____ 1. The cover letter needs to motivate the employer to read the attached résumé.

_____ 2. The cover letter should list everything on the résumé.

_____ 3. Never let the employer know if you want to check on the status of the job opening.

_____ 4. The cover letter should be addressed to a specific contact person.

_____ 5. One cover letter should be sufficient to send to all prospective employers.

THE INTERVIEW

If the cover letter and résumé were successful, an interview will follow. The **interview** is the most important step toward employment. It is informative for both the interviewer and applicant. By gathering information from the interviewer, the applicant can gain more information about the prospective position. He or she must decide whether this office and position are a good fit. Before the interview, there will be much to prepare for.

A Professional Presentation

The following can be helpful to an applicant to determine if the job is right:

- Is this job a good fit for me?
- Is the office location right?
- Will the job have growth potential?

By keeping these in mind, a good professional fit can be made. A professional presentation is essential. First impressions are always important in an interview. The potential employer will make a judgment in the first minutes of the interview. Being prepared for each aspect of the interview will make it a great experience.

Do not be nervous. This is a hard emotion to overcome, but it is important when interviewing. How does one overcome nervousness? Everyone is nervous in an interview situation, and the employer realizes this. It is how the interviewee handles that nervousness that is important. Some people will simply fall apart and presume it is normal. An employer will judge emotional reactions and it may mean not getting the position, even if the person is the best candidate on paper. A professional reimbursement specialist will be working with both patients and staff members. He or she must be capable of handling stress in an appropriate manner. As was discussed in the first chapters of this book, communication is one of the most important skills needed in the health care office. An interview is the first chance to demonstrate that skill.

Preparing for the Interview

It is necessary to practice, practice, and practice. It is helpful to prepare for interview nervousness by rehearsing. A novice can enlist the help of anyone and everyone to practice. Many health claims programs will include a class in preparing for this interview process. It is a very valuable class and should not be taken lightly. A wise learner will prepare. Take advantage of your academic time to ask a teacher unknown to you to help with a practice interview.

Preparations for the interview includes:

- Always arrive on time for the interview.

- Bring an extra copy of your résumé with you.

- Dress in a professional manner, no fad clothing, piercing, or outlandish hair style. Remember, you are applying to work in a medical office.

- Light or no perfume or cologne would be best in an interview.

Interview Questions

There are many resources to help in the interview process. There are books and there is online information. There are common questions asked in an interview. Figure 14-3 will list many of the common questions. A list of some appropriate answers can be practiced before the interview.

The applicant must be very familiar with his or her résumé. If an answer in the interview does not match the résumé, the employer will wonder if the applicant is being honest. By being themselves and answering any unexpected questions with honesty and calmness the applicant will have the best chance to obtain the desired position. If a question is confusing, the interviewer can clarify it before answering. By repeating the question, the applicant will have time to formulate an answer.

Unsuitable questions do not require answers. Examples of unsuitable questions could include questions regarding your health or any disabilities, questions regarding your family, and questions regarding your age. Some questions will give the applicant an indication that he or she may not want to work for this particular employer. If the job is a preferred position, there are some ways around these inappropriate questions. It is possible to change the direction of the question by simply saying the question is not appropriate, or "this is not an issue." The applicant can ask why the question is important to the job listed.

General Interview Questions

Expect questions regarding your qualifications, academics, career interests, experience, and your personality.

1. Tell me about yourself. (Remember, this question is work-related.)

2. What experience do you have in the field?

3. Why did you leave your last job?

4. What do co-workers say about you?

5. What do you know about this organization?

6. Why do you want to work for this organization?

7. Are you a team player? (Expand on the answer to this.)

8. What is your philosophy towards work?

9. Why should we hire you?

10. Explain how you would be an asset to this organization.

11. What is your greatest strength?

12. What are your weaknesses?

13. Tell me about your dream job.

14. What kind of person would you refuse to work with?

15. Tell me about your ability to work under pressure.

16. Tell me about a time when you helped resolve a dispute between others.

17. What have you learned from mistakes on the job?

18. Describe your work ethic.

19. What motivates you to do your best on the job?

20. How do you propose to compensate for your lack of experience?

Figure 14-3. Sample interview questions

The interviewer might ask if the applicant has any questions about the position. This is where research becomes valuable, by preparing some questions for the interviewer.

1. Can you describe a typical day in your billing department?
2. Is this a new job position or would I be replacing someone?

It is never appropriate to ask about salary on the first interview, that topic will be discussed later in the hiring process.

Remembering to glean information during the interview will help the applicant find the perfect position. He or she may feel the energy from the interviewer regarding the job, the office, and other staff members.

The Interview Process

Let's look at the interview from start to finish. The prepared applicant has his or her goals set, his or her résumé memorized, and his or her interview questions in mind. It could be helpful to drive to the office to determine the time needed to arrive.

When waiting for the interview to start, an employer may ask applicants to fill out their application form. This may be a duplicate of the résumé, but many companies require an official application. It would be helpful to have a generic practice application filled out ahead of time to make sure all the correct information can be copied to the employer's application. A cheerful attitude will help the atmosphere. It will also help to dissipate nervousness. Having a résumé to hold will help keep nervous hands from shaking. When meeting the interviewer, a firm handshake and a smile will leave a good impression. An applicant should wait for permission to take a seat, and let the interviewer lead the interview. The questions should be answered with confidence and be to the point.

Some interviews are conducted with more than one interviewer. An applicant should make eye contact with all present in the room. Body language is important. Fidgeting is a sign of nervousness. The body, especially the hands, should be kept still. Having appropriate posture and a smile shows confidence.

Knowledge is the best preparation in the interview process. If the applicant has the solid knowledge of what it takes to be a medical reimbursement specialist, he or she will be a success.

At the end of the interview, it is important to thank the employer for his or her time and ask what the next step is in the hiring process. Knowing the time line of the hiring process will help the follow-up process.

STOP AND PRACTICE

Exercise 14-3

Fill in the blank for each statement.

1. The interview should be informative for both the _____ and the _____.

2. In preparing for the interview, set some _____ and find out if the job is a good professional fit for you.

3. Being _____ for the interview will help alleviate nervousness.

4. Dressing, talking, and acting _____ will ensure a great interview.

5. _____ by having friends and family interview you before the actual professional interview.

Short answer: Answer each question with a short statement.

6. List some goals the applicant would have regarding the possible employment.

   _____

   _____

   _____

7. Explain how the applicant would prepare for the interview.

   _____

   _____

   _____

   _____

8. List some possible questions the applicant could ask the employer.

   _____

   _____

   _____

   _____

9. List some possible questions the employer would ask in an interview.

   _____

   _____

   _____

10. Why is knowledge the best preparation in the interview process?

   _____

   _____

   _____

THE THANK YOU LETTER

Many prospective employees do not send a **thank you letter** for the interview. A thank you note may quietly help with the interview follow-up. Many employers do not want calls from all the applicants, but a thank you letter will accomplish a follow-up.

The thank you letter should be sent promptly after the interview (within 24 hours). This will accomplish a couple of things. The employer will recognize and appreciate the interest. If the employer has multiple résumés, he or she will pull your résumé to attach the thank you letter, thus pulling your résumé to the top of the pile.

When writing the thank you letter, it is essential to be as specific as possible. It must be addressed to the interviewer by name and title. Use the specific job title, description, and time of the interview. This letter should be brief but should also include a quick summary of your qualifications for the job. Mentioning information regarding the office will show interest and enthusiasm for the job. End the thank you letter with a statement of interest in the job.

Figure 14-4 shows an example of a thank you letter.

Congratulations, you have landed that all-important first job as a reimbursement specialist!

STOP AND PRACTICE

Exercise 14-4

Fill in the blank for each statement.

1. A thank you letter will quietly help with the _____ to the job opening.

2. The thank you letter should be sent within _____ of the interview.

3. The thank you letter may pull the _____ to the top of the employer's list of applicants.

4. It is essential to be _____ when sending a thank you letter.

5. The thank you letter should include a brief _____ for the job.

2020 Smith Road
Smith, NC 27777
333-222-1111

June 1, 20XX
Ms. Jane Doe
Billing Manager
City, NC 27777

Dear Ms. Doe:

I'd like to thank you for the time you spent talking with me about the reimbursement specialist position with Dr. Goodnow. I am very excited about this position and convinced that my knowledge and reimbursement certification more than equips me for the job.

Please contact me if you have any other questions regarding my qualifications. As you know, my work-study internship at the New Clinic provided me with excellent experience in the reimbursement environment.

I look forward to hearing from you soon about this position, and again I thank you for meeting with me.

Sincerely,

Jana Smith

Figure 14-4. Sample thank you letter

CHAPTER SUMMARY

- A résumé is the first important step toward employment in the job market.

- A résumé is a document that outlines the reimbursement specialist's experiences and job skills.

- The résumé should not be too lengthy, but long enough to describe your accomplishments.

- The headings used on the résumé are important for the employer to get a quick overview.

- The professional résumé should be simple and easy to read.

- Honesty is a must when writing a professional résumé.

- Be specific and knowledgeable regarding the job applied for.

- The cover letter is written to grab the attention of the employer, making him or her want to read the attached résumé.

- The thank you letter should be sent soon after the interview and can call attention to your interest in employment.

- For the job interview, dress, talk, and act professionally at all times.

- Be calm and prepared for the employment interview.

- Practice interview techniques with family, friends, and teachers.

REVIEW QUESTIONS

Define the following key terms.

1. Résumé

   _____

   _____

2. Cover letter

   _____

   _____

3. Soft skills

   _____

   _____

4. Objective

   _____

   _____

5. Spell-check

   _____

   _____

6. Action verb

   _____

   _____

True or False: Choose the correct answer for each question.

_____ 7. The résumé should outline the applicant's experiences and accomplishments at a quick glance.

_____ 8. The résumé should show flair with unusual fonts and scripts.

_____ 9. Researching the prospective employer and addressing the résumé to the specific personnel is imperative in a writing a professional résumé.

_____ 10. The cover letter is always sent with the résumé.

_____ 11. The interview process is designed to allow the applicant to practice job skills.

_____ 12. The prospective employer will understand any nervousness, focusing more on how the applicant handles the nervousness.

_____ 13. Modern, stylish clothes, hair, and cosmetics are what the employer expects to see in the interview process.

_____ 14. Experience is the best preparation for the interview process.

_____ 15. It is unprofessional to ask questions of the interviewer.

Short answer: Answer each question with a short statement.

16. Write an objective for an opening as a reimbursement specialist in a cardiology office.

_____

_____

_____

17. List some soft skills.

_____

_____

_____

18. Explain the steps in preparing for a job interview.

_____

_____

_____

19. Explain the importance of body language in an interview.

_____

_____

_____

20. Explain why the thank you letter is so important to landing that great job.

_____

_____

_____

PRACTICAL APPLICATION

Research local job openings and write a résumé, cover letter, and thank you letter for a job you have found. Pair up and proofread each others' documents.

Have the instructor set up a mock interview setting. Have teachers, administrative personnel, and local employers interview you. Make time for constructive comments from the interviewers. Practice always makes perfect.

Appendix

Case Studies

These case studies provide additional practice completing CMS-1500 claims. The case studies printed here are the same case studies that appear in the SimClaim software in the back of your textbook, provided here for convenience. CMS-1500 claim forms may be completed for these case studies either electronically using the SimClaim software, or manually using a blank CMS-1500 form. Check with your instructor before beginning.

CASE STUDY 1
David Downs

Nathan Aspen, M.D.
26 Cascade Road • Green, NC 22771 • (335) 111-2525
Tax ID# 22-2345678
NPI# 3312345678

Case Study

PATIENT INFORMATION:

Name:	David Downs
Social Security #:	007-25-1212
Address:	1018 Oak Street
City:	Green
State:	NC
Zip Code:	22771
Home Telephone:	(335) 111-3321
Date of Birth:	05-12-1987
Gender:	Male
Occupation:	Firefighter
Employer:	City of Green
Spouse:	Jennifer Downs
Spouse's SSN:	007-31-5545
Spouse's Employer:	Green Memorial Hospital
Spouse's Date of Birth:	01-30-1987

INSURANCE INFORMATION:

Patient Number:	Downs252
Place of Service:	Office
Primary Insurance Plan:	Aetna
Primary Insurance Plan ID #:	MNM1238746
Group #:	0012
Primary Policyholder:	David Downs
Policyholder Date of Birth:	05-12-1987
Relationship to Patient:	Self
Secondary Insurance Plan:	
Secondary Insurance Plan ID #:	
Secondary Policyholder:	

Patient Status   ☒ Married   ☐ Divorced   ☐ Single   ☐ Student   ☐ Other

---

DIAGNOSIS INFORMATION

	Diagnosis	Code		Diagnosis	Code
1.	Carpal tunnel syndrome	354.0	5.		
2.			6.		
3.			7.		
4.			8.		

PROCEDURE INFORMATION

	Description of Procedure or Service	Date	Code	Charge
1.	Level 2 office visit - new patient	02-03-YYYY	99202	$75.00
2.				
3.				
4.				
5.				
6.				

SPECIAL NOTES:

CASE STUDY 2

Joy Johnson

Nathan Aspen, M.D.
26 Cascade Road • Green, NC 22771 • (335) 111-2525
Tax ID# 22-2345678
NPI# 3312345678

Case Study

PATIENT INFORMATION:

Name:	Joy Johnson
Social Security #:	004-25-1133
Address:	1244 Grove Street
City:	Green
State:	NC
Zip Code:	22771
Home Telephone:	(335) 111-9813
Date of Birth:	07-15-1960
Gender:	Female
Occupation:	Real Estate Agent
Employer:	Cedar Real Estate Agency
Spouse:	
Spouse's SSN:	
Spouse's Employer:	
Spouse's Date of Birth:	

INSURANCE INFORMATION:

Patient Number:	Johns1212
Place of Service:	Office
Primary Insurance Plan:	Blue Cross Blue Shield of NC
Primary Insurance Plan ID #:	XXN9876543
Group #:	M123
Primary Policyholder:	Joy Johnson
Policyholder Date of Birth:	07-15-1960
Relationship to Patient:	Self
Secondary Insurance Plan:	
Secondary Insurance Plan ID #:	
Secondary Policyholder:	

Patient Status ☐ Married ☐ Divorced ☒ Single ☐ Student ☐ Other

DIAGNOSIS INFORMATION

	Diagnosis	Code		Diagnosis	Code
1.	Mass, breast	611.72	5.		
2.			6.		
3.			7.		
4.			8.		

PROCEDURE INFORMATION

	Description of Procedure or Service	Date	Code	Charge
1.	Level 3 office visit - new patient	03-25-YYYY	99203	$100.00
2.				
3.				
4.				
5.				
6.				

SPECIAL NOTES:

CASE STUDY 3

Christopher Cunningham

Jan Moore, M.D.
13 Route 233 • Poplar, NC 22762 • (335) 123-9897
Tax ID# 54-8526541
NPI# 5564138795

Case Study

PATIENT INFORMATION:

Name:	Christopher Cunningham
Social Security #:	004-52-2121
Address:	15 Lexington Ave
City:	Poplar
State:	NC
Zip Code:	22762
Home Telephone:	(335) 123-9154
Date of Birth:	08-26-1955
Gender:	Male
Occupation:	Carpenter
Employer:	Lexington Builders Inc.
Spouse:	Cathy Cunningham
Spouse's SSN:	004-63-9898
Spouse's Employer:	
Spouse's Date of Birth:	04-25-1955

INSURANCE INFORMATION:

Patient Number:	Cunni003
Place of Service:	Office
Primary Insurance Plan:	Prudential
Primary Insurance Plan ID #:	MXN5834568
Group #:	0199
Primary Policyholder:	Christopher Cunningham
Policyholder Date of Birth:	08-26-1955
Relationship to Patient:	Self
Secondary Insurance Plan:	
Secondary Insurance Plan ID #:	
Secondary Policyholder:	

Patient Status ☒ Married ☐ Divorced ☐ Single ☐ Student ☐ Other

---

DIAGNOSIS INFORMATION

	Diagnosis	Code		Diagnosis	Code
1.	Urinary tract infection	599.0	5.		
2.			6.		
3.			7.		
4.			8.		

PROCEDURE INFORMATION

	Description of Procedure or Service	Date	Code	Charge
1.	Level 2 office visit - new patient	06-15-YYYY	99202	$75.00
2.	Urinalysis	06-15-YYYY	81002	$25.00
3.				
4.				
5.				
6.				

SPECIAL NOTES:

Jan Moore, M.D.
13 Route 233 • Poplar, NC 22762 • (335) 123-9897
Tax ID# 54-8526541
NPI# 35564138795

Case Study

PATIENT INFORMATION:

Name:	Melissa Mason
Social Security #:	005-23-5599
Address:	922 Glen Ave
City:	Poplar
State:	NC
Zip Code:	22762
Home Telephone:	(335) 123-6633
Date of Birth:	08-30-1955
Gender:	Female
Occupation:	Sales Associate
Employer:	Poplar Hardware Store
Spouse:	Mark Mason
Spouse's SSN:	005-66-1122
Spouse's Employer:	Self
Spouse's Date of Birth:	03-2-1955

INSURANCE INFORMATION:

Patient Number:	Mason008
Place of Service:	Office
Primary Insurance Plan:	Connecticut General
Primary Insurance Plan ID #:	005235599
Group #:	0125
Primary Policyholder:	Melissa Mason
Policyholder Date of Birth:	08-30-1955
Relationship to Patient:	Self
Secondary Insurance Plan:	
Secondary Insurance Plan ID #:	
Secondary Policyholder:	

Patient Status   ☒ Married   ☐ Divorced   ☐ Single   ☐ Student   ☐ Other

DIAGNOSIS INFORMATION

Diagnosis	Code	Diagnosis	Code
1. Fatigue	780.79	5.	
2. Irregular periods	626.4	6.	
3.		7.	
4.		8.	

PROCEDURE INFORMATION

Description of Procedure or Service	Date	Code	Charge
1. Level 3 office visit - new patient	06-25-YYYY	99203	$100.00
2. Venipuncture	06-25-YYYY	36415	$40.00
3.			
4.			
5.			
6.			

SPECIAL NOTES:

CASE STUDY 5
Gretchen Grant

John Jones, M.D.
625 Acorn Street • Willis, NC 22735 • (335) 652-1199
Tax ID# 31-5689135
NPI# 2356891578

Case Study

PATIENT INFORMATION:

Name:	Gretchen Grant
Social Security #:	004-63-9898
Address:	87 Lindsay Ave
City:	Willis
State:	NC
Zip Code:	22735
Home Telephone:	(335) 652-1479
Date of Birth:	09-15-1938
Gender:	Female
Occupation:	Retired
Employer:	
Spouse:	Gary Grant
Spouse's SSN:	004-11-2222
Spouse's Employer:	Retired
Spouse's Date of Birth:	01-26-1938

INSURANCE INFORMATION:

Patient Number:	Grant008
Place of Service:	Office
Primary Insurance Plan:	Medicare
Primary Insurance Plan ID #:	004-63-9898A
Group #:	
Primary Policyholder:	Gretchen Grant
Policyholder Date of Birth:	09-15-1938
Relationship to Patient:	Self
Secondary Insurance Plan:	AARP
Secondary Insurance Plan ID #:	1235A2589H
Secondary Policyholder:	Gretchen Grant

Patient Status ☒ Married   ☐ Divorced   ☐ Single   ☐ Student   ☐ Other

DIAGNOSIS INFORMATION

	Diagnosis	Code		Diagnosis	Code
1.	Coronary Artery Disease	414.9	5.		
2.			6.		
3.			7.		
4.			8.		

PROCEDURE INFORMATION

	Description of Procedure or Service	Date	Code	Charge
1.	Level 2 office visit - new patient	07-12-YYYY	99202	$60.00
2.				
3.				
4.				
5.				
6.				

SPECIAL NOTES:
Referred by Steven Springer, M.D. NPI# 0259873510

John Jones, M.D.
625 Acorn Street • Willis, NC 22735 • (335) 652-1199
Tax ID# 31-5689135
NPI# 2356891578

Case Study

PATIENT INFORMATION:

Name:	Thomas Trevor
Social Security #:	005-66-1122
Address:	1298 Neal Street
City:	Willis
State:	NC
Zip Code:	22735
Home Telephone:	(335) 652-4569
Date of Birth:	02-03-1937
Gender:	Male
Occupation:	Retired
Employer:	
Spouse:	Tracey Trevor
Spouse's SSN:	005-33-2222
Spouse's Employer:	Retired
Spouse's Date of Birth:	02-18-1937

INSURANCE INFORMATION:

Patient Number:	Trevo5510
Place of Service:	Office
Primary Insurance Plan:	Medicare
Primary Insurance Plan ID #:	005-66-1122A
Group #:	
Primary Policyholder:	Thomas Trevor
Policyholder Date of Birth:	02-03-1937
Relationship to Patient:	Self
Secondary Insurance Plan:	
Secondary Insurance Plan ID #:	
Secondary Policyholder:	

Patient Status   ☒ Married   ☐ Divorced   ☐ Single   ☐ Student   ☐ Other

DIAGNOSIS INFORMATION

Diagnosis	Code	Diagnosis	Code
1. pneumonia	486	5.	
2.		6.	
3.		7.	
4.		8.	

PROCEDURE INFORMATION

Description of Procedure or Service	Date	Code	Charge
1. Level 3 office visit - est patient	01-22-YYYY	99213	$65.00
2. Chest X-ray, two views	01-22-YYYY	71020	$75.00
3.			
4.			
5.			
6.			

SPECIAL NOTES:
pt referred to Peter Potter, M.D. NPI # 8523697415   for respiratory consultation

CASE STUDY 7
Dale Davidson

Robert Raider, M.D.
17 Raider Park • Walker, NC 22735 • (335) 358-9911
Tax ID# 01-3214321
NPI# 1593572584

Case Study

PATIENT INFORMATION:		INSURANCE INFORMATION:	
Name:	Dale Davidson	Patient Number:	David111
Social Security #:	001-66-2323	Place of Service:	Office
Address:	52 Richards Street	Primary Insurance Plan:	Oxford
City:	Brooks	Primary Insurance Plan ID #:	001662323
State:	NC	Group #:	M231
Zip Code:	22791		
Home Telephone:	(335) 333-1111	Primary Policyholder:	Dale Davidson
Date of Birth:	10-13-1966	Policyholder Date of Birth:	10-13-1966
Gender:	Male	Relationship to Patient:	Self
Occupation:	Appliance Sales		
Employer:	Jones Appliance Center	Secondary Insurance Plan:	
Spouse:		Secondary Insurance Plan ID #:	
Spouse's SSN:			
Spouse's Employer:		Secondary Policyholder:	
Spouse's Date of Birth:			

Patient Status ☐ Married ☒ Divorced ☐ Single ☐ Student ☐ Other

DIAGNOSIS INFORMATION

Diagnosis	Code	Diagnosis	Code
1. finger pain	729.5	5.	
2.		6.	
3.		7.	
4.		8.	

PROCEDURE INFORMATION

Description of Procedure or Service	Date	Code	Charge
1. Arthrocentesis, small joint	11-16-YYYY	20600	$125.00
2. Depo-medrol, up to 40 mg	11-16-YYYY	J1030	$35.00
3.			
4.			
5.			
6.			

SPECIAL NOTES:
Left hand, fourth digit injected

Robert Raider, M.D.
17 Raider Park • Walker, NC 22735 • (335) 358-9911
Tax ID# 01-3214321
NPI# 1593572584

Case Study

PATIENT INFORMATION:

Name:	Edward English
Social Security #:	002-33-3321
Address:	10 Maple Street
City:	Brooks
State:	NC
Zip Code:	22791
Home Telephone:	(335) 358-3000
Date of Birth:	12-14-1935
Gender:	Male
Occupation:	Retired
Employer:	
Spouse:	Evelyn English
Spouse's SSN:	002-33-9988
Spouse's Employer:	Retired
Spouse's Date of Birth:	11-25-1935

INSURANCE INFORMATION:

Patient Number:	Engli4444
Place of Service:	Office
Primary Insurance Plan:	Medicare
Primary Insurance Plan ID #:	002-33-33212A
Group #:	
Primary Policyholder:	Edward English
Policyholder Date of Birth:	12-14-1935
Relationship to Patient:	Self
Secondary Insurance Plan:	Anthem
Secondary Insurance Plan ID #:	XVV1234567
Secondary Policyholder:	Edward English

Patient Status [X] Married ☐ Divorced ☐ Single ☐ Student ☐ Other

DIAGNOSIS INFORMATION

	Diagnosis	Code		Diagnosis	Code
1.	Chest pain	786.50	5.		
2.			6.		
3.			7.		
4.			8.		

PROCEDURE INFORMATION

	Description of Procedure or Service	Date	Code	Charge
1.	Level 3 office visit - new patient	02-06-YYYY	99203	$75.00
2.	Chest X-ray, two views	02-06-YYYY	71020	$55.00
3.				
4.				
5.				
6.				

SPECIAL NOTES:
Referred to Charles Conroy, M.D.   cardiology consult

CASE STUDY 9

Kristin Kruger

Jason Jones, D.O.
233 Route 152 • Urban, NC 22766 • (335) 852-3311
Tax ID# 02-9876543
NPI# 1112323568

Case Study

PATIENT INFORMATION:

Name:	Kristin Kruger
Social Security #:	001-11-2222
Address:	99 Richardson Ave
City:	Urban
State:	NC
Zip Code:	22766
Home Telephone:	(335) 852-3535
Date of Birth:	11-25-1982
Gender:	Female
Occupation:	Waitress
Employer:	Urban Diner
Spouse:	Kevin Kruger
Spouse's SSN:	006-22-3333
Spouse's Employer:	TLC Trucking
Spouse's Date of Birth:	08-13-1982

INSURANCE INFORMATION:

Patient Number:	Kruge456
Place of Service:	Office
Primary Insurance Plan:	Aetna
Primary Insurance Plan ID #:	006223333
Group #:	TLC01
Primary Policyholder:	Kevin Kruger
Policyholder Date of Birth:	08-13-1982
Relationship to Patient:	Spouse
Secondary Insurance Plan:	
Secondary Insurance Plan ID #:	
Secondary Policyholder:	

Patient Status [X] Married   ☐ Divorced   ☐ Single   ☐ Student   ☐ Other

---

DIAGNOSIS INFORMATION

	Diagnosis	Code		Diagnosis	Code
1.	Laceration, hand	882.0	5.		
2.			6.		
3.			7.		
4.			8.		

PROCEDURE INFORMATION

	Description of Procedure or Service	Date	Code	Charge
1.	Level 2 office visit - est patient	10-02-YYYY	99212	$85.00
2.				
3.				
4.				
5.				
6.				

SPECIAL NOTES:

Jason Jones, D.O.
233 Route 152 • Urban, NC 22766 • (335) 852-3311
Tax ID# 02-9876543
NPI# 1112323568

Case Study

PATIENT INFORMATION:		INSURANCE INFORMATION:	
Name:	Lisa Lowe	Patient Number:	Lowe0011
Social Security #:	002-33-4545	Place of Service:	Office
Address:	859 Lowell Road	Primary Insurance Plan:	Medicare
City:	Urban	Primary Insurance Plan ID #:	002-33-4545B
State:	NC		
Zip Code:	22766	Group #:	
Home Telephone:	(335) 852-5050	Primary Policyholder:	Lisa Lowe
Date of Birth:	12-25-1933	Policyholder Date of Birth:	12-25-1933
Gender:	Female	Relationship to Patient:	Self
Occupation:	Retired		
Employer:		Secondary Insurance Plan:	AARP
Spouse:	Leon Lowe		
Spouse's SSN:	002-14-1010	Secondary Insurance Plan ID #:	01212358G
Spouse's Employer:	Retired		
Spouse's Date of Birth:	02-03-1933	Secondary Policyholder:	Lisa Lowe

Patient Status	☒ Married	☐ Divorced	☐ Single	☐ Student	☐ Other

DIAGNOSIS INFORMATION

	Diagnosis	Code		Diagnosis	Code
1.	Bladder infection, cystitis	595.9	5.		
2.			6.		
3.			7.		
4.			8.		

PROCEDURE INFORMATION

	Description of Procedure or Service	Date	Code	Charge
1.	Level 1 office visit - est patient	04-15-YYYY	99211	$50.00
2.	Urinalysis	04-15-YYYY	81002	$25.00
3.				
4.				
5.				
6.				

SPECIAL NOTES:

CASE STUDY 11

Danielle Dayton

Martin Miles, M.D.
4310 Horton Ave • Sunshine, NC 22633 • (335) 321-6515
Tax ID# 03-2586543
NPI# 0226587012

Case Study

PATIENT INFORMATION:

Name:	Danielle Dayton
Social Security #:	003-33-3214
Address:	51 Florida Ave
City:	Sunshine
State:	NC
Zip Code:	22633
Home Telephone:	(335) 321-9999
Date of Birth:	11-22-1998
Gender:	Female
Occupation:	Customer Service Rep
Employer:	Sunshine Medical Center
Spouse:	
Spouse's SSN:	
Spouse's Employer:	
Spouse's Date of Birth:	

INSURANCE INFORMATION:

Patient Number:	Dayto555
Place of Service:	Office
Primary Insurance Plan:	United Healthcare
Primary Insurance Plan ID #:	TRS3698495
Group #:	Sun01
Primary Policyholder:	Susan Dayton
Policyholder Date of Birth:	05-05-1965
Relationship to Patient:	Parent
Secondary Insurance Plan:	Aetna
Secondary Insurance Plan ID #:	XXY1234567
Secondary Policyholder:	Daniel Dayton

Patient Status ☐ Married ☐ Divorced ☐ Single ☒ Student ☐ Other

---

DIAGNOSIS INFORMATION

	Diagnosis	Code		Diagnosis	Code
1.	ankle injury	959.7	5.		
2.			6.		
3.			7.		
4.			8.		

PROCEDURE INFORMATION

	Description of Procedure or Service	Date	Code	Charge
1.	Level 1 office visit - est patient	06-21-YYYY	99211	$45.00
2.	Ankle X-ray, three views	06-21-YYYY	73610	$55.00
3.				
4.				
5.				
6.				

SPECIAL NOTES:

Martin Miles, M.D.
4310 Horton Ave • Sunshine, NC 22633 • (335) 321-6515
Tax ID# 03-2586543
NPI# 0226587012

Case Study

PATIENT INFORMATION:

Name:	Patrick Poole
Social Security #:	005-55-5454
Address:	35 Marion Street
City:	Sunshine
State:	NC
Zip Code:	22633
Home Telephone:	(335) 321-1111
Date of Birth:	01-30-1925
Gender:	Male
Occupation:	Retired
Employer:	
Spouse:	Patricia Poole
Spouse's SSN:	003-33-1313
Spouse's Employer:	Retired
Spouse's Date of Birth:	02-03-1925

INSURANCE INFORMATION:

Patient Number:	Poole123
Place of Service:	Office
Primary Insurance Plan:	RR Medicare
Primary Insurance Plan ID #:	R005-55-5454
Group #:	
Primary Policyholder:	Patrick Poole
Policyholder Date of Birth:	01-30-1925
Relationship to Patient:	Self
Secondary Insurance Plan:	Blue Cross Medigap
Secondary Insurance Plan ID #:	MDG9871258
Secondary Policyholder:	Patrick Poole

Patient Status: ☒ Married ☐ Divorced ☐ Single ☐ Student ☐ Other

DIAGNOSIS INFORMATION

Diagnosis	Code	Diagnosis	Code
1. Trochanteric fracture of femur	820.01	5.	
2.		6.	
3.		7.	
4.		8.	

PROCEDURE INFORMATION

Description of Procedure or Service	Date	Code	Charge
1. Level 3 office visit - new patient	09-20-YYYY	99203	$75.00
2. Hip X-ray, two views	09-20-YYYY	73510	$85.00
3.			
4.			
5.			
6.			

SPECIAL NOTES:
Referred by Jennifer James, M.D. NPI# 8523579514

CASE STUDY 13

Roy Rancourt

Lynn Landry, M.D.
22 Juniper Lane • Ash, NC 22655 • (335) 669-3321
Tax ID# 04-8523579
NPI# 9998745556

Case Study

PATIENT INFORMATION:

Name:	Roy Rancourt
Social Security #:	004-65-3214
Address:	999 Richardson Road
City:	Ash
State:	NC
Zip Code:	22655
Home Telephone:	(335) 321-6213
Date of Birth:	10-11-1965
Gender:	Male
Occupation:	Transportation Dispatcher
Employer:	ABBA Trucking
Spouse:	Rowena Rancourt
Spouse's SSN:	004-33-1425
Spouse's Employer:	ACTION Accounting
Spouse's Date of Birth:	03-12-1965

INSURANCE INFORMATION:

Patient Number:	Ranco001
Place of Service:	Office
Primary Insurance Plan:	United Healthcare
Primary Insurance Plan ID #:	004331425
Group #:	ACT1597535
Primary Policyholder:	Rowena Rancourt
Policyholder Date of Birth:	03-12-1965
Relationship to Patient:	Self
Secondary Insurance Plan:	
Secondary Insurance Plan ID #:	
Secondary Policyholder:	

Patient Status   ☒ Married   ☐ Divorced   ☐ Single   ☐ Student   ☐ Other

DIAGNOSIS INFORMATION

	Diagnosis	Code		Diagnosis	Code
1.	gastric ulcer, chronic without hemorrhage without obstruction	531.70	5.		
2.			6.		
3.			7.		
4.			8.		

PROCEDURE INFORMATION

	Description of Procedure or Service	Date	Code	Charge
1.	Level 3 office consultation	02-17-YYYY	99243	$225.00
2.				
3.				
4.				
5.				
6.				

SPECIAL NOTES:
Referred by Leonard Loring, M.D.   NPI# 8523579516

Lynn Landry, M.D.
22 Juniper Lane • Ash, NC 22655 • (335) 669-3321
Tax ID# 04-8523579
NPI# 9998745556

Case Study

PATIENT INFORMATION:

Name:	Bonnie Boland
Social Security #:	002-22-1212
Address:	88 College Ave
City:	Ash
State:	NC
Zip Code:	22655
Home Telephone:	(335) 321-1212
Date of Birth:	06-25-1940
Gender:	Female
Occupation:	Retired
Employer:	
Spouse:	Bruce Boland
Spouse's SSN:	002-39-2525
Spouse's Employer:	MOP Plumming
Spouse's Date of Birth:	04-13-1945

INSURANCE INFORMATION:

Patient Number:	Bolan005
Place of Service:	Office
Primary Insurance Plan:	Oxford
Primary Insurance Plan ID #:	002392525
Group #:	MOP0025
Primary Policyholder:	Bruce Boland
Policyholder Date of Birth:	04-13-1945
Relationship to Patient:	Spouse
Secondary Insurance Plan:	Medicare
Secondary Insurance Plan ID #:	002-22-1212A
Secondary Policyholder:	Bonnie Boland

Patient Status   ☒ Married   ☐ Divorced   ☐ Single   ☐ Student   ☐ Other

DIAGNOSIS INFORMATION

Diagnosis	Code	Diagnosis	Code
1. Diabetes mellitus without complications	250.00	5.	
2.		6.	
3.		7.	
4.		8.	

PROCEDURE INFORMATION

Description of Procedure or Service	Date	Code	Charge
1. Level 2 office visit - est patient	08-12-YYYY	99202	$50.00
2. Influenza vaccine	08-12-YYYY	90658	$20.00
3. Administration of influenza vaccine	08-12-YYYY	G0008	$10.00
4.			
5.			
6.			

SPECIAL NOTES:
Medicare is secondary payer

CASE STUDY 15

Tammy Topper

Steven Searles, M.D.
250 Route 125 • Turner, NC 22722 • (335) 357-4564
Tax ID# 01-3589614
NPI# 1123556789

Case Study

PATIENT INFORMATION:		INSURANCE INFORMATION:	
Name:	Tammy Topper	Patient Number:	Toppe68
Social Security #:	005-36-6363	Place of Service:	Office
Address:	37 Clipper Lane	Primary Insurance Plan:	Blue Cross Blue Shield of NC
City:	Turner		
State:	NC	Primary Insurance Plan ID #:	WXY1112223
Zip Code:	22722		
Home Telephone:	(335) 357-9999	Group #:	POP11
Date of Birth:	07-04-1966	Primary Policyholder:	Tammy Topper
Gender:	Female	Policyholder Date of Birth:	07-04-1966
Occupation:	Bank Teller	Relationship to Patient:	Self
Employer:	Green Bank		
Spouse:		Secondary Insurance Plan:	
Spouse's SSN:		Secondary Insurance Plan ID #:	
Spouse's Employer:			
Spouse's Date of Birth:		Secondary Policyholder:	

Patient Status   ☐ Married   ☒ Divorced   ☐ Single   ☐ Student   ☐ Other

DIAGNOSIS INFORMATION

	Diagnosis	Code		Diagnosis	Code
1.	Back pain	724.5	5.		
2.			6.		
3.			7.		
4.			8.		

PROCEDURE INFORMATION

	Description of Procedure or Service	Date	Code	Charge
1.	Level 3 office consultation	02-15-YYYY	99243	$250.00
2.	Lumbosacral X-ray, three views	02-15-YYYY	72100	$125.00
3.				
4.				
5.				
6.				

SPECIAL NOTES:
Referred by Mary Meadow, D.O.   NPI# 5465456585

Steven Searles, M.D.

250 Route 125 • Turner, NC 22722 • (335) 357-4564
Tax ID# 01-3589614
NPI# 1123556789

Case Study

PATIENT INFORMATION:

Name:	Jeremy Jeffreys
Social Security #:	002-22-8888
Address:	65 Lee Street
City:	Turner
State:	NC
Zip Code:	22722
Home Telephone:	(335) 357-8978
Date of Birth:	12-20-1968
Gender:	Male
Occupation:	Mechanic
Employer:	John's Filling Station
Spouse:	Jackie Jeffreys
Spouse's SSN:	003-66-5410
Spouse's Employer:	Unemployed
Spouse's Date of Birth:	01-01-1967

INSURANCE INFORMATION:

Patient Number:	Jeffr009
Place of Service:	Office
Primary Insurance Plan:	James Company
Primary Insurance Plan ID #:	W/C File #0259632
Group #:	002-22-8888
Primary Policyholder:	Jeremy Jeffreys
Policyholder Date of Birth:	12-20-1968
Relationship to Patient:	Self
Secondary Insurance Plan:	
Secondary Insurance Plan ID #:	
Secondary Policyholder:	

Patient Status ☒ Married   ☐ Divorced   ☐ Single   ☐ Student   ☐ Other

DIAGNOSIS INFORMATION

Diagnosis	Code	Diagnosis	Code
1. Magnetic foreign body in eye	871.5	5.	
2.		6.	
3.		7.	
4.		8.	

PROCEDURE INFORMATION

Description of Procedure or Service	Date	Code	Charge
1. Level 2 office visit - new pt	07-29-YYYY	99202	$225.00
2.			
3.			
4.			
5.			
6.			

SPECIAL NOTES:

Workers Compensation   injury date 07-28-YYYY

CASE STUDY 17

Mark Moses

Leonard Loving, M.D.
33 Elm Street • Pebble, NC 22654 • (335) 321-9876
Tax ID# 07-3589412
NPI# 5587912358

Case Study

PATIENT INFORMATION:		INSURANCE INFORMATION:	
Name:	Mark Moses	Patient Number:	Moses009
Social Security #:	007-44-8727	Place of Service:	Office
Address:	125 Paton Ave	Primary Insurance Plan:	Tricare Standard
City:	Pebble	Primary Insurance Plan ID #:	007-44-8727
State:	NC		
Zip Code:	22654	Group #:	
Home Telephone:	(335) 321-9876	Primary Policyholder:	Mark Moses
Date of Birth:	02-03-1979	Policyholder Date of Birth:	02-03-1979
Gender:	Male	Relationship to Patient:	Self
Occupation:	U.S. Navy		
Employer:	U.S. Navy	Secondary Insurance Plan:	
Spouse:		Secondary Insurance Plan ID #:	
Spouse's SSN:			
Spouse's Employer:		Secondary Policyholder:	
Spouse's Date of Birth:			

Patient Status   ☐ Married   ☐ Divorced   ☒ Single   ☐ Student   ☐ Other

DIAGNOSIS INFORMATION

	Diagnosis	Code		Diagnosis	Code
1.	Sinus polyp	471.8	5.		
2.	Deviated septum, nasal	470	6.		
3.			7.		
4.			8.		

PROCEDURE INFORMATION

	Description of Procedure or Service	Date	Code	Charge
1.	Level 2 office consultation - new pt	03-16-YYYY	99242	$200.00
2.				
3.				
4.				
5.				
6.				

SPECIAL NOTES:

Leonard Loving, M.D.
33 Elm Street • Pebble, NC 22654 • (335) 321-9876
Tax ID# 07-3589412
NPI# 5587912358

Case Study

PATIENT INFORMATION:

Name:	Penelope Peoples
Social Security #:	004-35-1526
Address:	928 Lindsay Court
City:	Pebble
State:	NC
Zip Code:	22654
Home Telephone:	(335) 321-3333
Date of Birth:	08-30-1930
Gender:	Female
Occupation:	Retired
Employer:	
Spouse:	Deceased
Spouse's SSN:	
Spouse's Employer:	
Spouse's Date of Birth:	

INSURANCE INFORMATION:

Patient Number:	Peopl004
Place of Service:	Office
Primary Insurance Plan:	Medicare
Primary Insurance Plan ID #:	004-35-1526
Group #:	
Primary Policyholder:	Penelope Peoples
Policyholder Date of Birth:	08-30-1930
Relationship to Patient:	Self
Secondary Insurance Plan:	Medicaid
Secondary Insurance Plan ID #:	MCD3984212210
Secondary Policyholder:	Penelope Peoples

Patient Status ☐ Married ☐ Divorced ☐ Single ☐ Student ☒ Other

DIAGNOSIS INFORMATION

	Diagnosis	Code		Diagnosis	Code
1.	Pneumonia	486	5.		
2.			6.		
3.			7.		
4.			8.		

PROCEDURE INFORMATION

	Description of Procedure or Service	Date	Code	Charge
1.	Level 3 office visit - est patient	01-01-YYYY	99203	$60.00
2.				
3.				
4.				
5.				
6.				

SPECIAL NOTES:
Referred to Howard Hopkins, M.D. for respiratory consult

CASE STUDY 19
Cody Cobble

Catherine Crane, M.D.
88 Franklin Street • Long Beach, NC 22769 • (335) 221-8888
Tax ID# 01-3693691
NPI# 5551212354

Case Study

PATIENT INFORMATION:

Name:	Cody Cobble
Social Security #:	007-84-7278
Address:	333 Graves Street
City:	Long Beach
State:	NC
Zip Code:	22769
Home Telephone:	(335) 221-1155
Date of Birth:	09-29-1998
Gender:	Male
Occupation:	Student
Employer:	
Spouse:	
Spouse's SSN:	
Spouse's Employer:	
Spouse's Date of Birth:	

INSURANCE INFORMATION:

Patient Number:	Cobbl2585
Place of Service:	Office
Primary Insurance Plan:	Medicaid
Primary Insurance Plan ID #:	2222333344
Group #:	
Primary Policyholder:	Cody Cobble
Policyholder Date of Birth:	09-29-1998
Relationship to Patient:	Self
Secondary Insurance Plan:	
Secondary Insurance Plan ID #:	
Secondary Policyholder:	

Patient Status ☐ Married ☐ Divorced ☐ Single ☒ Student ☐ Other

DIAGNOSIS INFORMATION

Diagnosis	Code	Diagnosis	Code
1. Mumps	072.9	5.	
2.		6.	
3.		7.	
4.		8.	

PROCEDURE INFORMATION

Description of Procedure or Service	Date	Code	Charge
1. Level 1 office visit - est patient	05-18-YYYY	99201	$55.00
2.			
3.			
4.			
5.			
6.			

SPECIAL NOTES:
Mother's Name: Cathy Cobble
Father's Name: Chad Cobble

Catherine Crane, M.D.
88 Franklin Street • Long Beach, NC 22769 • (335) 221-8888
Tax ID# 01-3693691
NPI# 5551212354

Case Study

PATIENT INFORMATION:		INSURANCE INFORMATION:	
Name:	Wyatt Watkins	Patient Number:	Watki56
Social Security #:	006-52-8884	Place of Service:	Office
Address:	897 Neal Street	Primary Insurance Plan:	United Healthcare
City:	Long Beach	Primary Insurance Plan ID #:	003529991
State:	NC		
Zip Code:	22769	Group #:	MTV1235894
Home Telephone:	(335) 221-5555	Primary Policyholder:	Wilma Watkins
Date of Birth:	11-02-2005	Policyholder Date of Birth:	09-29-1988
Gender:	Male		
Occupation:		Relationship to Patient:	Parent
Employer:			
Spouse:		Secondary Insurance Plan:	Medicaid
Spouse's SSN:		Secondary Insurance Plan ID #:	2852232112
Spouse's Employer:			
Spouse's Date of Birth:		Secondary Policyholder:	Wyatt Watkins

Patient Status	☐ Married	☐ Divorced	☐ Single	☐ Student	☒ Other

DIAGNOSIS INFORMATION

	Diagnosis	Code		Diagnosis	Code
1.	Cystic congenital kidney disease	753.10	5.		
2.			6.		
3.			7.		
4.			8.		

PROCEDURE INFORMATION

	Description of Procedure or Service	Date	Code	Charge
1.	Level 3 office visit - est patient	09-10-YYYY	99203	$75.00
2.				
3.				
4.				
5.				
6.				

SPECIAL NOTES:
Mother's insurance United Healthcare, Medicaid secondary

Appendix II

Internet Links

- American Medical Association (AMA) www.ama-assn.org
- American Academy of Professional Coders (AAPC) www.aapc.com
- American Health Information Management Association (AHIMA) www.ahima.org
- American Medical Billing Association (AMBA) www.ambanet.net
- Blue Cross Blue Shield www.bcbsa.com
- Center for Medicare and Medicaid (CMS) www.cms.gov
- Federal Blue Cross Blue Shield www.fepblue.org/
- Federal Register www.archives.gov/federal-register
- HCPCS information www.cms.hhs.gov go to Medicare, then to HCPCS
- Medicaid www.cms.hhs.gov go to Medicaid link
- Medicare www.medicare.gov
- National Committee for Quality Assurance (NCA) www.ncqa.org
- National Correct Coding Initiative Edits Manual www.cms.hhs.gov/NationalCorrectCodInitEd/
- National Workers' Compensation www.workerscompensation.com
- TRICARE www.mytricare.com
- US Dept of Labor www.dol.gov/esa/whd/
- World Health Organization (WHO) www.who.int/

Appendix III

Forms

[Street Address]
[City, ST Zip Code]
[phone]
[fax]
[Web address]

[Company Name]

Fax

To: _____   From: _____

Fax: _____   Pages: _____

Phone: _____   Date: _____

Re: _____   cc: _____

☐ Urgent   ☐ For Review   ☐ Please Comment   ☐ Please Reply   ☐ Please Recycle

_____

● Disclaimer: This facsimile transmission contains information that is confidential and/or privileged. This information is intended for use only by the addressee indicated above. If you are not the intended recipient, please be advised that any disclosure, copying, distribution, or use of the contents of this information is strictly prohibited, and that any misdirected or improperly received information must be returned to this company immediately. Your cooperation in phoning us of erroneous receipt is requested.

Figure AIII-1. Fax cover sheet

Authorization for Release of Medical Record Information

Name: _____   Date of Birth: _____

Address: _____   Medical Record No.: _____

City: _____   State: _____ Zip: _____

Telephone No.: _____

I hereby authorize:

Name: _____   Address: _____

City: _____   State: _____ Zip: _____

to disclose information from my/my minor child's medical records to (name and address):

Name: _____   Address: _____

City: _____   State: _____ Zip: _____

I hereby authorize redisclosure of this information to:

Name: _____   Address: _____

City: _____   State: _____ Zip: _____

This information is needed for the following reason:

The specific information I wish to have released is (included dates of treatment):

I understand that I may revoke this consent at any time, except where information has already been released. This authorization is valid for a sixty (60) day period from the date it is signed.

Signature: (Parent or Legal Guardian if Minor Child)   Date:

Expires:

Witness:

This medical record may contain information about drug abuse, alcoholism, alcohol abuse, venereal disease, abortion, or mental health treatment. Separate consent must be given before this information can be released.

☐ DO consent to have this information disclosed.
☐ DO NOT consent to have this information disclosed.

Signature: (Parent or Legal Guardian if Minor Child)   Date:

This medical record may contain information concerning HIV testing and/or AIDS diagnosis treatment. Separate consent must be given before this information can be released.

☐ DO consent to have this information disclosed.
☐ DO NOT consent to have this information disclosed.

Signature: (Parent or Legal Guardian if Minor Child)   Date:

Figure AIII-2. Authorization for release of medical information

1500

HEALTH INSURANCE CLAIM FORM

APPROVED BY NATIONAL UNIFORM CLAIM COMMITTEE 08/05

◻◻◻ PICA   PICA ◻◻◻

1. ☐ MEDICARE ☐ MEDICAID ☐ TRICARE ☐ CHAMPVA ☐ GROUP ☐ FECA ☐ OTHER   1a. INSURED'S I.D. NUMBER   (For Program in Item 1)
   (Medicare #) (Medicaid #) CHAMPUS   (Member ID#) HEALTH PLAN BLK LUNG
                 (Sponsor's SSN)   (SSN or ID) (SSN) (ID)

2. PATIENT'S NAME (Last Name, First Name, Middle Initial)   3. PATIENT'S BIRTH DATE   SEX   4. INSURED'S NAME (Last Name, First Name, Middle Initial)
                                                              MM   DD   YY   M☐ F☐

5. PATIENT'S ADDRESS (No., Street)   6. PATIENT RELATIONSHIP TO INSURED   7. INSURED'S ADDRESS (No., Street)
                                                              Self☐ Spouse☐ Child☐ Other☐

CITY   STATE   8. PATIENT STATUS   CITY   STATE
                                                              Single☐ Married☐ Other☐

ZIP CODE   TELEPHONE (Include Area Code)   ZIP CODE   TELEPHONE (Include Area Code)
                  (   )   Employed☐ Full-Time☐ Part-Time☐   (   )
                                                                       Student   Student

9. OTHER INSURED'S NAME (Last Name, First Name, Middle Initial) 10. IS PATIENT'S CONDITION RELATED TO: 11. INSURED'S POLICY GROUP OR FECA NUMBER

a. OTHER INSURED'S POLICY OR GROUP NUMBER   a. EMPLOYMENT? (Current or Previous)   a. INSURED'S DATE OF BIRTH   SEX
                                                              ☐ YES ☐ NO   MM   DD   YY   M☐   F☐

b. OTHER INSURED'S DATE OF BIRTH   SEX   b. AUTO ACCIDENT?   PLACE (State)   b. EMPLOYER'S NAME OR SCHOOL NAME
   MM   DD   YY   M☐   F☐   ☐ YES ☐ NO

c. EMPLOYER'S NAME OR SCHOOL NAME   c. OTHER ACCIDENT?   c. INSURANCE PLAN NAME OR PROGRAM NAME
                                                              ☐ YES ☐ NO

d. INSURANCE PLAN NAME OR PROGRAM NAME   10d. RESERVED FOR LOCAL USE   d. IS THERE ANOTHER HEALTH BENEFIT PLAN?
                                                                                                    ☐ YES ☐ NO   If yes, return to and complete item 9 a-d.

READ BACK OF FORM BEFORE COMPLETING & SIGNING THIS FORM.
12. PATIENT'S OR AUTHORIZED PERSON'S SIGNATURE I authorize the release of any medical or other information necessary   13. INSURED'S OR AUTHORIZED PERSON'S SIGNATURE I authorize
to process this claim. I also request payment of government benefits either to myself or to the party who accepts assignment   payment of medical benefits to the undersigned physician or supplier for
below.   services described below.

SIGNED _____   DATE _____   SIGNED _____

14. DATE OF CURRENT: ☐ ILLNESS (First symptom) OR   15. IF PATIENT HAS HAD SAME OR SIMILAR ILLNESS.   16. DATES PATIENT UNABLE TO WORK IN CURRENT OCCUPATION
    MM   DD   YY   INJURY (Accident) OR   GIVE FIRST DATE MM   DD   YY   MM   DD   YY   MM   DD   YY
                         PREGNANCY(LMP)   FROM   TO

17. NAME OF REFERRING PROVIDER OR OTHER SOURCE   17a.   18. HOSPITALIZATION DATES RELATED TO CURRENT SERVICES
                                                 17b. NPI   MM   DD   YY   MM   DD   YY
                                                                          FROM   TO

19. RESERVED FOR LOCAL USE   20. OUTSIDE LAB? $ CHARGES
                                                                          ☐ YES ☐ NO

21. DIAGNOSIS OR NATURE OF ILLNESS OR INJURY (Relate Items 1, 2, 3 or 4 to Item 24E by Line)   22. MEDICAID RESUBMISSION
                                                                                                   CODE   ORIGINAL REF. NO.
1. └___.___   3. └___.___

                                                                                               23. PRIOR AUTHORIZATION NUMBER
2. └___.___   4. └___.___

24. A. DATE(S) OF SERVICE						B. PLACE OF SERVICE	C. EMG	D. PROCEDURES, SERVICES, OR SUPPLIES (Explain Unusual Circumstances)		E. DIAGNOSIS POINTER	F. $ CHARGES	G. DAYS OR UNITS	H. EPSDT Family Plan	I. ID. QUAL.	J. RENDERING PROVIDER ID. #
From			To					CPT/HCPCS	MODIFIER						
MM	DD	YY	MM	DD	YY										
1														NPI	
2														NPI	
3														NPI	
4														NPI	
5														NPI	
6														NPI	

25. FEDERAL TAX I.D. NUMBER   SSN ☐ EIN ☐   26. PATIENT'S ACCOUNT NO.   27. ACCEPT ASSIGNMENT? (For govt. claims, see back)   28. TOTAL CHARGE   29. AMOUNT PAID   30. BALANCE DUE
                                                                           ☐ YES ☐ NO $ $ $

31. SIGNATURE OF PHYSICIAN OR SUPPLIER   32. SERVICE FACILITY LOCATION INFORMATION   33. BILLING PROVIDER INFO & PH # (   )
INCLUDING DEGREES OR CREDENTIALS
(I certify that the statements on the reverse
apply to this bill and are made a part thereof.)

SIGNED _____ DATE _____   a. NPI   b.   a. NPI   b.

NUCC Instruction Manual available at: www.nucc.org   APPROVED OMB-0938-0999 FORM CMS-1500 (08-05)

Figure AIII-3. CMS-1500 form. For instructional use only.

Patient Registration Form

Patient's Name:_____ SS #:_____

      First Name   Middle   Last Name

Date of Birth:_____ ☐Male ☐Female ☐Single ☐Married ☐Widowed ☐Divorced ☐Separated

Street Address: _____

City/State/Zip Code: _____ Home Phone w/Area Code: _____

     Cell Phone w/Area Code: _____ Fax w/Area Code: _____

Spouse's Name: _____ SS #:_____

Spouse's Employer: _____ Spouse's Work Phone #:_____

Patient's Employer:_____ Work Phone w/Area Code:_____

Credit: (Circle) MC Visa # _____ Exp __/__/___ Name on card _____

Responsible Party: _____ Relationship: ☐Self ☐Spouse ☐Parent ☐Other

If patient is a Minor, are parents ☐Married ☐Divorced Custodial Parent:_____

     Custodial Parent's Home Phone w/Area Code: _____ Work Phone w/Area Code:_____

     Custodial Parent's SS #:_____ Date of Birth: _____

In case of emergency, contact (not living with you): _____

     Phone Number w/Area Code: _____ Relationship to Patient:_____

Is this injury work-related?☐Yes☐No If yes, date of injury? _____ Claim #:_____

     How did this injury happen? _____

Referring Physician's Name & Phone Number:_____

<u>PLEASE PRESENT INSURANCE CARD(S) & PHOTO ID FOR COPYING AND COMPLETE THE REQUESTED INFORMATION</u>

Insurance Company # 1:_____ Phone Number: _____

     Primary Insured's Name: _____ Date of Birth:_____

     Policy #:_____ Group #: _____ Relationship:_____

Insurance Company # 2:_____ Phone Number: _____

     Primary Insured's Name: _____ Date of Birth:_____

     Policy #:_____ Group #: _____Relationship:_____

If you do not have insurance, have you applied for Medicaid?☐Yes ☐No If yes, what is the name and phone number of the social worker with whom you are working?

_____

- I hereby authorize the payment of medical benefits to _____ for services rendered. I understand that I am financially responsible for any services not covered by my insurance carrier.
- I further agree to pay all collections costs, attorney fees, and other collections costs that may be incurred to enforce the collection of any amounts outstanding.
- I hereby authorize _____to release any medical information necessary to complete and process my insurance claims.

Patient's OR Insured's Signature (If patient is a Minor, must have Responsible Party Signature)   Date

I authorize Dr._____ to treat me and use my personal health information for healthcare operations.

Patient's Signature (OR Parent if patient is a Minor)   Date

Figure AIII-4. Patient registration form

Outpatient Encounter Form

Patient Information		Payment Method		Visit Information	
Patient ID number		**Primary**		Visit date	
Patient name		Primary ID number		Visit number	
Address		Primary group number		Rendering physician	
City/State		**Secondary**		Referring physician	
Social Security number		Secondary ID number		Reason for visit	
Phone number		Secondary group no.			
Date of birth		Cash/credit card			
Age		Other billing			

E/M Modifiers	Procedure Modifiers	Other Modifiers
24 — Unrelated E/M service during postop.	22 — Unusual, excessive procedure	
25 — Significant, separately identifiable E/M	50 — Bilateral procedure	
57 — Decision for surgery	51 — Multiple surgical procedures in same day	
	52 — Reduced/incomplete procedure	
	55 — Postop. management only	
	59 — Distinct multiple procedures	

CATEGORY	CODE	MOD	FEE	CATEGORY	CODE	MOD	FEE
Office Visit — New Patient				**Wound Care**			
Minimal office visit	99201			Debride partial thick burn	11040		
20 minutes	99202			Debride full thickness burn	11041		
30 minutes	99203			Debride wound, not a burn	11000		
45 minutes	99204			Unna boot application	29580		
60 minutes	99205			Unna boot removal	29700		
Other				Other			
Office Visit — Established				**Supplies**			
Minimal office visit	99211			Ace bandage, 2"	A6448		
10 minutes	99212			Ace bandage, 3"–4"	A6449		
15 minutes	99213			Ace bandage, 6"	A6450		
25 minutes	99214			Cast, fiberglass	A4590		
40 minutes	99215			Coban wrap	A6454		
Other				Foley catheter	A4338		
General Procedures				Immobilizer	L3670		
Anascopy	46600			Kerlix roll	A6220		
Audiometry	92551			Oxygen mask/cannula	A4620		
Breast aspiration	19000			Sleeve, elbow	E0191		
Cerumen removal	69210			Sling	A4565		
Circumcision	54150			Splint, ready-made	A4570		
DDST	96110			Splint, wrist	S8451		
Flex sigmoidoscopy	45330			Sterile packing	A6407		
Flex sig. w/biopsy	45331			Surgical tray	A4550		
Foreign body removal—foot	28190			Other			
Nail removal	11730			**OB Care**			
Nail removal/phenol	11750			Routine OB care	59400		
Trigger point injection	20552			OB call	59422		
Tympanometry	92567			Ante partum 4–6 visits	59425		
Visual acuity	99173			Ante partum 7 or more visits	59426		
Other				Other			

Vitals:
B/P _____
Pulse _____
Temp. _____
Height _____
Weight _____

Other Visit Information:
Lab Work to Order: _____
Referral to: _____
Provider Signature: _____
Next Appointment: _____

Fees:
Total Charges: $_____
Copay Received: $_____
Other Payment: $_____
Total Due: $_____

Company Name, Street Address, City, State ZIP Code, phone number

Figure AIII-5. Encounter form

Medicare Secondary Payer Questionnaire

All Medicare patients must complete this questionnaire before this medical office can submit your Medicare claim. Medicare law requires this information to determine if your Medicare coverage is your primary or secondary insurance policy.

1. I am working full time _____, part time _____.

2. I retired on this date _____.

3. I had a job-related injury _____ Date _____.

4. I have had treatment for an injury relating to a car accident _____ Date _____.

5. I have had treatment for another kind of accident (liability) _____ Date _____.

6. I am on kidney dialysis _____ Dates _____.

7. I have had an organ transplant _____ Date _____.

8. I am enrolled in Medicare HMO _____ Date _____.

9. I am a veteran _____ I have a fee card _____.

10. I have Black Lung Benefits _____ Date _____.

11. I am covered by an employer group policy by a company with more than 20 employees, by either myself or my spouse _____ Insurance company _____.

12. I have an insurance policy to supplement my Medicare _____ Insurance company _____.

13. I am covered by an employer-sponsored health plan for retirees _____ Insurance company _____.

14. I am covered by Medicaid _____ Date _____ ID # _____.

Patient signature _____ Date _____.

Figure AIII-6. Medicare Secondary Payer Questionnaire

(A) Notifier(s):

(B) Patient Name: _____ **(C) Identification Number:** _____

ADVANCE BENEFICIARY NOTICE OF NONCOVERAGE (ABN)

**NOTE**: If Medicare doesn't pay for **(D)**_____ below, you may have to pay.

Medicare does not pay for everything, even some care that you or your health care provider have good reason to think you need. We expect Medicare may not pay for the **(D)** _____ below.

(D) _____	**(E) Reason Medicare May Not Pay:**	**(F) Estimated Cost:**

WHAT YOU NEED TO DO NOW:

- Read this notice, so you can make an informed decision about your care.
- Ask us any questions that you may have after you finish reading.
- Choose an option below about whether to receive the **(D)** _____ listed above.
  Note: If you choose Option 1 or 2, we may help you to use any other
      insurance that you might have, but Medicare cannot require us to do this.

(G) OPTIONS: **Check only one box. We cannot choose a box for you.**

❑ **OPTION 1.** I want the **(D)** _____ listed above. You may ask to be paid now, but I also want Medicare billed for an official decision on payment, which is sent to me on a Medicare Summary Notice (MSN). I understand that if Medicare doesn't pay, I am responsible for payment, but **I can appeal to Medicare** by following the directions on the MSN. If Medicare does pay, you will refund any payments I made to you, less co-pays or deductibles.

❑ **OPTION 2.** I want the **(D)** _____ listed above, but do not bill Medicare. You may ask to be paid now as I am responsible for payment. **I cannot appeal if Medicare is not billed.**

❑ **OPTION 3.** I don't want the **(D)** _____ listed above. I understand with this choice I am **not** responsible for payment, and **I cannot appeal to see if Medicare would pay.**

(H) Additional Information:

This notice gives our opinion, not an official Medicare decision. If you have other questions on this notice or Medicare billing, call **1-800-MEDICARE** 1-800-633-4227/**TTY**: 1-877-486-2048).

Signing below means that you have received and understand this notice. You also receive a copy.

(I) Signature:	**(J) Date:**

According to the Paperwork Reduction Act of 1995, no persons are required to respond to a collection of information unless it displays a valid OMB control number. The valid OMB control number for this information collections is 0938-0566. The time required to complete this information collections is estimated to average 7 minutes per response, including the time to review instructions, search existing data resources, gather the data needed, and complete and review the information collections. If you have comments concerning the accuracy of the time estimate or suggestions for improving this form, please write to: CMS, 7500 Security Boulevard, Attn: PRA Reports Clearance Officer, Baltimore, Maryland 21244-1850.

Form CMS-R-131 (03/08)   Form Approved OMB No, 0938-0566

Figure AIII-7. Advance Beneficiary Notice (ABN). _Courtesy of the Centers for Medicare & Medicaid Services._ http://www.cms.hhs.gov

Medicare Surgical Disclosure Notice

Medicare beneficiary:

Name _____ Date _____

Medicare regulations require that all non-participating physicians provide the following

information to patients having elective surgery with a cost of $500.00 or more. I am a

non-participating physician and will not be accepting assignment on your surgery charge.

Surgery _____

Name of physician _____

Estimated charge _____

Estimated Medicare reimbursement _____

Patient's estimated payment _____

Acknowledged and agreed by:

_____ signature of Medicare beneficiary or legal representative

_____ date

_____ signature of physician

_____ date

Figure AIII-8. Medicare Surgical Disclosure Notice

INSTRUCTIONS

1. Type answers to ALL questions and file original with the Worker's Compensation Commission within 72 hours after first treatment.
2. DO NOT FAIL to forward to the Worker's Compensation Commission PROGRESS REPORTS and FINAL REPORT upon discharge of patient.

WORKERS' COMPENSATION COMMISSION

6 NORTH LIBERTY STREET, BALTIMORE, MD 21201-3785
SURGEON'S REPORT

This is First Report ☐   Progress Report ☐   Final Report ☐

DO NOT WRITE IN THIS SPACE

WCC CLAIM #

EMPLOYER'S REPORT   Yes ☐   No ☐

1. Name of Injured Person:		Soc.Sec.No.	D.O.B.	Sex M ☐ F ☐

2. Address: (No. and Street)   (City or Town)   (State)   (Zip Code)

3. Name and Address of Employer:

4. Date of Accident or Onset of Disease: Hour: A.M. ☐   P.M. ☐   5. Date Disability Began:

6. Patient's Description of Accident or Cause of Disease:

7. Medical Description of Injury or Disease:

8. Will injury result in:
    (a) Permanent defect?   Yes ☐   No ☐   If so, what?   (b) Disfigurement?   Yes ☐   No ☐

9. Causes, other than injury, contributing to patient's condition:

10. Is patient suffering from any disease of the heart, lungs, brain, kidneys, blood, vascular system or any other disabling condition not due to this accident? Give particulars.

11. Is there any history or evidence present of previous accident or disease? Give particulars.

12. Has normal recovery been delayed for any reason? Give particulars.

13. Date of first treatment: Who engaged your services?

14. Describe treatment given by you:

15. Were X-rays taken?   By whom? – (Name and Address)   Date:
Yes ☐   No ☐

16. X-rays Diagnosis:

17. Was patient treated by anyone else?   By whom? – (Name and Address)   Date:
Yes ☐   No ☐

18. Was patient hospitalized?   Name and Address of Hospital   Date of Admission:
Yes ☐   No ☐   Date of Discharge:

19. Is further treatment needed?   For how long?   20. Patient was ☐ will be ☐ able resume regular work on:
Yes ☐   No ☐   Patient was ☐ will be ☐ able resume light work on:

21. If death ensued give date: 22. Remarks: (Give any information of value not included above.)

23. I am a qualified specialist in: I am a duly licensed Physician in the State of: I graduated from Medical School: (Name)   Year:

Date of this report: (Signed)

(This report must be signed PERSONALLY by Physician.)

Address: Phone:

EVERY QUESTION MUST BE ANSWERED AND FORM SIGNED

Figure AIII-9. First report of injury form for Workers' Compensation claim

Medical Terminology Review by Marie A. Moisio, MA, RHIA

ROOTS, PREFIXES, AND SUFFIXES

Understanding the meaning of roots, prefixes, and suffixes provides a brief definition for many medical terms. A **root** is the foundation of a medical term and usually identifies a body part, color, and sometimes a condition. A **prefix** added to the beginning of a root modifies the meaning of the medical term. A **suffix** added to the end of the root identifies body processes, diseases, abnormal conditions, procedures, and treatments. To define the medical term, start with the meaning of the suffix, the prefix next, and the root last. For example, *hemigastrectomy* means excision of half of the stomach. The suffix -*ectomy* means excision; the prefix *hemi-* means half; and the root *gastr* means stomach. Although a brief definition is helpful, the best place to find the complete definition of all medical terms is in a medical dictionary.

ROOTS

Roots are usually listed with a combining vowel. The combining vowel, usually an *o* and sometimes an *i*, helps ease the pronunciation of medical terms. For example, *gastr/o* indicates that in some medical terms the root *gastr* uses the combining vowel *o*. Some commonly used roots with combining vowels are listed here.

Root	Meaning
abdomin/o	abdomen
aden/o	gland
adren/o; adrenal/o	adrenal gland
aneurysm/o	aneurysm
angi/o	vessel
appendic/o; append/o	appendix
arter/o; arteri/o	artery
arthr/o	joint
ather/o	fat; fatty plaque
bronch/o; bronchi/i	bronchus
burs/o	bursa; sac
cardi/o	heart
cephal/o	head
cerebr/o	cerebrum
cervic/o	cervix
cholangi/o	bile duct
cholecyst/o	gallbladder
choledoch/o	common bile duct
col/o; colon/o	colon
colp/o	vagina
cor/o; coron/o	heart
cost/o	rib
crani/o	cranium; skull
cut/o; cutane/o	skin
cyan/o	blue; bluish
cyst/o	sac; bladder
derm/o; dermat/o	skin
dipl/o	two; double
duoden/o	duodenum
encephal/o	brain
endocrin/o	endocrine
enter/o	intestines
erythr/o	red
esophag/o	esophagus
gastr/o	stomach
gingiv/o	gums
gyn/o; gynec/o	woman
hem/o; hemat/o	blood
hepat/o	liver
hyster/o	uterus
ile/o	ileum
ili/o	ilium; pelvic bone
ir/o; irid/o	iris
jejun/o	jejunum
lapar/o	abdominal wall
laryng/o	larynx
leuk/o	white
lith/o	stone
lymphaden/o	lymph gland
mamm/o; mast/o	breast

Root	Meaning
my/o	muscle
myel/o	bone marrow; spinal cord
myring/o	eardrum
nas/o	nose
nephr/o	kidney
neur/o	nerve
melan/o	black
metr/i; metr/o	uterus
ocul/o	eye
oophor/o	ovary
ophthalm/o	eye
orchi/o; orchid/o	testis; testicle
oste/o	bone
ot/o	ear
ovari/o	ovary
peritone/o	peritoneum
phac/o; phak/o	lens
pharyng/o	pharynx
phleb/o	vein
pleur/o	pleura
pneum/o	air; lung
prostat/o	prostate gland
pulmon/o	lung
pyel/o	renal pelvis
rect/o	rectum
ren/o	kidney
retin/o	retina
rhin/o	nose
salping/o	fallopian tubes; oviducts
scler/o	sclera; hard
sigmoid/o	sigmoid colon
spleen/o	spleen
spondyl/o	vertebral column
stomat/o	mouth
thorac/o	chest; thorax
thromb/o	clot; thrombus
thyr/o; thyroid/o	thyroid gland
trache/o	trachea
tympan/o	eardrum
ur/o	urine; urinary system
ureter/o	ureter
urethra/o	urethra
uter/o	uterus
vagin/o	vagina
vas/o	vessel; vas deferens
ven/o	ven
ventricul/o	ventricle
vertebr/o	vertebra
vesic/o	urinary bladder
xanth/o	yellow

PREFIXES

Prefixes are written with a hyphen following the prefix. Some commonly used prefixes are listed here.

Prefix	Meaning
a-; an-; ana-	no; not; without
ante-	forward
anti-	against
auto-	self
bi-	two; double; both
brady-	slow
dura-	hard
dys-	abnormal; painful
echo-	sound
hemi-	half
hyper-	above; excessive
hypo-	deficient; below
macro-	large
mal-	bad; poor; abnormal
micro-	small
mono-	one
multi-	many
neo-	new
non-	not
nulli-	none
pan-	all
para-	beside; around
per-	through
peri-	around; surrounding
retro-	backward; behind; upward
semi-	half
sub-	below; beneath; under
tachy-	fast
tri-	three
uni-	one

SUFFIXES

Suffixes are written with a hyphen preceding the suffix. Some commonly used suffixes are listed here.

Suffix	Meaning
-algia	pain
-cele	hernia; protrusion
-centesis	surgical puncture
-clasia; clasis	surgical breaking
-cytosis	condition of cells
-desis	binding; fixation
-dynia	pain
-ectasis	stretching; dilation
-ectomy	surgical removal; excision
-emesis	vomiting
-emia	blood condition
-gram	a picture, record; X-ray film
-graph	instrument for recording
-graphy	process of recording
-ia; -iasis	condition; abnormal condition
-itis	inflammation
-lysis; -lytic	destruction; breakdown
-malacia	softening
-megaly	enlarged; enlargement
-metry	measuring; to measure
-oid	like; resembling
-oma	tumor
-opia	vision
-osis	condition
-paresis	partial paralysis
-pathy	disease; illness
-penia	deficiency; decreased number
-pepsia	digestion
-pexy	surgical fixation
-phagia	eating; swallowing
-plasty	surgical repair
-plegia	paralysis
-pnea	breathing
-ptosis	drooping; sagging
-ptysis	spitting up
-(r)rhagia	hemorrhage
-(r)rhaphy	suture of
-(r)rhea	discharge; flow
-(r)rhexis	rupture
-sclerosis	hardening
-scopy	vizualization with a scope
-stenosis	narrowing

Suffix	Meaning
-(o)stomy	creating a new opening
-tomy	incision into
-therapy	treatment
-(o)tocia	labor; birth
-tonia	muscle tone
-tresia	opening
-tripsy	crushing
-uria	urine; urination

Glossary

Abuse: Abuse is unknowingly filling an improper health claim.

Accept assignment: This is an agreement by the physician to have reimbursement sent directly to the medical facility from an insurance company and accepts their payment in full.

Account receivable: Account receivable in the physician's office are monies owed to the physician from unpaid claims.

Action verb: It is important to remember to use action verbs in a résumé. The action verb will indicate a motivated applicant.

Add on codes: Some procedures are performed in addition to primary procedures. These additional procedures are listed as add on codes.

Adjustment: An adjustment is a percentage of the charge adjusted off a patient's account.

Advance Beneficiary Notice (ABN): An ABN is a document explaining that the service might not be a covered service, due to medical necessity.

Aged trial balance report: The aged trial balance report is produced by the medical billing software and reports all unpaid claims, the age of the unpaid claims, and what insurance company (or patient) is responsible for the balance.

Ambulatory facility: An ambulatory facility is one in which a patient is treated as an outpatient, not formally admitted to a facility overnight.

American Health Information Management Association (AHIMA): AHIMA is a professional association credentialing and regulating health information management.

Ancillary charges: These charges are additional charges for services and procedures rendered to a patient for clinical evaluation, such as x-ray, lab, and diagnostic testing.

Appeal: An appeal is a written request to the insurance company to research the health claim and reverse the previous denial on that claim.

Assignment of benefit: This statement authorizes the insurance company to pay the provider directly.

Audit: An audit involves the insurance company examining the medical records for the claim they are processing.

Audits: Audits is the process of checking the documentation of a patient's visit against the billed charges, for compliance reasons.

Authorization: Authorization is a document providing official permission to release specific protected health information to specific entities.

Balance billing: Balance billing is the billing of an unpaid balance to the patient when the physician has a contract with the patient's insurance company.

Batch proof: Data reported proving the amount of money entered on patient's accounts equals the checks sent by the insurance company.

Billing cycle: The billing cycle starts with collecting data for the health claim, producing a clean claim, submitting a clean claim, and collecting reimbursement for that claim.

Blue Cross Blue Shield: It is a health insurance covering both outpatient and inpatient benefits.

Capitation: Capitation is a uniform payment made for a predetermined group of patients, to the physician from an insurance company. This payment is usually made for a specific amount of time (month, year).

Centers for Medicare and Medicaid (CMS): Medicare is run by the Centers for Medicare and Medicaid Services (CMS). They set the regulations but allow independent Medicare carriers to administer the processing of claims.

Certificate and group numbers: The certificate number is issued to the policy holder by the insurance company as a method to recognize the benefits in the insurance contract for the patient. The policy holder's group number will help the insurance company identify benefits if the policy holder is covered under a group policy through their place of employment.

Certifications: Nationally recognized associations award certifications in many aspects of the medical reimbursement field. These certifications acknowledge expertise in reimbursement and coding within the ambulatory, hospital, and insurance company environments.

CHAMPVA: CHAMPVA is the governmental and civilian medical health program for the department of veteran affairs. This is health coverage for veterans with a 100% service-related disability and their families.

Charge entry: Charge entry is a step in the billing process, when the reimbursement specialist correctly enters codes for services and diagnoses into the medical billing software.

Chief complaint: Is the documentation of a patient's condition (in his own words) for determining the E&M code level.

Claim follow-up: Claim Follow Up is one of the most important steps in the reimbursement process. Once the claim has been submitted, the reimbursement specialist must track, or follow-up claims. The follow-up is knowing the status on every claim billed.

Claim status: The claim status is the reporting of where the claim is in the insurance company's processing cycle.

Claim submission: Sending a health claim or bill to a third party.

Clean claim: A clean claim is a claim that has all of the necessary and correct information the insurance company needs for a full and correct reimbursement.

Clearinghouse: A clearinghouse is a service that receives electronically submitted claims from the physicians' offices, checks the claims for technical errors, and sends the claims on to the correct insurance company in the correct electronic format.

CMS-1500 billing form: The CMS-1500 form is a universal billing form used by all insurance companies.

Co-insurance: A percentage of the charge, billed by the physician after the reimbursement comes from the insurance company to the patient.

Collate: A photocopy machine can collate, or arrange copies in the proper sequence.

Commercial insurance: It is a group of private insurance companies offering health care policies.

Compliance: Compliance is defined as a disposition to yield to a rule.

Consumer collections: Collections from patients are called consumer collections and are regulated by federal and state laws.

Contact information: Contact information should include a full name, a permanent address, pertinent telephone numbers, and e-mail addresses. This information should be centered at the top of the résumé.

Contractual payments: Is the predetermined reimbursement determined by a contract between the insurance company and physician.

Conventions: Conventions are symbols designed to help the coder gain more information about the codes.

Coordination of benefits (COB): Is a provision in health insurance policy that prevents multiple insurance companies from paying for the same benefits, and the sequence in which multiple insurance companies will pay.

Co-pay: Is a predetermined amount of money due by the patient at the time of service.

Corrective Coding Initiative (CCI): CCI is a system developed by CMS to promote correct coding methodologies.

Cover letter: A cover letter is a personalized, written document that is intended to introduce a résumé to a prospective employer.

Cover sheet: When sending any information via the fax machine, it is important to include a cover sheet. The cover sheet is the first page of any information sent.

Coverage termination: Coverage termination indicates the patient no longer has a policy with the insurance company.

Current Procedural Terminology (CPT): The Current Procedural Terminology manual is a set of codes used to describe procedures and services performed by the physician and other health professionals.

Deductible: A deductible is a pre-set amount of money the patient must pay before the insurance company will reimburse any charges.

Defense Enrollment Eligibility Reporting System (DEERS): DEERS is the eligibility reporting system for TRICARE insurance.

Demographics: The important information regarding the patient, which include the patient's name, date of birth, address, insurance information, marital status, employment information, and reason for treatment.

Denied claim: A denied claim is a kind of claim that is not reimbursed for a coverage issue.

Diagnosis: The process of determining and reporting a patient's disease, injury, or condition.

Disclaimer: A disclaimer should always be printed at the bottom of the cover letter. A disclaimer is a statement that disclaims responsibility for information sent to an incorrect source.

Durable medical equipment (DME): Equipment that can be used repeatedly, in the patient's home for medical conditions, such as wheel chairs, crutches, canes, etc.

E codes: E codes are used to describe the external causes, environmental events, circumstances, and conditions of the patient's injury.

Electronic Claim submission (ECS): Submitting or sending a medical claim (bill) electronically to an insurance company or responsible party.

Electronic data interchange (EDI): the process of exchanging data between two or more computers.

Electronic fund transfer (EFT): The electronic fund transfer is a kind of payment which is much faster and the reimbursement is directly deposited into the physician's bank account.

Electronic Medical Record (EMR): EMRs are medical records in digit format (paperless records).

Electronic swipe devices: Electronic swipe devices look very much like credit card point-of-service devices. This gives the physician's office the ability to check patient's insurance eligibility instantly and have an immediate overview of their benefits.

Encounter form: An encounter form is a document that defines the services and procedures performed for a patient at each visit.

Evaluation and management (E&M): E&M codes that describe physician services. This includes the patient history, the physical exam, and the medical decision making or physician management of the patient's problem.

Exam: The documentation of clinical findings by a physician.

Explanation of benefits (EOB): An explanation of benefits (EOB) is necessary for the payment entry to be accomplished. The EOB is a statement from the insurance company explaining how they reimbursed each claim.

Fax: The fax, or facsimile, machine utilizes a phone line and photo sensors to scan and send documents instantly over the telephone line.

Fee schedule: The amount of reimbursement the physician will expect for each service or procedure in the treatment of patients.

Fee-for-service: It is a payment system where the physician is paid for specific medical charges by an insurance company and the balance is due from the patient.

First party: In a contract with an insurance company, the policy holder is the first party in this contract.

First report of injury: It is a document for Workers' Compensation Insurance explaining the work related injury.

Follow-up: The follow-up is the process of checking the status on outstanding balances with insurance companies.

Font: Style of letters used on a computer.

Fraud: Fraud is knowingly billing incorrectly to inflate reimbursement.

Group policies: Policies that are offered to a large number of employees are called group policies.

Health Care Financing Administration (HCFA): The original system set up by Medicare to administer Medicare health benefits and regulations. It is now called CMS.

Health claim: The health claim or insurance bill is generated by a computer using specialized billing software, and is formatted to a CMS-1500 billing form.

Health Insurance Portability and Accountability Act (HIPAA): A compliance policy set by the U.S. Department of Health and Human Services that establishes national standards for the protection of health information.

Health insurance: Health insurance is a contract between an individual and an insurance company. This contract states the insurance company will pay a predetermined payment for medical costs when that person is sick or injured and requires medical treatment.

Health maintenance organization (HMO): HMO seeks to control medical costs and improve the quality of health care.

Healthcare Common Procedure Coding System (HCPCS): HCPCS is a coding system consisting of CPT and National Level II codes.

History: The documentation of the history of a patient's clinical problems.

Indemnity plans: This is a type of insurance plan that reimburses the physician for actual costs of specific charges.

Indented code: The indented code is a code with a description that refers back to a common stand-alone code with a slightly different description.

Indigent: Indigent implies no income available

In-house audit: The process of checking the patient's medical records against the medical code selected to be billed to the insurance company.

Insurance benefits: The insurance benefit or payment is determined by the insurance company as set by the contract each patient has within their policy.

Insurance commissioner: The insurance commissioner is with the Department of Insurance. The commissioner handles complaints that are filed with the Department of Insurance.

Insurance verification: Insurance verification involves checking the patient's eligibility for insurance benefits with their insurance company.

Insured: The person whose name is on the insurance policy.

International Classification of Diseases (ICD): ICD codes are three-five digit codes that reference standard descriptions of diseases, conditions, and injuries.

Invoice: It is a statement or a bill.

Limiting charge: The limiting charge is the highest amount of money a Medicare non-participating physician can charge. This is 15% over the Medicare approved amount for a service or procedure.

Local Coverage Determination Manual (LCD): Local Coverage Determination Manuals will link many CPT codes with medically necessary ICD-9-CM codes. This will help the medical billing office determine if a service or procedure will be deemed medically necessary, which will result in correct reimbursement. This manual sets rules and edits for local coverage determinations.

Managed care: Managed care provides subscribers with affordable health care while maintaining quality of care from the physician. Managed care plans offer reduced premiums for the patient who stays within a predetermined network of physicians who manage the patients' medical needs.

Medicaid: The Medicaid health care program was established on July 30, 1965 authorized by the Social Security Act. This program was set up to reimburse physicians for the treatment of patients with low income, few resources, and disabilities.

Medical codes: Each service and/or procedure performed on the patient then must be medically coded with nationally recognized numeric and alphanumeric medical codes to identify each service performed.

Medical decision making (MDM): The documentation by a physician of a patient's complexity of symptoms, conditions, and diseases which helps in determining a level of care code for E&M coding. This includes number of diagnoses, data reviewed, and risk of complications for the patient.

Medical record: The legal document of a patient in which all treatment and administrative processes is documented and saved.

Medical team: The team which consists of both the clinical and administrative departments in ambulatory facilities.

Medicare beneficiary: A person eligible to receive healthcare benefits.

Medicare Claims Processing Manual: It is a manual explaining the rules and regulations for submitting Medicare claims.

Medicare Remittance Advice (MRA): MRA is a document from Medicare outlining the reimbursement, rejections, or denials on a health claim. This document is sent to the physician.

Medicare Summary Notice (MSN): MSN is a document (EOB) from Medicare outlining the reimbursement, rejections, or denials on a health claim that is sent to the patient.

Medicare Surgical Disclosure Notice: It is a document outlining the costs associated with an elective surgery for the patient who is covered by Medicare.

Medicare: Medicare is the largest governmental health insurance program in the United States. Medicare is a federally funded health insurance program for people over the age of 65 and some qualified disabled patients.

Medicare's original fee-for-service plan: Medicare's original plan is the fee-for-service plan. Patients have a yearly deductible with billed services reimbursed according to the Medicare fee schedule.

Medigap: It is a secondary supplemental insurance to Medicare, covering any balance that Medicare does not pay "filling in the gap".

Modifier: A modifier is a two-digit alphanumeric or numeric code that alerts the insurance company of an unusual circumstance.

Morbidity: Pertaining to illness or disease.

Mortality: Pertaining to death.

National Center of Health Statistics: It is one agency of the US Dept of Health and Human Services responsible for changes made to the ICD-9-CM diagnosis codes.

National Committee for Quality Assurance (NCQA): NCQA evaluates all managed care organizations. The NCQA accredits the managed care organizations and shows that the plan meets the standards beyond what is required by law.

National Coverage Determination Manual (NCD): NCD is a data set by Medicare outlining the rules which determine under what clinical circumstances a service is a covered benefit. These rules determine what is considered reasonable and necessary, and what codes are correct.

National Provider Identifier Number (NPI): NPI is a unique numeric or alphanumeric identifier given every physician by Medicare for billing purposes.

National standard format (NSF): The format seen on the computer screen in the CMS-1500 format.

Objective: It is a short statement stating the goal of the applicant in applying for a specific job.

Outstanding balance: A non-paid balance on an account, from either an insurance company or patient.

Outstanding claim: The outstanding claim is an unpaid claim.

Overhead: The overhead is the cost of running an office, must be maintained as well as paying the physician and staff for the services rendered. The overhead would include the cost of the facility, facility maintenance, utilities, medical equipment and maintenance, medical supplies, office supplies, and much more.

Participating physician: Participating physician s a physician who contracts with an insurance company and agrees to accept what that insurance company reimburses for services.

Patient collections: It is a method of collecting money from the patients which is an essential process in the medical office and a difficult one.

Patient registration form: A patient registration form will help collect information for both the reimbursement specialist and the clinical staff.

Payer of last resort: Medicaid insurance program should always be billed last if the patient has multiple health care policies. It is called the payer of last resort.

Payment entry: The entry of the payment to the patient's account by reimbursement specialist after the payment is received by the physician's billing office.

Payment posting: Posting reimbursement payments to the patient's account.

Point-of-service (POS): The point-of-service (POS) system is a kind of managed care system that minimizes the restrictions to the patient in choosing a physician. They can choose physicians outside the provider network at a higher cost.

Policy holder: The person who enters into a contract with an insurance company.

Policy: The policy is a certificate of coverage that outlines what medical costs are covered and what services are not covered.

Preauthorizations: The administrative team (billing office) can receive or send referrals to specialists. They can acquire preauthorizations, which are approvals of reimbursement from an insurance company regarding medical necessity and appropriateness for services and procedures rendered.

Preferred provider organization (PPO): The PPO is a managed care plan that allows the patients to see network physicians at a discounted rate.

Premium: a monthly payment, which the policyholder pays the insurance company.

Primary care manager (PCM): PCM is the physician responsible for the management of a patient's health care.

Primary care physician (PCP): The physician who manages the patient's health care. The PCP's job is to provide efficient and effective health care while keeping the medical costs at a minimum.

Prior-authorization: The prior-authorization is the insurance company's permission to proceed with a specific service and receive reimbursement.

Professionalism: Professionalism is a standard of behavior in character and methods for a professional.

Reimbursement: Reimbursement is defined as: to compensate another for services rendered.

Rejected claim: A rejected claim is a denied reimbursement because of a technical error on a claim (not a clean claim).

Relative Value Unit (RVU): Medicare's fee schedule is based on relative value units (RVUs). The RVUs are based on physician work, practice expenses, and malpractice expense.

Release of information: A release of information is a document signed by the patient, giving the medical office authorization to send private medical information to the insurance company.

Remittance advice: Is a document from an insurance company outlining the reimbursement, rejections, or denials for a submitted medical claim.

Resubmitted: Resubmitting a claim is resending the claim after correction.

Résumé: The résumé is a document that outlines an applicant's skills and experiences at a glance.

Reverse chronological order: Data presented in order of most recent to the oldest.

Router: A name given to an encounter form by the Physician's offices.

Scrubber: When the claim is electronically submitted directly to the insurance company or through a clearinghouse, a scrubber report is generated. It reports all the claims submitted, total amount of the claims in dollar amounts, and any claims that were rejected and not submitted do to any edits for errors and missing information.

Second party: In a contract with an insurance company, the physician is the second party in this contract.

Soft collection: A method of collecting outstanding balances from patients through normal statement billing and friendly calls.

Soft skills: The applicant should include customer service skills, telephone skills, accounting skills, and computer skills. These are called soft skills.

Spell-check: Spell-check is a dictionary that is built into the computer. It will alert the user of a misspelled word.

Spend down: Some states have spend down programs for individuals who are medically needy but are slightly above the Medicaid eligibility. These individuals are asked to spend a certain amount of money on their health care before Medicaid will start reimbursement.

Sponsor: Sponsor is the policy holder for TRICARE Insurance.

Stand-alone code: The stand-alone code is a code with a full description of the procedure.

Statement: A statement is an invoice or bill explaining the money that is owed to the physician. Statements are commonly sent to patients on a monthly basis.

Summary of qualifications: The summary of qualifications is a heading for experienced professionals in a résumé. It should motivate the employer to call for an interview.

Super bill: a billing document used by the medical office to document clinical information on each patient at each visit or encounter.

Supporting documentation: Supporting documents are proof that the claim is a correct clean claim.

Symbols: The symbols next to the codes are important in the understanding of the code chose.

Thank you letter: A thank you letter is sent in response to an interview allowing the applicant to follow-up with the employer on the application process.

The American National Standard Institute (ANSI): ANSI approves the electronic formatted claim in encrypted form for security and confidentiality of patient information.

Third party: In a contract with an insurance company, the third party in the contract is the insurance company.

Time limit: The time limit gives the billing office a very specific amount of time to resolve the denial.

TRICARE: TRICARE is the health care coverage for active military personnel and their families.

Upcoding: Incorrectly coding what the physician has documented. Up-coding is coding a higher-level service than was performed.

V codes: V codes can be found in the main index of the ICD-9-CM manual. V codes describe patient encounters other than illness or injury.

Workers' Compensation (W/C): Workers' Compensation (W/C) is a program that covers individuals for the treatment of work-related injuries and illnesses.

World Health Organization (WHO): WHO is an international organization who developed the ICD classification of diseases, reported by coders world wide.

Write-off: Is an amount of money adjusted off a patient's account.

Index

IMPORTANT! READ CAREFULLY: This End User License Agreement ("Agreement") sets forth the conditions by which Cengage Learning will make electronic access to the Cengage Learning-owned licensed content and associated media, software, documentation, printed materials, and electronic documentation contained in this package and/or made available to you via this product (the "Licensed Content"), available to you (the "End User"). BY CLICKING THE "I ACCEPT" BUTTON AND/OR OPENING THIS PACKAGE, YOU ACKNOWLEDGE THAT YOU HAVE READ ALL OF THE TERMS AND CONDITIONS, AND THAT YOU AGREE TO BE BOUND BY ITS TERMS, CONDITIONS, AND ALL APPLICABLE LAWS AND REGULATIONS GOVERNING THE USE OF THE LICENSED CONTENT.

1.0 SCOPE OF LICENSE

1.1 <u>Licensed Content.</u> The Licensed Content may contain portions of modifiable content ("Modifiable Content") and content which may not be modified or otherwise altered by the End User ("Non-Modifiable Content"). For purposes of this Agreement, Modifiable Content and Non-Modifiable Content may be collectively referred to herein as the "Licensed Content." All Licensed Content shall be considered Non-Modifiable Content, unless such Licensed Content is presented to the End User in a modifiable format and it is clearly indicated that modification of the Licensed Content is permitted.

1.2 Subject to the End User's compliance with the terms and conditions of this Agreement, Cengage Learning hereby grants the End User, a nontransferable, nonexclusive, limited right to access and view a single copy of the Licensed Content on a single personal computer system for noncommercial, internal, personal use only. The End User shall not (i) reproduce, copy, modify (except in the case of Modifiable Content), distribute, display, transfer, sublicense, prepare derivative work(s) based on, sell, exchange, barter or transfer, rent, lease, loan, resell, or in any other manner exploit the Licensed Content; (ii) remove, obscure, or alter any notice of Cengage Learning's intellectual property rights present on or in the Licensed Content, including, but not limited to, copyright, trademark, and/or patent notices; or (iii) disassemble, decompile, translate, reverse engineer, or otherwise reduce the Licensed Content.

2.0 TERMINATION

2.1 Cengage Learning may at any time (without prejudice to its other rights or remedies) immediately terminate this Agreement and/or suspend access to some or all of the Licensed Content, in the event that the End User does not comply with any of the terms and conditions of this Agreement. In the event of such termination by Cengage Learning, the End User shall immediately return any and all copies of the Licensed Content to Cengage Learning.

3.0 PROPRIETARY RIGHTS

3.1 The End User acknowledges that Cengage Learning owns all rights, title and interest, including, but not limited to all copyright rights therein, in and to the Licensed Content, and that the End User shall not take any action inconsistent with such ownership. The Licensed Content is protected by U.S., Canadian and other applicable copyright laws and by international treaties, including the Berne Convention and the Universal Copyright Convention. Nothing contained in this Agreement shall be construed as granting the End User any ownership rights in or to the Licensed Content.

3.2 Cengage Learning reserves the right at any time to withdraw from the Licensed Content any item or part of an item for which it no longer retains the right to publish, or which it has reasonable grounds to believe infringes copyright or is defamatory, unlawful, or otherwise objectionable.

4.0 PROTECTION AND SECURITY

4.1 The End User shall use its best efforts and take all reasonable steps to safeguard its copy of the Licensed Content to ensure that no unauthorized reproduction, publication, disclosure, modification, or distribution of the Licensed Content, in whole or in part, is made. To the extent that the End User becomes aware of any such unauthorized use of the Licensed Content, the End User shall immediately notify Cengage Learning. Notification of such violations may be made by sending an e-mail to infringement@cengage.com.

5.0 MISUSE OF THE LICENSED PRODUCT

5.1 In the event that the End User uses the Licensed Content in violation of this Agreement, Cengage Learning shall have the option of electing liquidated damages, which shall include all profits generated by the End User's use of the Licensed Content plus interest computed at the maximum rate permitted by law and all legal fees and other expenses incurred by Cengage Learning in enforcing its rights, plus penalties.

6.0 FEDERAL GOVERNMENT CLIENTS

6.1 Except as expressly authorized by Cengage Learning, Federal Government clients obtain only the rights specified in this Agreement and no other rights. The Government acknowledges that (i) all software and related documentation incorporated in the Licensed Content is existing commercial computer software within the meaning of FAR 27.405(b)(2); and (2) all other data delivered in whatever form, is limited rights data within the meaning of FAR 27.401. The restrictions in this section are acceptable as consistent with the Government's need for software and other data under this Agreement.

7.0 DISCLAIMER OF WARRANTIES AND LIABILITIES

7.1 Although Cengage Learning believes the Licensed Content to be reliable, Cengage Learning does not guarantee or warrant (i) any information or materials contained in or produced by the Licensed Content, (ii) the accuracy, completeness or reliability of the Licensed Content, or (iii) that the Licensed Content is free from errors or other material defects. THE LICENSED PRODUCT IS PROVIDED "AS IS," WITHOUT ANY WARRANTY OF ANY KIND AND CENGAGE LEARNING DISCLAIMS ANY AND ALL WARRANTIES, EXPRESSED OR IMPLIED, INCLUDING, WITHOUT LIMITATION, WARRANTIES OF MERCHANTABILITY OR FITNESS FOR A PARTICULAR PURPOSE. IN NO EVENT SHALL CENGAGE LEARNING BE LIABLE FOR: INDIRECT, SPECIAL, PUNITIVE OR CONSEQUENTIAL DAMAGES INCLUDING FOR LOST PROFITS, LOST DATA, OR OTHERWISE. IN NO EVENT SHALL CENGAGE LEARNING'S AGGREGATE LIABILITY HEREUNDER, WHETHER ARISING IN CONTRACT, TORT, STRICT LIABILITY OR OTHERWISE, EXCEED THE AMOUNT OF FEES PAID BY THE END USER HEREUNDER FOR THE LICENSE OF THE LICENSED CONTENT.

8.0 GENERAL

8.1 <u>Entire Agreement</u>. This Agreement shall constitute the entire Agreement between the Parties and supercedes all prior Agreements and understandings oral or written relating to the subject matter hereof.

8.2 <u>Enhancements/Modifications of Licensed Content</u>. From time to time, and in Cengage Learning's sole discretion, Cengage Learning may advise the End User of updates, upgrades, enhancements and/or improvements to the Licensed Content, and may permit the End User to access and use, subject to the terms and conditions of this Agreement, such modifications, upon payment of prices as may be established by Cengage Learning.

8.3 <u>No Export</u>. The End User shall use the Licensed Content solely in the United States and shall not transfer or export, directly or indirectly, the Licensed Content outside the United States.

8.4 <u>Severability</u>. If any provision of this Agreement is invalid, illegal, or unenforceable under any applicable statute or rule of law, the provision shall be deemed omitted to the extent that it is invalid, illegal, or unenforceable. In such a case, the remainder of the Agreement shall be construed in a manner as to give greatest effect to the original intention of the parties hereto.

8.5 <u>Waiver</u>. The waiver of any right or failure of either party to exercise in any respect any right provided in this Agreement in any instance shall not be deemed to be a waiver of such right in the future or a waiver of any other right under this Agreement.

8.6 <u>Choice of Law/Venue</u>. This Agreement shall be interpreted, construed, and governed by and in accordance with the laws of the State of New York, applicable to contracts executed and to be wholly preformed therein, without regard to its principles governing conflicts of law. Each party agrees that any proceeding arising out of or relating to this Agreement or the breach or threatened breach of this Agreement may be commenced and prosecuted in a court in the State and County of New York. Each party consents and submits to the nonexclusive personal jurisdiction of any court in the State and County of New York in respect of any such proceeding.

8.7 <u>Acknowledgment</u>. By opening this package and/or by accessing the Licensed Content on this Web site, THE END USER ACKNOWLEDGES THAT IT HAS READ THIS AGREEMENT, UNDERSTANDS IT, AND AGREES TO BE BOUND BY ITS TERMS AND CONDITIONS. IF YOU DO NOT ACCEPT THESE TERMS AND CONDITIONS, YOU MUST NOT ACCESS THE LICENSED CONTENT AND RETURN THE LICENSED PRODUCT TO CENGAGE LEARNING (WITHIN 30 CALENDAR DAYS OF THE END USER'S PURCHASE) WITH PROOF OF PAYMENT ACCEPTABLE TO CENGAGE LEARNING, FOR A CREDIT OR A REFUND. Should the End User have any questions/comments regarding this Agreement, please contact Cengage Learning at Delmar.help@cengage.com.